PATHWAY TO GOD

IN

HINDI LITERATURE

PATHWAY TO GOD

IN

HINDI LITERATURE

R. D. RANADE

GYAN

Published by

GYAN

Gyan Publishing House
5, Ansari Road
Daryaganj, New Delhi-110002
Phone: 011-47034999, 9811692060
E-mail: books@gyanbooks.com

Distribution Network
gyanbooks.com
India, USA, Canada, UK, Australia

ISBN: 978-93-6920-463-2 (PB)

First Published, 1954

2nd Impression 2025

Printed at: Gyan Press, Delhi.

PATHWAY TO GOD IN HINDI LITERATURE
Author: R. D. RANADE

ॐ

PATHWAY TO GOD

IN

HINDI LITERATURE

R. D. RANADE.

1954

PUBLISHED BY ADHYATMA VIDYA MANDIR

SANGLI . NIMBAL (R. S.) . ALLAHABAD

Dr. Rajendra Prasad's Speech

at the end of

Dr. R. D. Ranade's lecture on 'The Sublime in Mystical Experience' at the Rashtrapati Bhavan, New Delhi, on 16th April 1954.

You have been so far hearing a discourse on a very abstruse subject, and it is Prof. Ranade's special field of work, in which he has studied not only the old Sanskrit philosophy, but also the philosophy of the West, and the philosophy that has been taught by people who have practical experience in their own life.

We have a large body of Literatures dealing with what is called the '*Sant Bani*'—the teachings of the Saints,—and you all know how Prof. Ranade has been devoting years of study to that particular kind of literature in the Indian languages. We know his book dealing with the '*Sant Bani*' in Marathi literature. The book in Hindi has just, I think, come out, and we are anticipating an equally good book for those who can understand it—the *Sant Bani* in Kannada literature, and of course Sanskrit is at the bottom of all these. So the philosophy which we have inherited from the past now lives in him, and I am very happy that it has been possible for us to have this second lecture of his in this house. We have had the privilege to listen to his another discourse, I think, about two years ago.

We had the pleasure of hearing a very elevating speech to-day. On behalf of you all, I desire to convey the thanks of all of us to Prof. Ranade.

ADDENDA

The order of the Padas and Dohas in the Paramartha Sopana has been generally maintained in the Pathway. But there are three major changes which are noted below :—

PADAS

Original order in the 'Paramartha Sopana'		Changed order in the 'Pathway'	
1. करनी बिन कथनी	II–10	करनी बिन कथनी	II–3
2. झीनी झीनी बीनी	II–8	झीनी झीनी बीनी	IV–12

DOHAS

3. हीरा तहाँ न खोलिए	V–6	हीरा तहाँ न खोलिए	V–28

As regards the minor changes, in the case of the Padas in the Paramatha Sopana, Nos.—I–10, IV–15, IV–17, V–17, V–16 become respectively in the Pathway I–9, IV–17; IV–19, V–16, V–17; and in the case of the Dohas in the Paramartha Sopana, Nos.—II–14, II–15, V–14, V–21, V–33, V–34 become respectively in the Pathway II–15, II–14, V–12, V–19, V–34, V–33.

ERRATA

Page	13	Line	26	read	सत्य एष प्रवोधे
,,	21	,,	28	,,	is one and a half
,,	39	,,	14	,,	cornered for concerned
,,	80	,,	23	,,	Surdas for Tulsidas
,,	88	,,	24	,,	enumeration
,,	139	,,	16, 24	,,	dɔes
,,	139	,,	12	,,	produces
,,	161	,,	4	,,	अव भी नहीं विगड़ा है कुछ
,,	170	,,	12	,,	अगर है शौक मिलनेका
,,	174	,,	3	,,	such
,,	177	,,	15–16	,,	onomatopoeically
,,	182	,,	25	,,	Chāṇakya
,,	183	,,	20	,,	buffets
,,	231	,,	27	,,	God-intoxication
,,	233	,,	17	,,	is psychic energy
,,	234	,,	3	,,	turmoil
,,	251	,,	29	,,	सुवर्नज्योतोः
,,	286	,,	6	,,	author
,,	307	,,	12	,,	identical
,,	319	,,	20	,,	Apsaras
,,	326	,,	1	,,	Vice-Chancellor's
,,	335	,,	1	,,	Reality
,,	346	,,	4	,,	proving
,,	380	,,	1	,,	by a sort of

General Introduction

I

CRITERIA OF MYSTICAL EXPERIENCE

Preliminary.

" These three Indian languages only I know in the original–Marathi, Kannada and Hindi – and I have planned out three volumes. I have already published one on Maharashtra Mysticism, the next is the present volume on Hindi Mysticism, and the third is in the course of preparation and publication, a couple of chapters of which have been published in the Karnatak University. " This was what the present writer said in his lecture on the Culmination of Spiritual Experience in Hindi Saints, at the Rashtrapati Bhavan, in March 1952. It has been a long-cherished aim of the present writer to gather the multi-coloured flowers of the mystic garden, and to present a garland of them to the Lord. It has been also his ambition to write a general work on the Pathway to God with reference to the Philosophies and Religions of the East and the West, to which subject he has devoted the major part of his life. The three volumes mentioned above, along with the three works, Upanishadic Philosophy, the Bhagvadgita, and the Vedanta, which have been either already produced or are in contemplation, will certainly supply material to that subject from the Indian side. The mystics of all ages and countries have spoken the same language, as they are denizens of the same spiritual world. There are no racial, no communal, no national prejudices among them. Time and Space have nothing to do with the eternal and infinite character of their mystical experience. These together constitute a band of divine musicians, each contributing his own note, and all together producing a harmony that is wonderful.

Intuitional Character.

Mysticism denotes that attitude of mind which involves a direct, immediate, intuitive apprehension of God. It signifies the highest attitude of which man is capable, namely, a beatific contemplation of God, and its dissemination in the Society and the World. The surest criterion of mysticism is the reality of the experience as enjoyed by the mystic himself. It is known only to him and to his Maker. Before it there is no appeal; for it there is no criterion. It is this personal-divine aspect of a mystic's spiritual realisation which stamps it with a peculiar halo and worth. It is in this sense that mystical experience has been regarded as ineffable. It has been very often supposed that, for mystical experience, no separate faculty like intuition need be requisitioned, but that intellect, feeling, and will might suffice to enable us to have a full experience of God. Now it is a matter of common knowledge that even for heights to be reached in artistic, scientific, or poetic activity, a certain amount of direct, immediate, intuitive contact with Reality is required. Far more is this the case in the matter of mystical experience. Intuition, far from contradicting intelligence, feeling, or will, does penetrate and lie at the back of them all. Intuition would not deny to Mysticism a title to philosophy if intellect requires it. As it connotes a determinative effort towards the acquisition of reality, it implies a definite, prolonged, and continuous exercise of the will. As feeling brings the subject and object into more intimate contact than any other psychological process, it also becomes a vital part of the process of realisation. Thus it seems that intelligence, will, and feeling are all necessary in the case of mystical endeavour. Only intuition must back them all. It is this unique character of mystical experience, namely, its intuitive and ineffable character which has served to make all God-aspiring humanity "a common and hidden society", the laws of which are known to themselves, if at all.

The Intellectual aspect.

We have seen above how mystical experience involves the full operation of the intuitive faculty which subsumes under it the operations of intellect, will, and feeling and is not contradictory of them. We must say that that kind of mystical experience must be invalid, which does not tend to an intellectual clarification of thought. A man who is labouring under delusions, a man who is likely to suffer from hallucinations, a man who is pathologically neural, can never hope to attain to real mystical experience. A man who aspires after the mystical life must have a penetrating and unfaltering intellect; he must also have a powerful philosophic imagination. It is not without reason that great mystics like Śankaracharya and Yajnavalkya, Plotinus and Spinoza, St. Paul and Augustine, Jnaneshwar and Kabir have produced the great intellectual works that have lived after them. We must say about these works that they enjoy a certain amount of immortality, and they can never perish so long as the world prizes their inner mystic fibre. Accurate intellectual thought, among other things, which will compel philosophical assent and admiration, is a sure accompaniment of mystical experience. It is true that there are temperamental differences between mystics, as there are temperamental differences between ordinary men. Not all mystics need be philosophers; not all mystics need lead a life of emotion; not all mystics be activists; but wherever true Mysticism is, one of these faculties must predominate; and unless we see in a mystic a full-fledged exercise of at least one of these faculties, we may not say that he is entitled to the name of a mystic at all. Hence intellectual power and absolute clarity of thought seem to be the primary criterion of mystical experience.

The moral aspect.

Another criterion of the reality of mystical experience is its capacity for the definite moral development of the individual and society. It has been urged by critics of Mysticism that it tends on the one hand to a life of a-moralism, and on the other, to a life of quietism. Dean Inge has said that those schools of Philosophy which are most in sympathy with Mysticism have been, on the whole, ethically weak; and he instances as a case in point what he calls Oriental Pantheism,–as if it stands in a category apart,–which regards all things as equally divine, and obliterates the distinction between right and wrong (Studies of English Mystics, p. 31). Also Dean Inge's denial of the title of a Mystic to Thomas à Kempis, because the latter teaches quietism, can be hardly justified. Now it is to be remembered that this criticism of Mysticism comes from Dean Inge who is more of a mystic than anything else; and a mystic saying that Mysticism starves the moral sense is only throwing stones at a glass-house in which he is himself living. On the other hand, we find that a true life of Mysticism teaches a full-fledged morality in the individual, and a life of general good in the world. If we go to Plotinus, we find the same perfection of moral virtues in mystical life insisted on. "The vision", he tells us, "is not to be regarded as unfruitful. In this state the perfect soul begets – like God himself – beautiful thoughts and beautiful virtues" (Enneads, 6.9.9).

St. John of the Cross teaches that "in a truly mystical life, a knowledge of God and His attributes overflows into the understanding from the contact with Him, and the soul is admitted to the knowledge of wisdom and grace, and the gifts and powers of God, whereby it is made so beautiful and rich" (Cant. 14.16.24.2). So far as the utility of the mystic to the society is concerned, we may almost take it to be a truism, and a mystic who is not of supreme service to the society is not a mystic at all. It is true that here again there are temperamental differences among mystics. One mystic may choose more or less to be of a Quietistic, and another of an Activistic type. But the fact remains that in either case he is of supreme service to humanity by calling their attention from moment to moment to the perfection and greatness of God. There have been mystics, who, like Aristotle's God, have moved the world by their divine contemplation. Unmoved themselves, they have become men of a world-shaking type. Rufus Jones narrates how Mystics have their consciousness invaded by the inrush of a large life : "Sometimes they have seemed to push a door into a larger range of being with vastly heightened energy. Their experience has been always one of joy and rapture. In fact, it is probably the highest joy of which a man is capable. Energy to live by actually does come to them from somewhere, and the Universe backs the experience" (Studies in Mystical Religion. p. xxx).

It has been occasionally contended by certain writers that mysticism has got nothing to do with a life of emotions. If, by a life of emotions, these people, on the one hand, mean a sombre and melancholy, or on the other, a buoyant and boisterous sentimentalism, we entirely agree with what these people say. But if they deny to a mystic the possession or use of emotions in their refined, pure, and "Deiform" state, we entirely disagree with them. In fact, if we take the trouble of reading the account of emotions given by Tulsidas, or Surdas and Eknath or Tukaram, we may be sure that the life of emotions is almost a *sine quâ non* of mystical experience. In fact, no mystical experience is possible unless we have a plenitude of finer emotions, all turned to the experience of God. A mystical life so far from being un-emotional is, we must say, supremely emotional; only the emotions ought to be exercised and kept under control by intellect. Otherwise, a mystic would tend either to be an extreme L'Allegro, or on the other hand, an extreme Il Penseroso. When Spinoza said that emotions must be transmuted into an intellectual love of God, he said most accurately what is needed in a true life of Mysticism.

The Emotional aspect.

We cannot close this section, however, without touching upon a point of vital importance, namely, that of the epistemological character of the reality of mystical experience. This of course would require a

Universality and Validity.

fuller treatment than we can afford to give it in this brief introduction but we can at least see how this criterion would work. The cumulative experience of the mystics of the East and the West would prove that there is a certain amount of universality in their mystical experience. They have the same teaching about the Name of God, the fire of Devotion, the nature of Self-realisation, and so forth, and it is due only to an overweening superciliousness that certain people might regard the mystics of one country or religion, as different from, or superior to, the mystics of other lands or faiths. If all men are equal before God, and if men have got the same ‘ Deiform faculty ’, which enables them to ‘ see God face to face ’, then there is no meaning in saying that there is a difference between the quality of God-realisation in some, as contrasted with the quality of God-realisation in others. It is true that there may be physical, mental and temperamental differences, but there is no difference in the quality of their mystical or intuitive realisation. It is this element of Universality, which, as Kant contends, would confer upon mystical experience objectivity, necessity and validity. We suppose that the objectivity and necessity conferred by mystical experience is even of a higher order than that of any other kind of human experience just because it is ‘ Deiform ’. It is this element of divinity in it that makes it so supremely compelling and valid.

II

CHIEF CHARACTERISTICS OF THE GREAT HINDI SAINTS.

Summary View.

It will not be out of place to give here a short account of the chief mystical teachings of the great Hindi saints treated of in this volume. We may conveniently divide these Saints into the following groups for our treatment in this brief introduction. We shall begin with the account of Kabir, Tulsidas, Surdas and Mirabai separately in that order, as these four constitute the major Hindi saints. After discussing the chief contributions to mystical experience which they have made, we shall proceed to another group, namely, that of Ramanand, Raidas and Nanak. Ramanand is evidently connected with Kabir, and Raidas was his disciple. Nanak comes in next, because he seems to have been influenced by the teachings of Kabir, as is evident from the large number of songs from Kabir which he has quoted in his Granth-Sahib. We next come to the continuance of the Kabirite teaching in Dharamdas, Charandas and Dadu, each of whom seems to be revelling in his own form of mystical experience. We then proceed to the two great saints of the Natha School, Matsyendranath and Gorakhnath. These should have been taken up earlier, but we wanted to show first the development of the Kabirite tradition in a continuous way. Matsyendranath exactly like the criticism which Bunyan passes upon sleep. The robbers of Krishnanand and the doleful creatures of Bunyan might verily be our tumultuous and turbulent passions.

Krishnanand further tells us that we have come into this world for buying and selling merchandise — he means spiritual merchandise — but we have not been successful in our transaction :

जिस कारज को जो तू आया
सौदा वह कछु कर ना पाया
यही बड़ा अफसोस

This reminds us of the celebrated passage in Pythagoras, in which he speaks of the three kinds of vocation being open to us. In this fair of life, he says, some people come to buy and sell. These are the economists. Others come to engage themselves in games. These are the politicians. Still others come simply to look on (theorein). These are the philosophers. What is the use of coming into this world if we are not able to visualise God ? Bacon has also lent his support to this doctrine of Pythagoras saying that in this mortal fair, our only profit should be God. Everything, in other words, except the pursuit of God is a vanity.

Finally, Krishnanand tells us that our proper business here below is to go back to our Maker in the same pure condition in which we came. "Trailing clouds of glory do we come from God, who is freedom in the manner of William James, his acute observations in regard to the question of the forefulfilment of a devotee's desires, and his suggestion that the Saint might be regarded as the Personal, and God as the Impersonal aspect of Reality, might easily be taken to be his chief contributions to a Philosophy of Mysticism. Kabir surpasses other Hindi saints in his description of the spiritual Teacher with his moral, mystical and social qualities. He has laid great stress on the importance of the Name of God. He would require us to meditate in silence and not call upon God in a loud tone; he would also advise us to meditate internally and by the help of the breath, and one of the tests for the reality of our spiritual development would, according to him, be that the Name would reveal itself before our vision or audition. Kabir lays stress on intense concentration by the aspirant,—a point which he elaborates with many apt illustrations. In his account of the technique of meditational practice, he describes the spiritual Charkha, the sole intent of the plying of which is for the propitiation of the Master. It is noteworthy that Kabir illustrates in himself a combination of the tough-minded and the tender-minded types, so far as the description of the Dark Night of the Soul is concerned. Kabir's doctrine of the inter-communicativeness of the senses in the mystical sphere, as contrasted with their inter-incommunicativeness in the physiological sphere, marks him out as an acute physiological and mystical observer. His account of various supersensuous experiences, such as those of sound, light, form, and colour, in addition to motor and tactual experiences, is very illuminating. According to him, the end of spiritual endeavour should be to realise not only the divine music but the Musician also. Kabir had likewise that extraordinary experience, namely that of flavourism, which involves the enjoyment of divine juice during or after the state of meditation. Kabir's description of the allied state of God-intoxication is evidently the result of Sufistic influence on him. His concept of Māyā as a great temptress is ample proof of the influence of Vedanta on him. The great Māyā, who tempts everyone, cannot tempt Kabir, as he has caught hold of the rope of Shabda, and, by its help, has been able to cross the river of existence. The great stress which he lays on the metaphysical and epistemological significance of Shabda is highly philosophic. Finally, the highest watermark of liberation in Kabir, his concept of the बेहद or Infinite, marks him out as a philosophic mystic of the first order.

Tulsidas.

Tulsidas would take the first place among those who have enriched Hindi spiritual literature by their poetical imagination, moral and devotional fervour, and philosophic insight. It has been said that there is scarcely a house in Europe where there is no copy of the Bible. Similarly, it may be said that there is scarcely a house in U. P. or Northern India generally, where there is no copy of the Tulsi-Ramayana. The great philosophical insight of Tulsidas could be easily seen in his insistence on the impossibility of understanding fully the architectonic skill of God. His statement that we must transcend the considerations of reality, unreality, and real unreality is a very high watermark of philosophic speculation. Tulsidas narrates how the vision of God reacts on the Saints and binds them all together in a common bond of God-love. With extraordinary moral imagination, Tulsidas compares Jnana to a lamp which burns, and Bhakti to a jewel which illumines. Tulsidas is unique in his formulation of the new nine kinds of Bhakti, the apex of which all is Rama Bharosa. As a philosophy of Emergence based upon Gestalt would look upon the whole as more than the sum of its parts, similarly, Tulsidas views God as a Spiritual Gestalt, who is more than the sum of the different aspects in which he is viewed by his different devotees. His remarkable exposition of the relation between such fundamental conceptions as Nama, Rupa, Saguna, Nirguna and Dhyana, marks him out as a thinker of a very high order. His insistence on the Name as the symbol of ultimate Reality, even the "noumenon" itself, and his highly philosophic statement, in Spinozistic fashion, that Name and Form are only the Attributes of God may be regarded as Tulsidas's great contributions to Indian philosophic thought. Like many other philosophers he regarded God as अन्तर्यामिन्, but at the same time he has no difficulty in calling God a बहिर्यामिन् also, a word which he uses for the first time, and in a unique sense in the History of Indian Philosophy. He emphasises the impossibility of perceiving the unperceivable God. Hence his apostrophe to the Tongue to sing God's name, and his consequent contribution to physiology and psychology in this connection is highly remarkable. His insistence on one-pointed devotion to God, like that of a Chataka, which would brave all dangers for the sake of God, and in fact his whole Chataka Chautisā may be taken to be a remarkable contribution to the philosophy of devotion. Finally, though we do not find many great mystical utterances in Tulsidas, he sometimes uses expressions almost in a mystical sense, as in his transcendent description of God as moving without feet and touching without hands, seeing without eyes and hearing without ears.

Surdas.

Surdas, with powerful and appropriate analogies, discusses the question of Illusionism. The Kantian problem of the contradictions of merit and reward, the consideration of the ravages of Death, and his consequent prayer to God to save him from helpless submission to Death, become for Surdas the chief incentives to his spiritual life. Surdas is most remarkable for his lyrical and devotional poetry. Consider, for example, his analogies of the sparrow and the elephant, in the midst of their agonies, calling upon God for helpful succour. In Yajnavalkyan fashion, he advo cates a eudaemonistic combination of material and spiritual welfare. His doctrine of supersensuous experience, as, for example, in the case of a blind man being able to visualise as due to the power and grace of God, as well as his other two doctrines of the internal perception of God, and of God's being caught up in every fibre of the devotee's body, are excellent illustrations of spiritual experience.

Mirabai.

Mirabai's description of her Dark Night of the Soul, her offer to ascend the funeral pyre and reduce her body to ashes, if necessary, as well as her vivid account, after the spiritual dawn, of her having come into possession of the jewel of God, as well as her unexcellable description of the spiritual Holi with its riot of sound and colour, have left a deep impression on Hindi spiritual literature. To add to this, we might say that her two other doctrines, namely, the doctrine of the 'Theos' becoming a 'Pantheos' as in the case of the Gopis, as well as her doctrine of Approximationism are enough to outwit the intellect of any technical philosopher.

Ramanand, Raidas, Nanak.

The philosopher-mystic Ramanand in his brilliant discussion of the nature of God describes both the internal immanence and the universal pervasiveness of God. He may be taken to be one of the few mystics who combines in himself the experiences of smell and colour. The various poetical analogies which Raidas employs for describing the relation of Saint and God, his philosophic statement about the futility of waving lights before the Omnipresent Being, and above all his daring account of his sinlessness, which enables him to dispense with the forgiveness of God, have made him a thinker of almost the first magnitude. Nanak, whose collection of devotional songs in the Granth-Sahib is a permanent beacon-light of spirit, is at his best in earnest appeal for turning every moment of our life to spiritual use, as well as in his description of the multifarious efficacy of the company of the saints. By a philosophico-mystical insight, he sees the unity of the internal and the external God, as well as perceives God in all things and all things in God.

Dharamdas, Charandas, Dadu.

Dharamdas, who in his later life became the head of an important Kabirite centre, speaks of the different kinds of supersensuous experience, such as thunder and lightning, the spiritual bath and the mellifluous juice. Charandas describes the valuelessness of words without action. He next proceeds to depict the marks of Brahminhood, and says "he alone deserves to be called a Brahmin who has realised Brahman, and who spends all his time in spiritual contemplation." His experience of God as not merely appearing to his vision wherever the eye may be cast, but also as talking with him, moving with him, and eating with him, is something very peculiar in the history of mystical experience. Dadu, who is supposed to have been the disciple of Kamal, excels in his description of a Kafir, who, he says, is an embodiment of vices like untruth, deceit, and a disbelief in God. In a philosophico-moral spirit, he prays to the Lord to keep him ever on the right path. His prayer in this connection may be regarded as a philosophical instead of a lyrical prayer as in Surdas. We also see some high mystical elements in his conceptions of the spiritual Charkha and the Divine Juice.

Matsyendra and Gorakh.

Matsyendranath, the founder of the Natha School examines the bona fides of ritualism, the pursuit of mere Yoga, intellectualism and mere moralism, and determines their proper place in the meditational process. Gorakhnath has been regarded as the most famous of the Nath School because from him descended Gahininath and Jnaneshvar, one of the greatest mystics of India and the world. True to his lineage, Gorakhnath excels in describing various Yogic attainments, but also sees the limitations of them, and ultimately pants for the vision of God who is to him identical with his Guru Matsyendranath.

Mansur and Rahim.

We next proceed to the two great Muslim saints Mansur and Rahim. Mansur advises us to reject all ceremonial ritualism, and advocates the Anal-Haq method of meditation. His description of the travail of unison is most remarkable and pathetic, when he is having the vision of God in his anguish at the stake. Rahim, the famous poet-moralist of Akbar's time, who might probably be regarded as the greatest Doha writer of Hindi, barring of course Kabir, tells us how, in Herakleitian manner, 'flux' may be regarded as the most important incentive to spiritual life, how a morally acquired character is not capable of being influenced by any bad company, how in the alternative between egoism and devotionalism, between self and God, the latter is necessarily to the chosen, how the highest end of the accumulation of wealth-material or spiritual-is for the betterment and upliftment of humanity, how when the mind is full of the idea of God no rambling idea dare enter, and how in Upanishadic manner those who say they know do not know, and those who say they do not know are alone likely to know. As a lyrical Doha-writer Rahim does not seem to be inferior either to Tulsidas or Surdas. The Chataka of Tulsidas, the Sparrow of Surdas, and the Chakora of Rahim, which are their symbols as God's Elect, are on the same level so far as their intense and unfaltering devotion to God is concerned.

Gulal and Bahiro.

The poet-saint Gulal in his post-ecstatic ejaculation calls on us to sing the auspicious cradle song of self-realisation (*Anubhava Mangala*) in the Hindola Raga. Bahiro, using another significant Raga, the Pahāḍi, sings the song of Liberation with five different notes, each rising in pitch above the other, and all terminating in a crescendo of absolute self-surrender to the Will of God.

III
THANKS

I must thank very heartily His Highness Shrimant Chintamanrao Appasaheb, K. C. I. E., K. C. S. I., Rajasaheb of Sangli, for his great generosity in founding the Adhyatma Vidya Mandir in 1947, on behalf of the Ganapati Sansthana, to which is entirely due the credit for the preparation and printing of this and the companion volume. Adhyatma Parishads at various centres such as Allahabad, Sangli, Dharwar and Belgaum, were established on behalf of the Adhyatma Vidya Mandir, for bringing together all those who are interested in a philosophical investigation of the problem of God, irrespective of community or nationality, race or creed. Of course, it takes time for such institutions to gather momentum, and even though a good deal of lecturing work was accomplished in the interim at the different centres with the help of various scholars, works like these could be published only after a good deal of labour, and the passage of time. I have to express my most sincere thanks to Justice Shankar Sharan who helped us greatly as the President of the Adhyatma Parishad, Allahabad, and to Pandit Devi Prasad Shukla, the Convener of the Parishad, for putting so much life in the activities of the Adhyatma Parishad. Justice

S. K. Dar, Justice Mathur, Justice P. N. Sapru, Justice Harishchandra, Justice Agarwal, Dr. M. H. Syed, and Principal Sanjiva Rao, have greatly co-operated with the activities of the Adhyatma Parishad at Allahabad. Under the auspices of the Parishad many distinguished public men, amongst whom may be mentioned Dr. Radhakrishnan, Dr. K. N. Katju, Shri M. S. Aney, Shri R. R. Diwaker, Mr. S. S. Nehru, I. C. S., Dr. K. S. Krishnan, Swami Nikhilanand, Rt. Rev. Dr. Raymond, Bishop of Allahabad, and others, delivered learned and illuminating lectures. In the same series, and as Visiting Professor of the Madan Mohan Malaviya College, Allahabad, the present writer delivered lectures which constitute the major part of the present work. I owe more obligations than I can express to my respected friend Pandit Devi Prasad Shukla, Principal of the Madan Mohan Malaviya College, Allahabad, who read the entire type-script with me, and without whose continuous help and constant co-operation, not to speak of his incessant goading for the early completion of this work, the present volume could scarcely have seen the light of day so soon. The expositions of some of the Padas have been taken from the lectures I delivered at the Rashtrapati Bhavan and the Constitution Club in New Delhi in March 1952. Two chapters of this book, namely, Part I chapter III, and Part II chapter IV, were delivered as lectures in the All-India Radio, Allahabad, and then appeared in the Sunday issues of the Leader, for which I feel heartily indebted to both. My most sincere thanks are due to the late Shri Ram Nathan, who attended the Adhyatma Parishad Meetings, Allahabad, and prepared the reports of my lectures for the Press. I have also to thank heartily my nephew Prof. N. G. Damle, M. A., Poona, my friend Prof. T. K. Devlalkar, M. SC., Amalner, and my former student Prof. K. V. Gajendragadkar, M. A., Nasik, for rendering help of various kinds. I am greatly indebted to Shrimant Tatyasaheb Patwardhan, Rajasaheb of Miraj, for the kind interest he took in the publication of this volume. My sincere thanks are also due to Shri K. D. Sangoram, B. A., LL. B. Pleader, Athni, who helped towards the same purpose. I am much indebted to Shri D. P. Shintre, Stenographer, Nasik, for his untiring efforts and unabating zeal in taking down the dictation notes, and preparing the entire type-script for the Press. Mr. B. R. Kulkarni, M. A., my former student, and now Lecturer at the R. P. D. College, Belgaum, gave me help in the preparation of the Introduction, the Authorwise Index of Subjects, and the General Index. Mr. Pralhad H. Kulkarni, M. A., also a former student of mine, helped me in finally preparing, as well as checking, the Index of Sources of this volume. Shri Mohan Lal, M. A., Lecturer at Jasvant College, Jodhpur, has helped in preparing the Errata for this volume. The extraordinary pains which, with predominantly spiritual interest, Shri G. V. Tulpule, M. A., Secretary,

Adhyatma Vidya Mandir, Sangli, and Shri S. N. Deshpande, M. A., B. Sc., Manager, Ganapati Sansthan Press, Sangli, have taken in rendering help of all kinds, and carefully reading the proofs of the entire volume, are beyond all praise. Finally, I must express my hearty thanks to Shri S. J. Joshi, M. A., Retired Assistant Professor of the Banaras University, for reading the final proofs with me, and helping me in various other ways.

R. D. RANADE

PATHWAY TO GOD IN HINDI LITERATURE.

TABLE OF CONTENTS

1. General Introduction
   - (i) Criteria of Mystical Experience
   - (ii) Chief Characteristics of the great Hindi Saints
   - (iii) Thanks.
2. Table of Contents
3. Group–Headings

PART I

4. The Pathway in Pada Literature			1–265
Chapter	I	Incentives to Spiritual Life	1– 47
Chapter	II	The Necessity of Moral Preparation	48– 97
Chapter	III	The Relation of God to Saints	98–133
Chapter	IV	The Beginnings of the Pilgrimage	134–188
Chapter	V	The Highest Ascent	189–265

PART II

5. The Pathway in Doha Literature			269–405
Chapter	I	Incentives to Spiritual Life	269–280
Chapter	II	The Necessity of Moral Preparation	281–299

	Chapter III	The Relation of God to Saints	300–330
	Chapter IV	The Beginnings of the Pilgrimage	333–365
	Chapter V	The Highest Ascent	366–405
6.	Index of Sources		1—5
7.	Index of Subjects		6–10
8.	General Index		11ff.

GROUP-HEADINGS

PART I: PADAS

Group Numbers.			Source Numbers.

First Chapter

INCENTIVES TO SPIRITUAL LIFE

Group I	...	Illusion, Blindness and Sleep.	1—3
Group II	...	The Philosophical and the Ethical impetus.	4—5
Group III	...	Consciousness of Sin.	6—7
Group IV	...	Old age and Death.	8–10
Group V	...	Transmigration and Metempsychosis.	11–12
Group VI	...	Helplessness in Life's experience.	I3
Group VII	...	The way of escape.	14–15

Second Chapter

THE NECESSITY OF MORAL PREPARATION

Group I	...	Ungodliness, the root of all vice.	1—3
Group II	...	Who is a Kafir, a Fakir, and a Brahmin?	4—6
Group III	...	God, the source of all Virtue.	7—8
Group IV	...	Virtue in action.	9
Group V	...	God-devotion as superior to mere intellect or morality.	10–15

Third Chapter

THE RELATION OF GOD TO SAINTS

Group I	...	God in Ramanand and Kabir, Tulsidas and Mirabai, Raidas and Nanak.	1—8
Group II	...	Philosophical Prayers as in Dadu, Raidas, and Tulsidas.	9–11
Group III	...	Lyrical Prayers as in Surdas and Bahiro.	12–17

Fourth Chapter

THE BEGINNINGS OF THE PILGRIMAGE

Group I ... The Guru and his moral and spiritual characteristics. 1-3

Group II ... The Name and its relation to Form. 4-6

Group III ... Five points in the Methodology of Meditation. 7—12

Group IV ... The place of yoga and Absolutism in the Meditational Process. 13—14

Group V ... The two attitudes ; the militant and the submissive. 15—16

Group VI ... The Dark Night and the Dawn. 17—19

Fifth Chapter

THE HIGHEST ASCENT

Group I ... Varieties of Supersensuous Experience :

1. Mirabai. 1—3
2. Surdas and Tulsidas. 4—6
3. Gorakhanath, Dharamdas, and Yari. 7—10
4. Ekanath and Mahipati. 11—12

Group II ... Physiological, Psychological and Moral Effects of God-Realisation : Charandas. 13—14

Group III ... Sublimity and Ineffability of mystical experience : Kabir. 15—17

Group IV ... Flavourism and Beatification :

1. Kabir, 2. Dadu. 18—20

Group V ... God-intoxication :

Kabir. 21—24

Group VI ... Lifting of the cosmic deceit :

Kabir. 25—26

Group VII ... Ecstacy, and the sustenance of the world :
1. Maula, 2. Sakha. 27—28
Group VIII ... Post-ecstatic ejaculations :
1. Gulal, 2. Naraharinath, 3. Raidas. 29—32
Group IX ... Apostleship and prophethood :
Kabir. 33—34

PART II: DOHAS

First Chapter

INCENTIVES TO SPIRITUAL LIFE

Group I ... Perpetual Flux. 1—3
Group II ... Decrepitude and Death. 4—6

Second Chapter

THE NECESSITY OF MORAL PREPARATION

Group I ... Spiritual welfare and Material welfare. 1
Group II ... The place of Company in Spiritual Life. 2—4
Group III ... Fine arts and Mysticism. 5—6
Group IV ... Charity. 7—9
Group V ... Devotion to God in its Individual, Social, and Spiritual aspects. 10—12
Group VI ... Suffering as the ladder to God. 13—15

Third Chapter

THE RELATION OF GOD TO SAINTS

Group I ... Sainthood, a rare phenomenon. 1—2
Group II ... The immano-transcendence of God. 3—4
Group III ... The ascending stages of Tulsidas's philosophy of devotion. 5

Group IV ... The office of God for the Saints. 6—11
Group V ... The Saint as Personal and God as Impersonal Reality. 12—14

Fourth Chapter

THE BEGINNINGS OF THE PILGRIMAGE

Group I ... The nature and function of a Guru. 1—5
Group II ... Meditation by means of the Name. 6—10
Group III ... The function and power of the Name. 11—13
Group IV ... The physical requisites of Meditation. 14—16
Group V ... The mental requisites. 17—19
Group VI ... The moral requisites. 20—24
Group VII ... The mystical requisites. 25—27
Group VIII ... A devotee's passionate longing for God. 28—30

Fifth Chapter

THE HIGHEST ASCENT

Group I ... The Psychology of Spiritual Experience. 1—5
Group II ... The music and the Musician. 6—8
Group III ... Shabda as "Substance." 9—11
Group IV ... Visual experience : morphic and photic. 12—14
Group V ... Other super-sensuous experiences. 15—17
Group VI ... Realisation of the Self. 18—21
Group VII ... Motor and Tactual experience. 22—24
Group VIII ... The Travail of Unison. 25—26
Group IX ... The Moral marks of the God-realiser. 27—32
Group X ... Liberation, Beatification, and Infinitude. 33—35

PART ONE

Pathway to God in

PADAS

CHAPTER I

Incentives to Spiritual Life.

If we make a comparative study of the philosophies and religions of the world, and especially of the lives and teachings of those, who, in the various stages of humanity, and in different ages and lands, have walked on the path of God, we shall see that there are certain broad characteristics common to the pathway which they have all trodden in the attainment of God. These might for convenience sake be summarised under five heads. First, there are certain incentives which prompt men to spiritual life — philosophical, axiological and physiological. Then, there is the question of moral and spiritual preparation which they must tackle before they can hope to advance on the pathway. Thirdly, they have to keep before themselves certain exemplars of conduct and attainment, which they must necessarily follow. This they cannot do unless they have defined to themselves, both theoretically and practically, the nature and functions of God in relation to the exemplars above mentioned. When the relationship between the exemplars and God has been defined, they have to tread the path themselves, before they can be convinced about the reality of the experiences of those who have gone before them. Finally, after having walked on the pathway for a long time, and through travails and turmoils of body and mind, of nature and society, they can envisage to themselves certain landmarks, certain lamp-posts, which will help them to walk with courage and confidence on the pathway to God, and attain to the highest ideal they have been seeking.

In the present volume on the Pathway to God in Hindi Literature, we shall be concerned with these five chief topics which have characterised the pursuit, in the attainment of God, of seekers in the Hindi provinces, as they have also characterised that of the seekers in other provinces of India, as well as other parts of the world. We shall first state in brief the different incentives which have prompted the Hindi saints to the pursuit of the spiritual ideal. In the first place, there are the questions of the pursuit of illusions, of blindness to reality, and of sleeping while waking, which have been stressed by a number of thinkers all over the world. After this, comes the great philosophical question of the architechtonic skill which has been exhibited by God in the creation and governance of the world, and which fills the aspirant with wonder and awe and a sense of determination for the realisation of the ideal to which it points. This would be probably the cosmo-teleological approach to the determination of the nature of God. After this philosophical approach, we have to tackle the ethical approach also, especially from the side of the relationship of works to recompense. These questions have received the highest priority from philosophers and moralists, especially from Kant. After this philosophical and ethical approach, we have to consider the question of sin, whose existence we find in the lives of men and in society. Those, who want to evolve an incentive to spiritual life through the consideration of sin, are necessarily prompted to seek thenceforth a life which will be for ever beyond its pale. After the consideration of sin, come the questions of old age and death, which are very peremptory considerations, very positive facts, which lead a man Godward. Immediately after the question of death, we stand face to face with the questions of transmigration and metempsychosis, a determination of the nature of which, in Nachiketian fashion, also prompts us to pursue the spiritual ideal. The last incentive we shall discuss in the present chapter is the incentive of helplessness in life's experience, which will instil into the mind of man the conception of a Power altogether beyond the range of his own impotent reflection. A consideration of all these incentives may throw a gleam of light before the eye of the spiritual seeker, and he may find that unless he resigns himself completely to the will of this Omnipotent Being, it may not be possible for him to pursue the spiritual path steadfastly, courageously and successfully.

1. *Illusion, Blindness and Sleep.*— Coming to a detailed treatment of the incentives, we shall first discuss the question of illusionism as an incentive to spiritual life. Now, illusion is a simple word and has been made great use of by the Vedantic writers. What it fully implies, what its ultimate nature is, whether it may be justified in the last resort or not, are questions which we may not discuss here, but must leave to the Vedantists and Philosophers all over the world. We shall first discuss how Surdas deals with the question of illusion in his famous song धोखें ही धोखे डहकायो. If we analyse the song, we shall see that there are six ideas which Surdas stresses: sensuality, greed, pursuit of vanities, illusionism proper, loss of God, and subjection to death. Now, Surdas is a poet of great analogical imagination, and uses very powerful and appropriate analogies from facts of every-day experience to fix these ideas firmly in our mind. "I was inextricably caught up," he says in the first place, "like a fly in the honey of insatiable sensual desires." With all its effort, the fly cannot get out of the

honey, when it is once caught in the sticky juice. "Like a monkey", again, says Surdas, "I danced in every quadrivial for a few grains of corn at the behest of my master-juggler, showing my covetousness and greed for the most trivial things in life. My next fault has been the pursuit of vanities. I have been verily in the position of a parrot, which is attracted by the beauty of the Shālmali fruit, and when it goes and pecks at the fruit, the soft cotton flies away, and it is left with a mere void. Like a deer, again, I have gone in pursuit of vain mirages. Not having known the real nature of a mirage as due to refraction of the Sun's rays through different densities of hot air, I pursued the mirage in the hope that it would give me water, but it was not able to quench my thirst. If I had taken a scientific view of things, I might not have pursued such a vain mirage. As a consequence of my pursuit of vanities, I lost my diamond in the very centre of my house : हरि-हीरा घर माँझ गँवायो. God was the diamond and my heart (हृद्देश) was the centre of the house I was living in, and my great misfortune was that I was not able to know that there was that diamond inside me. Also, it was because I could not find God inside me that I deliberately made myself a morsel in the mouth of the Boa of Death. The big Boa is ready to engulf every creature that goes near its opened mouth, and it was no wonder that

I was devoured and digested by the big Boa." It was thus, says Surdas, that I have fallen a prey to illusion after illusion during the whole of my earthly career.

As Surdas stresses the conception of illusionism to prove the futility of a man's effort to search out the Real in the world, Kabir in his famous song केहि समुझावौं सब जग अन्धा is stressing the conception of blindness. We are reminded of the Seventh Book of Plato's Republic, wherein Plato says that those who have their faces turned towards the wall are blind to the existence of Reality, while he alone, who has the power to escape out of the cave and look out in the sun, can know what Reality is. In the poem under consideration, Kabir advances five different ideas to enable us to escape from the clutches of blindness, namely, self-control, self-abnegation, transcendence of intellect, search of the pathway, and the grace of God to crown all self-effort. In fact, Kabir's poem सब जग अन्धा might be taken to be almost an epitome of spiritual life. A skilled horseman riding an unruly horse might suffer a fall at any moment, says Kabir. He uses his famous analogy of water and wind to designate the horse and the horseman; also, body and mind are to him in the same relationship. The Bhagavadgita has also compared mind to wind in the famous verse :

चञ्चलं हि मनः कृष्ण प्रमाथि बलवद् दृढम् ।
तस्याहं निग्रहं मन्ये वायोरिव सुदुष्करम् ॥

Kabir likewise points out that an uncontrolled mind riding an unruly body might cause a dangerous fall at any moment. A second characteristic, which is required for the search of the Real according to Kabir, is the virtue of absolute self-abnegation. Naked we come into this world, he says, and naked we pass away : जाय लङ्गोटी झारिके बन्दा. The loin-cloth is merely a temporary vesture. It is only he, who can rid his mind of all sense of possession, that can rise to the sense of the Real. The third characteristic is the transcendence of intellect. Howsoever powerful the lamp a blind man may carry in his hand, he will never be able to search out what he desires. A greater instrument than that of intellect is required to search out a higher faculty which might give us the vision of the Real. Fourthly, says Kabir, like Jnaneshwar also, (*Vide* the last paragraph of this chapter) "in this miserable world, which may well be compared to a forest in conflagration, the fool rushes hither and thither without finding a clue to get out of it." What is this clue? That is the secret of the spiritual life. Unless one possesses the clue, one might not know what the way out might be. Finally, howsoever powerful the effort a man might make, if nature and destiny conspire against him, he will find himself helpless before them, and nothing can rescue him except the grace of God. An oarsman, plying his boat in a torrential midstream, will be in a dangerous predicament, from which nothing can rescue him except the grace and power of God. Many times during the life of a man he finds all his efforts of no avail. It is in such a plight that he must call upon God to rescue him from the dangerous situations in which he might be placed. In this way alone could he escape from his blindness into the light of the Real.

The incentive, which the poet Krishnanand has in view in his poem मुसाफिर सोता है बेहोस in seeking the Real in a world of unreality, is the incentive of freedom from sleep. We are all sleeping in this world, says Krishnanand, even though we seem to be awake. The poet wants us not to sleep to the extent of being unconscious; for, who knows whether, pilgrims as we are, we may not be attacked by robbers, and thus lose all the capital which we may have brought ? The poet tells us that we have brought a great capital with us while coming into the world — by capital, he means the spiritual capital. It is questionable whether every man is conscious of the spiritual capital which he has brought with him. It is customary to suppose that we do bring such a capital with us, but its nature nobody is able to define. It is too much to believe that a child can have a vision of God in the mother's womb, or cry सोऽहं सोऽहं in order to show its identity with its maker. It is wonderful that a child, having had a vision of God in the mother's womb, might come out entirely unconscious of that vision in a few months' time. The story of Parīkshit, as the derivation of the word itself shows, that he was seeing God all around himself in his mother's womb, protecting him with His mighty disc from the treacherous missiles of the enemy, is a story more for mythology than for history or experience.

We have referred above in Krishnanand to the possibility of the pilgrim being attacked during his unconscious sleep by robbers. In a celebrated passage of his Pilgrim's Progress, Bunyan is also bewailing his habit of sleeping into his mind, cursing his sinful sleep, and saying that during that state he might be attacked by doleful creatures also. " O wretched man that I am", he says, "that I should so indulge the flesh, as to use that rest for ease to my flesh, which the Lord of the hill hath erected only for the relief of the spirits of pilgrims. Oh thou sinful sleep! how, for thy sake, am I like to be benighted in my journey, I must hear the noise of doleful creatures ranging in the night for their prey, and if they should meet with me in the dark, how should I shift them? How should I escape being by them torn to pieces?" Krishnanand's criticism of sleep, which he regards as a state of pseudo-happiness, is exactly like the criticism which Bunyan passes upon sleep. The robbers of Krishnanand and the doleful creatures of Bunyan might verily be our tumultuous and turbulent passions.

Krishnanand further tells us that we have come into this world for buying and selling merchandise — he means spiritual merchandise — but we have not been successful in our transaction :

जिस कारज को जो तू आया
सौदा वह कछु कर ना पाया
यही वड़ा अफ़सोस

This reminds us of the celebrated passage in Pythagoras, in which he speaks of the three kinds of vocation being open to us. In this fair of life, he says, some people come to buy and sell. These are the economists. Others come to engage themselves in games. These are the politicians. Still others come simply to look on (theorein). These are the philosophers. What is the use of coming into this world if we are not able to visualise God? Bacon has also lent his support to this doctrine of Pythagoras saying that in this mortal fair, our only profit should be God. Everything, in other words, except the pursuit of God is a vanity.

Finally, Krishnanand tells us that our proper business here below is to go back to our Maker in the same pure condition in which we came. "Trailing clouds of glory do we come from God, who is our Home". Let us similarly go back to our Home as trailing clouds of glory. Is it not wonderful that this poet Krishnanand, who is not much known to fame, should remind us of some of the brilliant thoughts of Bunyan, Pythagoras and Wordsworth ?

2. *The philosophical and the ethical impetus :*—After a consideration of the incentives of illusion, blindness and sleep, let us now proceed to the philosophical and ethical approach to the spiritual life. In a very celebrated poem in the Vinaya Patrika,

केशव कहि न जाय का कहिए ? ॥

we are told by Tulsidas that it is impossible to understand fully the architechtonic skill of the Creator. "The way in which you have constructed the world, O Creator," says Tulsidas, "passes beyond our comprehension. If we just look at the handi-work of God either in the macrocosm or in the microcosm, our imagination reels, and our mind remains enwrapped within itself (समुझि मनहि मन रहिए), so that any philosophical discussion of Thy powers becomes impossible." The greatness of the work of God, in short, says Tulsidas, is in effable. In fact, this comes very near to the cosmo teleogical argument in Kant, viz. the contempla tion either of the cosmical process or of the end to which the whole creation moves.

In the second place, Tulsidas tells us that this ephemeral world is like a picture drawn by an artist without hands, and without colours, on a wall which does not exist. This evidently is a conglomeration of impossibilities. Students of philosophy know the familiar definition of philosophy as the search by a blind man of a black cat in a dark place where it is not. So also in Plato we know that famous utterance in the Seventh Book of the Republic : an archer and no archer, aiming and not aiming, at a bird and no bird, sitting and not sitting, on a tree and no tree, killed it and did not kill it with an arrow and no arrow. These are evidently a plethora of contradictions. So, the artist without hands, painting without colours on a wall which does not exist, in Tulsidas is exactly like these. But we might call the attention of our readers to other parallels, e. g. take the following famous verse from a great Kashmiri poet :

निरुपादानसम्भारमभित्तावेव तन्वते ।
जगच्चित्रं नमस्तस्मै कलाश्लाघ्याय शूलिने ॥

This looks exactly like the prototype of Tulsidas's utterance, or Tulsidas might have even derived it from Vidyāraṇya's Panchadashi from the celebrated chapter on Chitradīp. This shows, incidentally, that Tulsidas was a great Sanskrit scholar also.

Thirdly, we are told by Tulsidas how a crocodile, living in the waters of a mirage, swallows without mouth all the animate and inanimate objects that go to partake of the water :

रवि-कर-नीर बसइ अति दारुन
मकर रूप तेहि माहीं
बदन-हीन सो ग्रसइ चराचर
पान करन जे जाहीं

An unreal cause might strike terror in the minds of the percipients, (न मरइ भीति, दुख पाइय यहि तनु हेरे), and thus produce real effects. What great parallels has this conception of Tulsidas in other religious and philosophical systems! For example, look at Shankaracharya. In the great Bhashya, which he has written on the Vedanta Sutras, he gives us an idea which is exactly like that of Tulsidas; or Tulsidas's idea, we might say, is exactly like that of Shankaracharya. That may be a better way of putting it, because Shankaracharya was about six centuries earlier than Tulsidas. A thing might be unreal, but the effect might be real. Shankaracharya says that the रज्जुसर्प might be unreal; but it might create a real terror in the mind of the man who will thus be taking to his heels. On the other hand, we are told by Shankaracharya in his शतश्लोकी how an unreal cause might produce a real and yet beneficial effect :

स्वप्ने मंत्रोपदेशः श्रवणपरिचितः सत्यएवं प्रबोधे ।

The Mantra, which a Guru may give to his disciple in a dream, may become real and fructuous during his life, as it did in the case of Tukaram. So, both from the side of bad effects and good effects, unreality may lead to reality. We have thus seen that these great writers such as Plato, Vidyaranya, Shankaracharya and the Kashmiri Poet, in order to befool the understandings of people and to tell them of the limited power of their intellect, dwell on contradictions, and say it is not by intellectual endeavour alone that we can hope to reach the Absolute.

The next point in Tulsidas is a very philosophic one, and I think almost beyond the comprehension of a mere Hindi writer who is not conversant with Sanskritic philosophy. Tulsidas tells us we must transcend the considerations of reality, unreality and real unreality. Some people say that the world is real; others say that it is unreal; yet others say that it is both real and unreal:

कोउ कह सत्य झूट कह कोऊ जुगल प्रबल करि मानै ।

But Tulsidas says that he has transcended all these delusions because he has realised the self: जो आपहि पहिचानै. It may be seen that we are preferring the reading तुलसिदास परिहरै तीनि भ्रम जो आपहि पहिचानै to the reading तुलसिदास परिहरै तीनिभ्रम सो आपहि पहिचानै. According to the one, only he can transcend the three delusions who has realised the self; according to the other, unless we have transcended the three delusions we cannot realise the self. This raises a very important philosophic question. How are the two things related — Transcendence of delusions and the Realisation of the self? Which is the cause and which is the effect? It may be said that the two are interdependent like the obverse and the reverse sides of the same coin, that neither could be achieved without the other, and that, if at all, the two are achieved simultaneously. If we were, however, to choose between the two alternatives, we would rather say that he who has realised the self will alone be able to transcend the delusions and nobody else.

Those, however, who have been technical students of the Vedanta Sutras know that this three-fold distinction cf reality, unreality and real unreality has a firm grounding in the Vedantic systems. Reality was aimed at by Ramanuja, unreality by Shankaracharya, and real unreality by Nimbarka. Many great scholars have spent their brains on the correct interpretation of the Sutra of Badarayana अहिकुण्डलवत् and discussed *ad nauseam* whether the serpent is real, or the coil is real, or both the serpent and the coil are equally real. All these doctrines Tulsidas sets aside and preaches a doctrine of Self-realisation.

Let us now proceed to consider a song from Surdas which gives us the ethical approach to the spiritual life : ऊधो धनि तुम्हरो बेवहार. The Gopis here are addressing Uddhava or Krishna, they do not know whom. Literally, the song seems to be addressed to Uddhava, really, it is addressed to Krishna. In fact, their minds were so confounded by the devotion they bore to Krishna that they could not distinguish between Uddhava and his Master; and they wanted to accuse Krishna of certain things which imply an incentive to spiritual life which we shall explain just now. "In the first place," the Gopis say, "O Uddhava, you are cutting down mango trees and planting prickly thorns. Wherever there is sandle-wood to be found, you are consigning it to flames. Good things you despise, and bad things you encourage. You are rehabilitating the thieves, and making the good people run away, and you place reliance on those who bear tales to you : चोर बसावत साह भगावत, चुगलनि कौं एतबार. We cannot understand your threefold manner, O Uddhava, namely, कथनी, करनी and रहनी. "None of these can we understand in your case." So, we have to come to the conclusion, say the Gopis, thy Court, thy Assembly Hall, is merely chaotic: अंधाधुंद दरबार. "The good people are punished and the bad people prosper" – that is what in a sense the Gopis have said to Uddhava or Krishna. In Maharashtra, there was another poet, named Tatyaji, who has said the same thing. One does not know whether he knew the song of the Gopis. He is, in a sense, re-echoing the very words of the Gopis :

दाताओंको वंधन पड़े । भिखारियों को दौलत चढ़े ॥
चोरों को इमारत वढ़े । दुश्मनको मुक्ति सिद्धि ॥
सेवकको चिथड़ी । पतिव्रता की विपत पड़ी ॥
छिनाल जा वैकुंठ चढ़ी । तात्याजीकी ऐसी वानी है ॥
अंधाधुंद सरकार है ।

"Liberal donors are put into prison, and beggars are placed on the throne. Chaste women fall into adversity, and courtesans ascend to the heaven." Tatyaji says, "Verily, thy world-court is only full of anarchy." What is the philosophic consequence of this ?—that perturbed the intellect of such a great German philosopher like Kant ? Kant, who in his First Critique, the Critique of Pure Reason, could not by any intellectual arguments prove the existence of God, has discovered a very suitable argument in the second Critique, the Critique of Practical Reason, where he founds his proof of God upon this disparity between desert and fruit. Good people suffer in the world, and bad people prosper. How is an adjustment to be made between desert and fruit, asks Kant? He gives two answers. In the first place, he says, we have to posit an immortal life – a long life – through the course of which, the good people, who have suffered in this life, might be rewarded in a later; and the bad, who have been prosperous in this life, might receive due punishment. So this mal-adjustment in the world implies, says Kant, the proof of immortal life. Second, it requires a Judge who is to adjust the desert to fruit. That great Judge is God. It is only God who can adjust works to fruits. So, this proof of God, which is known as the moral proof, is very famous in the History of Philosophy. In the last Critique, namely, the Critique of Judgment, Kant comes to the teleological proof, which is next to this moral proof, but this moral proof stands highest in the case of Kant. According to Kant, this discrepancy between desert and fruit leads, on the one hand, to the proof of an immortal life, and, on the other, to the proof of God; but in our case, who are discussing the Nature of Spiritual life, how does it affect us ? Is it not our concern, as members of the Spiritual world, so to feel and pray within ourselves that Providence may bring about an adjustment between merit and reward ? If these are not righted, as we may see in the world, will it not be our spiritual endeavour so to will, that they are righted here and now ? At least, the endeavour will inspire us with a strong spiritual impulse for bringing about this very necessary desired adjustment.

3. *Consciousness of sin* :—Let us now pass on to the next incentive to spiritual life, namely that drawn from a consciousness of sin. In the case of sin, there seem to be three typical attitudes, namely those, for example of Surdas, Duryodhana and Indra. The first attitude is the

recognition of the responsibility of the Self, the second is that of vicarious responsibility on Nature, Society or God, and the third, the attitude to sin as a propaedeutic to spiritual life.

(1) The first attitude is exhibited by Surdas and Virgil. Surdas tells in a pitiful mood : कीजै प्रभु अपने बिरद की लाज. "I have seen, I have heard, I have known, and yet I have not been able to extricate myself from evil" : देखत सुनत सबै जानत हौं तऊ न आयौं बाज. The noteworthy feature about this attitude is that Surdas does not shake off his responsibility. Similar is case with Virgil. He says, "I see the better but follow the worse :" "Video meliors proboque, deteriora sequor." It is really a great attitude. A question, which incidentally arises in this connection, is the relation of self-effort to the Grace of God. Surdas knows that he is lacking in sufficient power of effort : दइ न जात केवट-उतराई; चाहत चढ़यौ जहाज, and therefore he asks for the Grace of God which alone can fill the deficiencies of self-effort.

(2) The second attitude to sin is that of vicarious responsibility exhibited by Duryodhana and Richard III. Duryodhana throws the responsibility of his bad actions on God. Take the following verse from the Pandava Gīta :

जानामि धर्मं न च मे प्रवृत्तिः, जानाम्यधर्मं न च मे निवृत्तिः ।
केनापि देवेन हृदि स्थितेन, यथा नियुक्तोऽस्मि तथा करोमि ॥

This is as much as to say, that a man may commit

sins, and throw the responsibility on God who is the maker of all things. Such an attitude to sin is absolutely irresponsible. It is only a facile way of escaping from one's own sins. This vicarious doctrine may take the shape of throwing the responsibility either on Nature, or on Society or on God. It is Nature which compels me to do bad actions, says Richard III. It is on account of the influence of Society, says another. It is God who makes me do all evil deeds, says Duryodhana. The real attitude of Duryodhana, however, is not simply that of throwing the responsibility on God, but that of giving a despising and defiant challenge to the power of God. Similar was the attitude of Richard III, so far as Nature was concerned. "Nature has sent me mis-shapen and before my time into the world, so that dogs bark at me when I halt by them. Therefore, it will be my endeavour to take vengeance upon Nature for this act of cruelty." This is the second attitude to sin, as exhibited by Richard III and Duryodhana.

(3) The third attitude would be that exhibited by Indra and Augustine. This attitude does recognise the compelling power of sin, but utilises the sin for rising into a life of spirit. "Had I not sinned," says Indra, "I would not have had that superb attitude of devotion to Rama, which other gods are jealous of in my case." Augustine also rises from a life of sin to a life of great spiritual achievement. This third attitude, therefore, concerns itself with the phenomenon of a rebound

from a life of sin into a life of spirit. This we shall consider in the song that follows.

It looks surprising, indeed, that a consciousness or a memory of our sins might lead us to a spiritual and holy life, and yet it did so in the case of Indra, as Tulsidas points out in his song शंकर रामरूप अनुरागे. Tulsidas begins by taking illustrations of four different deities—Shankara, Brahma, Kartikeya and Indra, and then passes on to the whole legion of the gods, in reference to their contemplation of Indra's glory. Tulsidas begins by considering the case of Shankara. Shankara had no axe to grind. His salvation came from Rama, and therefore he was full of love in looking at the 'Chabi' of Rama, and he drank of the beauty of Rama with fifteen eyes (5 × 3, पंचमुख and त्रिनयन). Unfortunately, the third eye burns. But it did not and could not do so in the case of Rama. Brahma enjoyed the beauty of Rama with eight eyes only (4 × 2, चतुर्मुख). But he repented that he had lost one of his heads, otherwise he could have enjoyed the 'Chabi' of Rama with ten eyes, instead of 8. One of his heads was cut off on account of his misdeeds. So, he enjoyed God with 8 eyes only with a sense of repentance. Kartikeya, who followed, and who is known as Shadanana, had six faces, and he enjoyed the 'Chabi' of Rama with twelve eyes, which, Tulsidas says, is one and a half times the number of eyes of Brahma (डेवढ़लोचन). So, he was very elated. There was the further reason for his joy because Kartikeya was a life-long Kumar, and Rama was a Kumar till that time. So, he took a particular pleasure in enjoying the 'Chabi' of Rama. And finally, we come to the case of Indra. Indra enjoyed the 'Chabi' of Rama with a thousand eyes. He had to thank his very sins, which led him to his great enjoyment of the form of God with a thousand eyes, instead either with fifteen, eight, or twelve. He was an अहिल्याजार, which expression is interpreted in the Vedas as equivalent to the Sun, who, being the paramour of Night, hides her face by day (अहिल्या); but, mythologically speaking, one might understand Indra as having had a thousand holes in his body on account of his most culpable sensuality. Now, Indra thanks himself for his previous sins because they enabled him to enjoy the 'Chabi' of Rama with a thousand holes or eyes in his body. And lastly, there was that host of gods who were jealous of Indra. "Oh, he is enjoying the beauty of Rama," they said, "with a thousand eyes; we cannot enjoy it even with two." There is a peculiar Bhojpuri word which Tulsidas uses in this connection (सिहाहीं), which means either praising, or being jealous. The gods either praised Indra or became jealous of him. Now, if we were to analyse psychologically the different emotions exhibited by all these great deities while enjoying the 'Chabi' of Rama, we can see, in the first place, the psychological attitude of Shankara was that of love; in the case of Brahma, it was repentance; in the case of Kartikeya, it was elation; in the case of Indra, it was gratefulness; and lastly, in the case of the gods, it was either jealousy or praise. So, all these psychological emotions have been brought out by Tulsidas in that simple incident of the gods looking at the 'Chabi' of Rama, as well as in his emphasis on Indra enjoying the beauty of Rama more than any other god or gods. That does not mean that we should lead a life of sin; that does not mean that. The story might have been either a historical or a merely allegorical anecdote. A consciousness of our own sins might also enable us to realise God, as it did in the case of Augustine. Augustine led a very sinful life in the beginning, and so his mother Monica went to her teacher, St. Ambrose, and asked him in what way her son could be saved, and she began to shed tears. Then, St. Ambrose replied, "Weep not my Sister; the child of these holy tears shall never perish." And we know that St. Augustine became the second founder of Christianity. Having led a life of sin in the beginning, he later became one of the great Saints of the world. So, even a consciousness of our own sins, provided we mend our ways and never return to the bad life again, provided we go forward courageously on the path of virtue, then, that consciousness will serve as a sure incentive to the consummation of our spiritual life.

4. *Old age and Death:*—After sin, comes the question of old age and death. Considerations of old age and death have always remained a powerful incentive towards spiritual life. Tulsidas gives an excellent illustration of the 'स्वभावोक्तिअलंकार' in his famous description of old age in the song ममता तू न गई मेरे मन तें. This description can be divided, for convenience sake, into four parts :

(1) "In general", says Tulsidas, "My body has become utterly exhausted, and I have lost all my vitality. All colour has disappeared from my face; my hair, which have been my companions from my very birth, have now become ripe ; also I feel no shame in either sitting or walking naked."

(2) Then, Tulsidas goes on to discuss how the sensory organs have become powerless. "Light has disappeared from my eyes, and my ears are refusing to hear sounds and words; my throat has been covered with phlegm and has become subject to paresis and bile."

(3) As regards motor organs, Tulsidas tells us, "My hands are suffering from continuous tremor, my teeth are either broken or have disappeared. My mouth cannot give out understandable words; unable to utter words, I call even my son by beckoning to him with my hand."

(4) Finally, "as the conclusion of all my physical and mental discomfiture," says Tulsidas, "my dear relatives and even my wife are turning me out of my own house. Even this has not prevented me from my personal attachment to them. As dark spots must remain the constant possessions of the Moon, so 'I and mine' have remained my constant possessions. Therefore, I surrender myself to Thee, O Lord, in the hope that that alone might enable me to extricate myself from thraldom to sense."

After the question of old age, let us now proceed to a very poetic description of the effects of death by Prabhudas, in his poem क्या तन माँजता रे. "Why dost thou forget", he asks, "that thou hast to mingle with dust some day? Dust thou art, and to dust thou shalt have to return. Thou art gaily strutting in the gardens with a flower in your turban; but when the God of Death will pounce upon you, you will lose all your gaiety and cease to leap on all fours." This reminds us of the famous description by Kalidāsa of a deer which, when pursued by King Dushyanta, ceased to leap gaily, and in terror seemed to move more in the air than upon earth:

पश्योदग्रप्लुतत्वाद्वियति बहुतरं स्तोकमुर्व्यां प्रयाति।

"So long as there are the wick and the oil in the lamp," continues Prabhudas, "the lamp glitters with brilliant luminosity; but as soon as the wick or the oil is finished, people will say 'take it away, take it away; we have no use for it any longer'." "The house-wife," the Poet tells us further, "weeps in streams. 'My mate has forsaken me for ever' she cries. Prabhudas gets up and says, 'Weep no longer, my sister, God has joined and God has separated.'" This is a sort of an eschatological optimism, for which the ordinary layman can have little value.

We shall now proceed to discuss how in Surdas a philosophic contemplation on death becomes a powerful incentive to the spiritual life. Many philosophers of antiquity, like the Stoics, made a continuous use of it. Even the Epicureans tell us not to be afraid of Death; for they say "When we are, Death is not; and when Death is, we are not." St. Paul, the great Christian apostle, used to say "I die daily". This is as much as to say, that only when we keep the fact of death every moment before us we may be encouraged to devote continuous attention to the spiritual life. There is a famous poem in Surdas (जा दिन मन पंछी उड़ि जैहै), in which he tells us in a didactic manner how this contemplation on death might be achieved. In the ordinary course of nature, when we look at a tree, we find that when the foliage of the tree has fallen down, then the bird which used to sit on it flies away. Surdas reverses this relation, and tells us by a sort of

विपर्ययालंकार that the bird flies away, and then the foliage of the tree falls down. Surdas has in mind the crumbling down of all sensations, affections, and passions as soon as the self has flown away. The reason for contrary experiences in nature and in man is evidently that, while in the latter case the connection between the bird and the foliage is organic, that in the former it is only accidental. In the case of the tree, the bird comes and perches on the tree, as if the tree is external to it. In the case of a human being, the bird, which is perching on the tree of the human body, makes the tree its organic vesture. This organic connection between the soul and the body might well be seen in the appearance of heat lingering in the body-cells even after the soul has departed and the man is dead. This of course occurs in the case of an old man, say a father; but in the case of a young child, Surdas tells us further, the lustre and colour of the body of the child, whom one had fondly loved in life, depart in addition, thus adding a poignant note to our contemplation on the ravages of death in general :

कँह वह नीर, कहाँ वह सोभा, कँह रंगरूप दिखै हैं।

"Let not the Dehi take pride", says Surdas, by a sort of a malapropism – for Surdas wants to use the word 'Dehi' in the sense of 'Deha' – "let not the body make you proud, O arrogant man; your only destiny is to fall an easy prey to jackals, crows and vultures (स्यांर काग गिध खैंहैं). If it does not become a coveted mouthful to these creatures, its next destiny would be either to be putrified, or be reduced to worms, or be turned into ashes and mingled with dust." Surdas, therefore, warns us to take thought that this contemplation on death should make one think early enough about turning the body to its proper use, long before the bird has flown away.

Surdas also adds a psychological element to this physical contemplation on the state of the body after death. "Those whom you have loved in life", says Surdas, "will begin to despise you as soon as you are dead. Others will be afraid of you, lest you might be turned into a ghost, catch hold of them and devour them. In either case, your relatives will insist upon your body being turned out of the house immediately after your death. Your sons, whom you had reared with so much affection through your life, and with fervent prayers to gods and goddesses for their welfare, will break your cranium with a bamboo stick when your body has been burnt, and throw the pieces to the four winds, lest a future grave-digger might catch hold of them and inspire a philosophic Hamlet to ponder as to whether the cranium belonged to a politician, a lawyer or a jester. It is time for you to think, therefore, O foolish man, and to seek the company of the

Saints, for it is only in their company that you will get something which will be worth your while. It is from them that you might learn to turn your own body and mind to their proper spiritual use." Surdas repents that he has wasted a very valuable life without attaining to God!

5. *Transmigration and Metempsychosis*:—After the questions of old age and death, the next incentives to attract the attention of the seeker are the questions of transmigration and metempsychosis. What happens to the soul of a man after it leaves the human body? That is the question which has taxed the brains of many philosophers and psychologists all the world over. The Christians and Mohamedans would deny transmigration. But the Buddhists and Hindus would assert it. The whole question turns upon what logical and empirical evidence is forthcoming to justify this doctrine. Kabir makes the following statement in this connection. Those who have gone from the world neither return to the world, nor send any message: जो जो गए बहुरि नहिं आए, पठवत नाहिं सँदेस. There are two points in this statement. In the first place, Kabir wants to say that those who have departed from the world will not return to it. In the second place, he tells us, it is not possible for them to send any message from where they have gone. The second point is easy enough. It definitely betokens Kabir's dis-

belief in either the planchette or psychical research. The first point is somewhat questionable. What does Kabir mean when he says that those who have gone from the world do not return to it? Are we to understand that he disbelieves transmigration, as he was born a Mohamedan ? It is likely that people might suppose from Kabir's statement that he did not believe in transmigration. Considering the utterances of Kabir in the whole poem, this would not be a correct interpretation. What Kabir means is that those who have gone from the world do not return to it in the same capacity, or as the same individuals. Otherwise, what justification would there be for the statement, which he makes immediately after this, namely, 'धरि धरि जनम सबै भरमे हैं ब्रह्मा विष्णु महेस' ? Even the Gods, Brahma, Vishnu and Mahesh, have to take on birth after birth and thus belong to the whirling community. Immediately after this, Kabir makes a still more precise and comprehensive statement, from which it would be understood that he does believe in transmigration. Look at the statement he makes indicating a perpetual round of births and deaths for every creature that is born in the world. He says, "Gods and Sages, spiritual teachers and saints; Yogins, itinerants and ascetics, naked Fakirs, tuft-haired men, shavelings, and doctors of letters; denizens of the upper, nether and other worlds; philosophers, artists, politicians and poets; kings and paupers, those who call out Adesh, and mendicants in variegated costumes roaming the earth in batches–everyone who is born in the world keeps on making a perpetual round of births and deaths." It would be very interesting to compare the above list with a similar list from Ramdas (Dasabodha III–9), which includes almost all the above categories of personalities, along with a few new ones such as "warriors and orators, doctors and magicians, clergymen and croesuses, poets and philologists, logicians and disputationists," to all of whom, the God of Death shows absolute impartiality in attacking all equally.

Kabir believes not merely in transmigration, but also in metempsychosis. Transmigration implies only the process of a soul's passage from the body, but metempsychosis further implies the taking on of another body after the passage. Kabir believes definitely in metempsychosis. He tells us, in a poem of surpassing irony and humour, reality and pathos, ethical and philosophical reflection—दिवाने मन भजन विना दुख पैहौ—how a man may take on birth after birth when he leaves his physical body. Kabir enumerates seven stages in this process of metempsychosis, almost as vividly as Shakespeare has done in the case of the Seven Stages of man's life in "As you like it".

There are Seven possibilities which Kabir predicates for the soul after the death of the body.

With a rearrangement, the possibilities may be said to belong to (1) the Eschatological realm – ghost; (2) Ornithological realm – crow and parrot; (3) the Intermediate realm (between the bird and the animal, in the sense that it flies like a bird and moves like an animal) – monkey; and (4) the Biological realm – ox, ass and camel. These complete the seven possibilities in which a man might be born after death. This does not, however, mean that all the categories of post-existence are exhausted. Kabir is selecting only these seven for illustration sake. The possibilities have been so vividly described by Kabir that we cannot do better than describe them in his own words :—

1. "After death you may be turned into a ghost," says Kabir, "and in that state of existence you will get only as little water as might suffice to cover the tip of a needle, and therefore you will have to 'die' of unquenchable thirst." We have only to imagine what the 'death' of a 'ghost' might mean.

2. "You may be next born as a crow so closely associated with a ghost or a departed spirit. Croaking and screeching all the while, you will fly and sit on putrid matter and take delight in plunging your beak deep into the filth."

3. "Then you may be born as a parrot, and, according to the wont of that species, take resort to some garden or other, and when the hawk will

hover in a circle over your head, in terror you will drop down, pinionless, fluttering through mid-air."

4. "You may next be born as the monkey of a juggler. Dancing to the motions of his baton, you will spread out your hands for alms before high and low, not being fortunate to get even a grain of corn."

After the death of a monkey, says Kabir, three more possibilities will open out before you — those of an ox, an ass and a camel.

5. "You may be born as an ox in an oil-man's house, and, with your eyes blinded with leather–flaps, you will be required to move hundreds of miles inside the house without being able to plant even a step outside it." In this connection, those who are conversant with either Greek or Indian philosophy might know that Pythagoras said he was born an ox in one of his former lives. Also Jayatīrtha was regarded to have been born the ox of his master Shri Madhvacharya in a former life, carrying on his back the philosophical manuscripts of his Master, which ultimately gave him the ability to comment on his great works.

6. "Next," says Kabir, "you may be born as an ass in a washerman's house, and will not be lucky to get even thorny grass to eat. He will place a heavy load on you and himself ride on

you, in addition, and you will have to carry both to the bank of a river ".

7. " Finally, your birth will be that of a camel, and you will be required to carry an immeasurably heavy weight on your back. At the end, you will not be able to get up when you have once sat down, and, continuously scraping and scratching on the ground, you will have to give up the ghost. " Those who have seen the Unta-khana at Allahabad near the Harijan Ashram can well bear testimony to this fact. In this connection, it is humorous to recall that an English friend of the present writer, a philosopher to boot, had come to Allahabad in connection with some University work, and while the present writer was taking him in his car round the city, he saw some camels on the streets and said that the most peculiar feature of Allahabad was the presence of so many camels.

Kabir deduces the following conclusion from the above account of the seven lives. " If you do not look out for, and avail yourself of, the everlasting Name of God (सत्नाम)" says Kabir, "you will have to repent deeply within yourself and descend by the downward ladder to the lowest rung of perdition."

It is important to remember that this great poem on metem-psychosis might be a poem to tell us that suffering also might be one of the powerful incentives to spiritual life. Of course, suffering is involved in metem-psychosis but it can also stand as an independent argument.

संसारदुःखें दुखवला । त्रिविधतापें पोळला ।
तोचि एक अधिकारी झाला । परमार्थासी ॥ says Ramdas.

दुःखत्रयाभिघाताज्जिज्ञासा तदवघातके हेतौ says the Samkhya philosopher.

बाप दुःखाचें केणें सुटलें । जेथ मरणाचे भरे लोटले । तिये मृत्युलोकींचे शेवटिले । हाटवेळें येणें जाहलें ॥ says Jnaneshwar.

From such-like utterances we can very well see how suffering can be a powerful incentive to spiritual life.

6. *Helplessness in Life's experience.*— The last incentive to spiritual life we may consider in this Chapter is the attitude of helplessness before an inscrutable Power which guides the destinies of the world. This inscrutability might take any of the following four forms. Either, it might concern itself with the indeterminateness of the power as such, and its consequent unpredictability and incalculability. This would be a reasonably scientific attitude. But it may also assume the metaphysical shape of a belief in fatalism, and may result in an unpurposive view of the universe. Even some of the great politicians sometimes express their belief in such a power, and call it fate. A third alternative might take the shape of a belief in a world-order or what the Stoics call 'Nature' and may result in some such utterance as " All that

is good to Thee, Oh Nature, is also good to me." A fourth might be a man's modest attitude — that of resignation or humility or submission to the will of God. Under this last head we shall, in a later Chapter, come to a poem from a Hindi saint who has expressed his idea in the famous lines जब हो तुम्हारी मर्जी तब प्राण तनसे निकले.

In the famous song of Kabir – करम गति टारे नाहिं टरी, we have been supplied with a number of illustrations to support this contention of the inscrutability of the unseen power. Kabir first tells us how the great sage Vashistha, with all his knowledge of the heavenly bodies, could not find out a suitable stellar conjuction for the coronation of Rama. What we find is, says Kabir, that Dasharatha died before the coronation took place, Rama was banished to the forest by his stepmother and Sita was later kidnapped by the Demon King. The course of events in history, says Kabir, is beyond any astronomical or scientific calculations.

The second illustration he gives is that of the famous king Nriga. It was customary to suppose that whoever gave a cow in charity was lifted to the heavens on account of the merit he had earned. In the case of Nriga, however, in spite of his having given crores of cows in charity, he had ultimately to be born as an ever-nodding lizard, because, once upon a time, he was obliged to nod his head when the question was put to him as to whether the cow he was offering in charity was not the one he had already given away before :

एक गौ जो देत विप्र को सो सुर लोक तरे ।
कोटि गौ राजा नृग दीन्हीं सो भव कूप परे ॥

The illustration which has been given by Surdas in the song 'दयानिधि तेरी गति लखि न परे ।' which is very similar to that of Kabir, tells us how God very often reconciles himself with the wrong course of events. Prahlad disobeyed his father. Disobedience is a crime. The crime led Prahlad to a state of bondage. In order to release him from bondage, God was obliged to take on the form of a man-lion and kill the father. Now how does this action of God rhyme with the moral principle? It might rhyme with the will of God to punish the wicked, but the principle of morality, that is obedience to the father, is here set at naught. God could afford not to obey the dictates of morality, because he is probably a super-moral Being. In any case, this involves a certain incalculability in the achievement of a particular end.

Krishna was, on the other hand, a great friend of the Pandavas, and yet the Pandavas were subjected to all sorts of adversities and humiliations : पाण्डव जिनके आप सारथी, तिनपर विपति परी । At every point during their warfare with the Kauravas, they were subjected to critical situations through which only his transcendent power could lift them. What happened at the time when Bhīshma was almost on the point of vanquishing the Pandavas? Krishna had to bring Shikhandi to kill the renowned warrior. What happened when Drona was told falsely that his son Ashwatthama was dead? Dhrishtadyumna had to come forward to kill the great Brahmin preceptor of archery. What happened at the time when Karna who was about to throw the deadliest atom-bomb of ancient times, namely, his Shakti on Arjuna? Krishna had to take resort to get the chariot of Karna stuck up in the earth, in order that Arjuna might be free to discharge his killing arrow at his invincible enemy. Was not Ashwatthaman successful in killing all the progeny of the Pandavas when Krishna by an artifice had taken away the Pandavas from the clutches of misfortune?

Another illustration which Kabir gives is that of a deer. It is customary to understand the line कहँ वह फंद कहाँ वह पारधी, कहँ वह मिरग चरी। as referring to the Hema Mriga which Rama pursued. Why was not Rama able to keep an unclouded intellect when he pursued the deer of gold? The Sanskrit poet says —

> असम्भवो हेममृगस्य जन्म तथापि रामो लुलुभे मृगाय ।
> प्रायः समापन्नविपत्तिकाले धियोऽपि पुंसां मलिनीभवन्ति ।।

It does not seem that the juxtaposition of the words in this line supports such an interpretation. On the other hand, we can legitimately go to an interpretation of this line in the spirit of the famous Sanskrit verse attributed to मुक्तापीड by वल्लभदेव in his सुभाषितावली :—

> छित्वा पाशमपास्य कूटरचनां भङ्क्त्वा बलाद्वागुराम् ।
> पर्यन्ताग्निशिखाकलापजटिलान्निःसृत्य दूरं वनात् ॥
> व्याधानां शरगोचरादति जवेनोत्प्लुत्य धावन्मृगः ।
> कूपान्तः पतितः करोति विमुखे किंवा विधौ पौरुषम् ॥

The verse tells us how a man might push successfully through a chain of calamities with courage and fortune, but ultimately succumb to the inevitable. We are told, in the above famous verse, how a deer escaped from the meshes and traps that had been set for him, escaped from the hide-outs where it was intended to be concerned by the pursuing hounds, escaped from the poisonous arrows of invincible archers, escaped also from the fire which was lit up on all sides of the forest in which it was pent, and when it had escaped all these catastrophes, dancing with joy as it did, it went and fell into the waters of a well and there gave up the ghost. The deer died and its vaunted conquest of calamities came to naught. The inescapable law of destiny was too strong for him.

Do we not know in contemporary history how and to what ultimate fate Hitler was subjected, in spite of his great and continuous conquests through a number of years after the late War broke out ? Did he not conquer France in eight days ? Did he not subject England to unimaginable fire and travail, and particularly London which he almost reduced to ashes ? Did he not intend to descend into Asia from the Caucasus, and did he not succeed in getting India bombed from the other side by his ever-watchful ally ? Was he not almost successful in subjugating Russia, but only Stalingrad held him ? Did not Hitler lift away Mussolini from the clutches of his enemies when he had already been taken prisoner in Italy itself? And ultimately was he not obliged, when he was cornered in Berlin from all sides, to shoot himself and his mistress for fear that he might otherwise be caught alive and become a butt of ridicule to the whole world ? He laughs best who laughs last ; and it is the ultimate conquest that matters. As the great master of literary style, Mr. Churchill, said a few years ago, England always lost battles, but always won the war.

Kabir shows himself to be almost a fatalist in the song we were considering, namely,— करम गति टारै नाहि टरी. ...... होनी होके रही. Surdas, however, is more submissive to the will of God. His great anxiety is how God might relieve him from a whirlpool of disasters. His only recourse is an utterance like this :

सूरदास वलि जात चरन की कैसे सूर तरै ।

To him, resignation or submission to the will of God would be a more potent instrument of achieving the end than either belief in an unseen power or a philosophic reconciliation with a world-order. Who, ever, in the course of history has emerged successful except through an alliance with God?

7. *The way of Escape*— We have hitherto discussed the different incentives that lead us to the pursuit of spiritual life. We shall now close this chapter by discussing two songs— one by Surdas and the other by Kabir – which tell us that the pursuit of God alone will enable us to transcend the evils implied in these incentives. In the song रे मन जनम अकारथ जात, which contains ideas reminiscent of those already advanced by Kabir, Tulsidas, as well as himself, Surdas points out that when your dear old relatives have once passed away, you will never, by any means, be able to get into contact with them. "Is it possible for leaves that have dropped down," asks Surdas, "to get stuck up again to their parent tree or to one another?" Continuing the idea of helplessness, Surdas tells us, "You will have to look on in helpless frenzy when death is snatching away your only dear child." "In your own case, finally," says Surdas, "when towards the end of your life you will be in your delirious state, caused by the morbid condition of the bodily humours, your throat will be choked up by phlegm, your tongue will falter and fail, and

you will not be able to utter a single word. One moment in such a state will appear to you as an aeon of time." Surdas here is pointing out the fallacies of psychological time. Time, it is well known, travels differently with different men, and and in different conditions of health and mind. It is lengthened in grief and shortened in joy. One moment in the departing state of a man, says Surdas, will appear to him like an eternity. On the other hand, we are told by Kabir that when a man is joyous, the ten incarnations of God will present themselves in a cinematographic fashion to the vision of the mystic in a single night : दश अवतार एक रत राजै अस्तुति सहज से आनी हो । In that case aeons of time will dwindle into a single night's experience. If you want to translate your grief into joy, says Surdas, you must necessarily take recourse to the contemplation of God. "Leave away your arrogance, Oh foolish man," says Surdas, "spiritual life alone will save you from helpless submission to death. Let your mind rest steadfastly on the feet of God."

This was exactly what Kunti had asked of Krishna, in the Mahābhārata :

> कृष्ण त्वदीयपदपङ्कजपञ्जरान्ते ।
> अद्यैव मे विशतु मानसराजहंसः ॥
>
> प्राणप्रयाणसमये कफवातपित्तैः ।
> कण्ठावरोधनविधौ स्मरणं कुतस्ते ॥

It is only a contemplation on the Gracious Lord that will enable one to transcend the evils of life.

We now pass on to the final song of the Chapter : रे दिल गाफिल गफलत मत कर, by Kabir. There are three points to be noted in this connection. In the first place, Kabir tells us " Pilgrim as you are, you have not been able to reach even the outskirts of the City of Devotion (प्रेमनगर का अन्त न पाया), and you will have to return as you came. " Then he tells us two further points which are of great significance from a comparative point of view as we shall presently see. " You have taken an extremely heavy load on your head and are sitting on a wrecked boat. You are sure to get drowned in the river of life. " Again he says " Your friend, God, is standing on the other side of the river. Why do you not make Him the pole-star of all your attention and effort ? "

Now those who have read the literature of Maharashtra Saints will recollect how very similar these last two points are to the famous utterances of Jnaneshwar. Let us quote two verses from the Jnaneshwari here :—

१) या लागि शतजर्जर नावे । रिगोनि केंवि निश्चित होआवें ।
... ...
तेंवि लोका येऊनि सोपद्रवा । केंवि न भजिजे मातें ।।

२) तरी झडझडोनि वहिला निघ । इये भक्तीचिये वाटे लाग ।
जिया पावसी अव्यंग । निजधाम माझें ।।

These lines express ideas which are extremely similar to the lines of Kabir in the following stanza of the song we are considering :

परली पार तेरा मीता खड़िया,
उस मिलने का ध्यान न धरिया,
टूटी नाव ऊपर जा बैठा,
गाफ़िल गोता खावेगा ॥

How is this similarity to be explained ? The question arises whether Jnaneshwar and Kabir had ever met. We know that Jnaneshwar and Namadeo had gone on a pilgrimage to Northern India and particularly to Kashi. But it is not definitely known whether they had met Kabir. As regards Namadeo, historians of Hindi literature say there was a definite gap between the passing away of Namadeo and the birth of Kabir, the first event having taken place in 1350 A. D. (Shake 1272), and the second in 1368 A. D. (Samvat 1425). According to the Maharashtra tradition, however, Namadeo who lived many years after the passing away of Jnaneshwar, who was Namadeo's senior contemporary, might have met Kabir during one of his later pilgrimages to Northern India. Even if this be not a fact, nothing would prevent us from supposing that Kabir had known Namadeo as a great spiritual saint. There are two definite references in Kabir to Namadeo in his famous work, the Beejak :—

(१) सनक सनंदन जयदेव नामा । भक्ति हेतु मन उनहू न जाना ।

(२) ब्रह्मा वरुण .... नामदेव जयदेव दासा । इनकी खबर कहत नहीं कोई किधर कियो है वासा ॥

We may, however, note that though there is no reference in Namadeo to Kabir, there are two very good references to Kabir in Janabai, the maid-servant and contemporary of Namadeo :

(१) कबिराच्या बैसोनि पाठी । शेले विणितां सांगे गोष्टी ॥

(२) नाचतां नाचतां देवाचा गळला पितांबर । सावध होजी देवा, ऐसें बोले कबीर ॥

Also we understand from a song of Kamal, which is to be found both in Hindi and Maharashtra recensions, that Kabir and Namadeo were the two great saints of the time, who were the subject-matter of the world's praise :—

दक्खन म्याने नामा दरजी उनोका बन्दा विठ्ठल है ।
और सेवा कछु नहीं जाने अन्दर भीतर केशव है ।
उत्तर म्याने भयो कबीरा रामचरनका बन्दा है ।
उनो का पूत कहै कमाल दोनोंका बोलबोला है ।

Whatever, therefore, the case may be so far as Namadeo is concerned, it would be hard to believe in the absence of reliable evidence that Jnaneshwar and Kabir had met. The similarity of ideas between the two might be explained either as due to an independent parallelism of thought or to the prevalence of the same spiritual ideas in the community of Saints from Kashi to Pandharpur.

We have already quoted a few lines from Jnaneshwar in comparison to the utterances of Kabir in the song we are considering. Let us end the chapter by giving a few further ideas from the passage in Jnaneshwar, not merely because the beginning and the end of the passage are almost identical with the ideas expressed by Kabir, but also because the passage would serve as an independent commentary on the different incentives that have been dealt with in the present chapter. "You are indeed sitting in a wrecked boat with a hundred holes," says Jnaneshwar, "how can you hope to get comfort on the perilous journey? Life is indeed a fair, where the wares of misery are being spread out and allocated by fate. When you are seeing that a conflagration is surrounding you in a forest, would it not be an act of prudence on your part to get out of it as early as possible?" Further, Jnaneshwar tells us, "You are indeed sleeping on a bed of scorpions. How can you ever hope to sleep in comfort? Avaricious and inconsiderate, you are like a frog which is trying to eat a fish while it is itself being devoured by a big boa." Jnaneshwar goes on to tell us, "All things in this world are transitory. The moon of this world is proverbially consumptive. Stars rise in this world only in order to set, and birth only means death. Knowing as they do that a child as it grows is making a nearer approach to death every day, they still raise auspicious flags in joy. Death indeed is like a lion's den to which all steps point, but from which none return : परतलें पाउलची नाहीं फिरीटी." Finally, Jnaneshwar tells us, "Histories and mythologies are merely stories of dead men. Why do not these considerations prompt you, Oh! vile man, to the pursuit of spiritual life? The whole world is full of misery. Who has ever heard a tale of happiness in this mortal world? If you have been so unfortunate as to have been born in this world, your first endeavour should be to get out of it as early as possible by making God the only cynosure of your devotion and effort." In this way, Jnaneshwar and the Saints of Hindustan are giving us an identical message.

CHAPTER II

The Necessity of Moral Preparation.

In our last Chapter we have taken a review of the various incentives that lead to the desire for the spiritual life. Now we must proceed to consider what moral virtues have to be cultivated before such a spiritual life could be realised. Cultivation of the moral virtues also implies an avoidance of bad qualities. Hence arises the necessity of the consideration for the avoidance of vices, along with the cultivation of moral virtues. The first great vice is the company of the wicked; for, it is the mother of all the vices. In the initial paragraphs of the present chapter, we shall discuss, with reference to relevant songs from Surdas, Dadu, Kabir and Charandas, the main vices that are to be avoided, and the main virtues that are to be cultivated. One of the most important of such virtues is the company of the good. A real welfare state is the company of the Saints. In this connection, Nanak tells us how the company of the Saints might enable us to have a vision of God. Tulsidas also tells us how all the Saints are tied together by the bond of God-love. That, according to Tulsidas, seems to be the highest virtue. We are further told by Tulsidas, in a सांगरूपक, how God-love is the charioteer who leads the chariot of life to spiritual victory. In a couple of other सांगरूपकs, Tulsidas gives us a vivid description of the distinction between Jnana and Bhakti, the one being compared to a dazzling light, the other to a brilliant jewel. Further, we hear from Surdas the opposition between the way of knowledge and the way of devotion and then a reconciliation of the two from Tulsidas. Finally, in a fine सांगरूपक, we are told by Tulsidas how this devotion to God might be compared to a diamond with nine facets, each representing one aspect of God-devotion, and all being present in an ideal Saint. After we have discussed these topics, we shall end the present chapter with a review of the various virtues that are to be cultivated, and the various vices that are to be avoided, which might be regarded as a distinct contribution of Hindi saints to ethical literature — a contribution which might well be compared to that made by the great moral philosophers of ancient and modern times, such as Aristotle and Plato, Sidgwick and Green.

1. *Ungodliness, the root of all vice* — In the first place, we are asked to avoid the company of the wicked. We should have no concern with such ungodly men. They are like serpents whose

venom-teeth would not give up secreting poison even if they are fed on milk. Surdas gives a number of metaphors to pursue this idea. The wicked man is like a crow which will not give up its black colour even if it be made to pick up camphor. This is a sort of अतद्गुण अलंकार. Students of rhetoric will not fail to call to mind an illustration of the opposite sort, when a Rajhansa is described as never becoming black even if it takes bath after bath in the waters of the Jumna (राजहंस तव सैव शुभ्रता). We should never try to please an ungodly man. There is no use in covering the body of an ass with a saffron or sandle paste, which suggests to our mind a similar idea from the Kanarese Saint-poet Purandardas, who describes an ass as not knowing the fragrance of the musk whose load it is carrying on its dull back. A monkey cannot be made beautiful, says Surdas, by being adorned with precious ornaments. He has no value for precious ornaments, as Hanuman had none for the diamonds in the necklace which Sita had presented to him, for the simple reason that the form of Rama could not be seen inside them. An elephant, again, we are told, will continue to cover its body with dust even if it is administered a bath in the limpid waters of a river. An arrow cannot penetrate to the inside of a hard stone even if the whole quiver be made empty : even so, the advice, which a spiritual teacher might give to a fallen man, would only be wasted on him.

We have another very famous illustration from Surdas, describing the voluptuous dance which everyone of us is carrying on in this Samsara. We are all doing a कत्थक dance, showing all sorts of sensual and voluptuous manifestations in every part of our limbs and dress. Fine arts are a double-edged sword. They might help the moral and spiritual path, as they might also excite sensual passions. It is not without reason that the National Radio Department should so manipulate its activities as to help the moral tendencies of the people, and check the immoral ones. A dancer is exactly like a singer, a poet or an artist. We do not want him to encourage the evil side of life. Surdas describes how a dancer puts on a long robe of passions over his body, and covers his neck with a garland of carnal desires. He tells us how he wears the decorative mark of attraction and covetousness. His mind is like a double-faced drum of illusion, beating to two opposite tunes. If we examine his heart, we shall see that it is beating with continuous sounds of insatiable greed. Such a dancer also swaddles his waist with a tight band of infatuation, and shows on his hips and buttocks the infinite arts of sexual imagery and action. The bells of his anklets are producing sounds of delicious scandals. And, finally, his one business is to dance on the steps of the foregone evil-doers without consideration of time and place. To see the exhibition of such vicious acts is to imbibe their seeds within ourselves.

In a similar spirit, Charandas describes the valuelessness of speech without action : करनी बिन कथनी इसी. It is simply the business of a braggart to talk, and do no action. A hypocrite could not do worse. What is wanted, says Charanadas, is that a good man should act as he speaks. Ramdas and Tukaram have already said : क्रियेवीण वाचाळता व्यर्थ आहे and बोले तैसा चाले, त्याची वंदावीं पाऊलें. It is much better not to talk at all, than to talk and not to do. It was for this reason that "mauna" was regarded as the highest virtue by ancient seers. But, if we talk, our actions should follow our words. Words without action, says Charandas, are like the night without the moon, like a so-called brave man who has no spirit of adventure in him, like a damsel without ornaments, and finally like the cradle of a barren woman which contains no child. Action, says Charanadas, is the cradle of God. The saints act as they speak, and it is for this reason that they attain to divinity.

2. *Who is a Kafir, a Fakir and a Brahmin*—Closely following upon some of the vices that have been discussed in the previous paragraphs is the description of a Kafir by Dadu Dayal. Look

at his mastery of Urdu words such as काफ़, मिसकीन and दोज़ख which he uses in his poem सो काफ़िर जो बोलै काफ़. Unfortunately, this line, सो काफ़िर जो बोलै काफ़, is open to two interpretations. Dadu Dayal might either mean that a Kafir is he who regards the world as unreal, or else he might also mean that the Kafir is one who tells an untruth. The first, however, is to be preferred as it has more philosophical import and agrees with later lines which deny the existence of God. Any one, who regards the world as unreal, is to Dadu the type of Kafir. Such a man's mind is always polluted (दिल अपणा नाहिं राखै साफ़) and he is festered with deceit, (कपट कूड़ सब उस हि माहीं). We are further told by Dadu Dayal that such a Kafir looks at his own shadow, just as a beautiful or a strong man might look at his image in a mirror. Now, one who regards the world as unreal should not regard the shadow as real, and it is exactly this, says Dadu Dayal, that a Kafir does. In other words, false to his doctrine of the unrealism of the world, he regards his shadow as real, and is proud of it. Also he has no esteem for God. Is there any God, he asks? If not, where is the necessity of obeying His laws? Such a person may be regarded, says Dadu, as a Kafir. Look at the very close analogy which exists hetween this description of a Kafir by Dadu and the description of the demoniac heritage in the sixteenth Chapter of the Bhagwad

Gita. Any one who knows the Bhagwadgita may remember the famous line असत्यमप्रतिष्ठं ते जगदाहुरनीश्वरम् — the world is unreal; it has no basis; in fact, it has no God either to create it or to control it. Probably, Dadu Dayal did not know anything about the Bhagwad Gita and yet it is interesting to see how two similar minds may work alike.

After having discussed some of the vices that have been mentioned by Hindi saints, let us now proceed to consider the virtuous life. In the first place, we shall begin with Kabir's description of a Fakir. A Fakir is he who, says Kabir, always remains merged in the happiness of God-contemplation. The happiness of God-contemplation he regards as higher than the happiness of Royalty or Sovereignty : जो सुख पावो राम भजनमें सो सुख नाहिं अमीरीमें. His one resting place is in the city of Devotion : प्रेम नगर मे रहनि हमारी. The moral characteristics of such a Fakir are described by Kabir as being poverty, patience and sufferance. It is only the virtue of सबूरी which will bring him to the attainment of his spiritual goal. An earthen pot in one hand and a wooden rod in the other is all the paraphernalia he possesses. This, he thinks, brings to him the empire of all the worlds. It was his consistent refusal to accept any paraphernalia of what the world regards as greatness that brought Mahatma Gandhi the sarcastic title of a Naked Fakir from Mr. Winston Churchill, as well as the honour and the high esteem in the eyes of the world, scarcely attained by any person in India in recent times. He despised the riches of the world and the riches of the world came to him. Look at the sublime appearance of the Rajghat upon which his remains lie buried. What greater example can be given of a more sublime appearance than that of Rajghat in which Mahatma Gandhi rests for ever on the banks of the Jumna!

Charanadas's description of a Brahmin is a metaphysical and mystical advancement on the moral and social doctrine of a Fakir in Kabir, which we have hitherto discussed. A Brahmin, according to Charanadas, is one who has realised Brahman. This seems to be almost a derivative explanation of the word. We may even convert the proposition and yet the proposition would be right. One who has realised Brahman is entitled to the name of a Brāhmaṇa. In fact, a Brāhmaṇa and a realiser of Brahman are convertible terms. These doctrines must be carefully remembered by those who might regard a Brāhmaṇa as one who belongs to a particular social caste. On the other hand, anyone of the lower classes — the backward class, the depressed classes and Harijans — who might realise God might equally be entitled to the name of a Brāhmaṇa or Brahman-knower. Charanadas tells us that such a Brāhmaṇa intro, verts the outgoing senses. Everyone knows that all our senses are extratropic, and it requires a great moral and spiritual power to turn them inward. Anyone who is able to do this, says Charanadas, should well be called a Brāhmaṇa. Sex and anger have no place in the being of such a man. Compassion is the chief insignia of his Brāhmaṇhood (जनेऊ). A Brāhmaṇa, according to Charanadas, is one who has gained both moral and mystical perfection. In this connection, we are told by Charanadas that the one principal function of a Brāhmaṇa is to learn आतमविद्या and to teach it. A Brāhmaṇa must spend the major part of his time in the contemplation of God. It is his business always to be merged in God. If, however, any time remains on hand, he must, as Plato recommends, learn and teach philosophy, which would enhance his intellectual grasp and make him socially useful. The present writer was wonder-struck to read a signboard called शब्द-प्रतापाश्रम when he last visited Gwalior. When he went inside, he saw that it was an Ashram which was devoted to the practice and propagation of Kabir's doctrine of शब्द. Even in this spirit, a Brāhmaṇa, says Charanadas, must learn आतमविद्या for himself, and teach it to others.

This description of a Brāhmaṇa by Charanadas brings to our mind a similar description of a Brāhmaṇa by Purandaradas which runs thus ;

ब्राह्मणनेंदरे ब्रह्मन तिळिदव. It is neither desirable nor possible to discuss this latter poem at length at this place. This will be done when the work on Karnatak Mysticism may come to be written. In the meanwhile, the following five points of spiritual experience may be noted, upon which Purandardas insists in his poem as being the chief marks of Brahminhood— (1) Anahata sound, (2) Rain of pearls, (3) Vision of moonlight, (4) Partaking of nectar, (5) Entrance into the ring of a thousand circles as well as into the expanse of शिशुमार, thus summarising in the experience of a saint both the microcosmic and the macrocosmic aspects of spiritual experience.

3. *God, the source of all virtue*— Let us now go to a direct treatment of the effects of the company of the saints on the progress of the aspirant. In a very celebrated poem, Nanak tells us the extreme value of the company of the good. The first chief effect of the company of the saints, says Nanak, is that it enables us to forget the difference between the self and the not-self— ethically (बिसरगई सब आप पराई), and therefore metaphysically. There is no enemy and no friend to such a man, no national no foreigner. He belongs to the city of the world, and, for the matter of that, the city of the spiritual world. He would not be satisfied with a mere Cosmopolis, but must be a member of the Theopolis. Another effect of

the company of the saints is that it puts in the mind of the aspirant an attitude of reconciliation with the highest reality – call it Nature or call it God. In the history of thought, we have had many instances to support this reconciliation between the developing aspirant and the order of nature. All that is good to thee, O Nature, says the great Stoic philosopher, Marcus Aurelius, is good to me. Job in the Old Testament reiterates the same idea in another fashion when he exclaims, "God hath given, and God hath taken away. Blessed be the name of the Lord". All prosperity, all adversity, all good and bad happenings in the world take place on account of the will of God. In a philosophical way, Leibnitz has explained the same idea in his doctrine of optimism enunciated in his Law of Sufficient Reason. Whatever is, says Leibnitz, has sufficient reason for its occurrence 'जो प्रभु कीनो सो भल मानो' says Nanak. Also we have in a great modern philosophic poet, Robert Browning, an expression of the same idea when he says, " God is in the heaven and all is right with the world. " To such a reconciliation, therefore, either with the order of the nature or with the will of God, does the progressing mystic arrive on account of the company of the saints. Nanak tells us what influence this company had made on his own mind. He says it was on account of the saints that he was able to have a continuous and unceasing vision of the one Sporting Lord, who is immanent both in man and in nature, thus illustrating what Green has said about the unity of the spiritual principle in nature and in man. This mystical vision makes Nanak laugh and blossom like a lotus. Every movement in the world of Nature and of man is to him a miracle worked by God.

There is, again, another very famous poem in Tulsidas, जाके प्रिय न राम बैदेही, in which he points out how this vision of God reacts on the saints, and binds them together with the vinculum of God-love. This verse is regarded as Tulsidas's reply to a letter which Mirabai wrote to him concerning some difficult situations in her family. Mirabai was troubled at home; her husband was dead; her brother-in-law was giving her every imaginable trouble. Everybody regarded her almost as an outcast; and so, being very much dissatisfied with her own life, she wrote a letter to Tulsidas as to what she should do, as to whether she should go out of the house and renouuce all claims to the kingdom. The song is supposed to be the reply which Tulsidas gives. The question has been debated as to whether this may be taken as a historical event. On the whole, however, the conclusion among scholars is that it may be so taken.

Another special feature of the poem is that Tulsidas gives his own personal opinion in the matter : 'एतो मतो हमारो '. Whenever any important idea comes up, Tulsidas gives his own personal opinion : Compare his utterances मोरे मत बड़ नाम दुहूँ ते and निज विचार अनुसार. In this case, likewise, he gives his personal opinion about God-love being the vinculum substantiale.

To prove this point Tulsidas first gives certain illustrations. For example, he tells us how, for the sake of God, Bharata left off his mother, Prahlada left his father, the Gopis left their husbands and Bibhishana left his brother. In spite of these things, however, says Tulsidas, their names have become symbols of auspiciousness in the world, 'भे जग मंगलकारी' ; in spite of their derelictions of duty their names have become mementos of universal respect and praise.

Tulsidas goes on to say, in this connection, that if anyone comes in the way of our God-devotion, we must renounce him. Says Christ also, in a similar manner, "leave off thy father and thy mother and follow me." Ramdasa has said that we should not mind renouncing our very dearest relatives, provided we can secure the friendship of God : देवाच्या सख्यत्वासाठी । पडाव्या जिवलगासी तुटी । Carlyle also expressed the same sentiment: "He who does not believe in God is our enemy. Our only business is to fight him to the death." We may see by reference to the Bhagwadgita also how it regards God-devotion as the supreme virtue. If we follow the argument of the Twelfth Chapter of the Bhagwad Gita, we shall find that in the last eight verses, Bhakti is regarded as supreme among all virtues, other virtues being only aspects of it. In the poem we are considering, Tulsidas tells us unreservedly that between any two friends or relatives, such as husband and wife, father and son, brother and sister and so on, God-devotion is the only link of real love – not any carnal love, nor any physical love, nor even any intellectual love. It is the spiritual love – the love of God – which binds all people together.

The present writer takes the liberty of calling the attention of his readers to a philological point here. Let us take the two lines—

> नातो नेह रामके मनियत, सुहृद सुसेव्य तहाँ लौं ।
> अंजन कहाँ आंखि जेहि फूटइ, बहुतक कहउँ कहाँ लौं ॥

Now, this is the reading that we have adopted in our text. Instead of the word तहाँ, two of the readings suggested are जहाँ and कहाँ. The present writer has discussed in his annotations to the poem that the reading जहां लौं is not of much value, because it makes सुहृद सुसेव्य the antecedent, and नेह से नाता मानना the consequent. In the case of the reading तहाँ लौं this difficulty is avoided. राम के नेह से नाता मानना becomes the antecedent, of which सुहृद सुसेव्य becomes the consequent. But, according to this interpretation, the first line नातो नेह............तहाँ लौं

would become an indicative statement and the second line अंजन..........कहाँ लौं an interrogative statement. Also, it involves a प्रतीप दृष्टान्त instead of a direct दृष्टान्त, which should certainly have been better. On the other hand, if we adopt the reading कहाँ लौं in the first line, the questions in the two lines become parallel with one another and there is no प्रतीप दृष्टान्त but a direct दृष्टान्त. There is, however, one difficulty in this, namely that the word नातो will have to be split up into ना and तो, so that the interpretation would be, 'how can you call a man, a friend or a relative unless he has an affection for God. What is the use of that collyrium which would only destroy our vision?' On the whole, the point of the two most important lines in Tulsidas is that God-love must be regarded as the only bond of union between any two relatives or friends.

This reminds us of the famous doctrine of Leibnitz in his Monadology that the monads, which are all indepedent, have no direct relationship with one another, except through the Central Monad, and that the only relationship that can subsist between any two monads is the indirect relationship through God. God thus becomes the Vinculum Substantiale. God, according to Leibnitz, is the Monas Monadum, and all the other monads are bound to this central monad by the bond of substantiality. Similarly, God–devotion, according to Tulsidas, is the bond of substantiality between any two relatives or friends.

This idea is also otherwise expressed in an Upanishad, which tells us that the spokes of a wheel are connected with each other not directly, but only through the central hub which is God : अरा नाभा विवार्पिताः. Also one can easily recall to mind the famous Upanishadic utterance

न वाऽरे सर्वस्य कामाय सर्वं प्रियं भवति ।
आत्मनस्तु कामाय सर्वं प्रियं भवति ॥

The mother should be dear to us not for her own sake but through God; the son should be dear to us not for his own sake but through God; everything should be dear to us not for its own sake but only through God. Love for God thus becomes the central and the highest virtue.

We have referred, at the beginning of the discussion of our present poem जाके प्रिय न राम बैदेही, to the story which connects the names of Tulsidas and Mirabai. It seems, however, that the same poem has even a more important feature about it, namely the connection it brings out between Tulsidas and Narsi Mehta, the famous poet saint of Gujrat. This point has not attracted the attention of scholars; so the present writer is taking the liberty of placing it before them. There are such great resemblances in the teachings of Tulsidas and Narsi Mehta on this head that one is kept wondering how the resemblances may be explained. Let us quote the poem of Narsi Mehta here in the original :

नारायणनुं नाम जे लेतां वारे तेने तजियेरे ।
मनसा वाचा कर्मणा करीने लक्ष्मीवरने भजियेरे ।
कुळनें तजिये, कुटुंबने तजिये, तजिये माने बापरे ।
भगिनीसुतदाराने तजिये, जेम तजे कंचुकी सापरे ।
प्रथम पिता प्रह्लादे तजियो न व तजियुं हरिनुं नाम रे ।
भरत शत्रुघ्ने तजि जनेता न व तजिया श्रीराम रे ।
ऋषिपत्नी श्रीहरीने काजे, तजिया भरथार रे ।
तेमां तेनु कांइए न गयुं पामी पदारथ चार रे ।
व्रजवनिता विठ्ठलने काजे सरव तजि वन चाली रे ।
भणे नरसैयो वृंदावन मां ते नो घणुं माहली रे ॥

It is not necessary for the poem to be translated because Gujrati like Marathi is alike to Hindi, and Hindi scholars may be able to understand it with a little trouble. It may be seen that the main points brought out in the poems of Tulsidas and Narsi Mehta are exactly similar. Tulsidas tells us that if anybody stands in the way of our God-devotion, we should brush him aside. In the same style, Narsi Mehta speaks about our rejection of all those who have no love towards God. It matters little whether it is the father, or the mother, or the brother, or the Guru, or the husband who stands in the way. They should all be rejected is the doctrine which both Tulsidas and Narsi Mehta propound. The illustrations which Narsi Mehta and Tulsidas give are almost identical. Bharata as having renounced his mother, and Prahlad as having renounced his father for the sake of God-love, are illustrations common to both. Bibhishana as having abjured his brother, and Bali as having left off his teacher, have been mentioned by Tulsidas. The ऋषिपत्नीs as having renounced their husbands are mentioned by Narsi Mehta. Finally the व्रजवनिताs as having forsaken their husbands for the sake of Krishna are mentioned both by Tulsidas and Narsi Mehta. We may note the word व्रजवनिता. Neither Tulsi nor Narsi use the word Gopis, but use alike the word व्रजवनिता in this connection. One is kept wondering whether Narsi Mehta may have influenced Tulsidas in this matter, especially as Narsi Mehta lived about a hundred years before Tulsidas. That was the question that troubled the present writer, but he consoled himself by remembering that the doctrine of the renunciation of the relatives is common, and almost the same illustrations occur in Tukaram also, though no influence has been traced between him and Narsi Mehta on the one hand, and between him and Tulsidas on the other. Tukaram tells us in a famous Abhanga :—

> नारायणीं घडे जेणें अंतराय । होत बाप माय वर्जावीं तीं ॥
> येर प्रिया पुत्र धना कोण लेखा । करिति तीं दुःखा पात्रशत्रु ॥
> प्रह्लादें जनक विभीषणें बंधु । राज्य माता निंदु भरतें केली ॥
> तुका ह्मणें सर्व धर्म हरिचे पाय । आणीक उपाय दुःखमूळ ॥

Here, like both Narsi Mehta and Tulsidas, Tukaram has mentioned Prahlada, Bharata and Bibhishana, though he has not mentioned the व्रजवनिताs. On the whole, therefore, so far as our present problem is concerned, it may not be impossible to believe that there was an independent parallelism of thought between Narsi Mehta and Tulsidas in this matter, though the parallelism remains wonderful. Further, the idea of Narsi Mehta पामी पदारथ चार रे has an echo in Tulsidas in चार ही चनक की in another connection. This implies that all the four पुरुषार्थs are attained in our pursuit of God. There is, however, one original feature both in Narsi Mehta and Tulsidas in connection with their doctrine of God-love. Narsi Mehta tells us that the rejection of our relatives should be like the casting of a slough by a serpent. जेम तजे कञ्चुकी साप रे is the trump card of Narsi Mehta. On the other hand, as we have seen, the most characteristic feature of Tulsidas is the bond of God-love, which binds all the devotees of God together. The Vinculum Substantiale is the trump card of Tulsidas.

4. *Virtue in action*— Tulsidas was maddened with God-love, and he repeats this idea, time after time, in a number of great continued metaphors or साङ्गरूपकs, which might adorn any literature of the world. We shall first consider the साङ्गरूपक on the chariot of spiritual victory. The

central idea of this सांगरूपक of the chariot is that the place of the charioteer is occupied by God-love, which leads the warrior to spiritual victory which is his aspiration and goal. " The wheels of his chariot, " says Tulsidas, " are the virtues of valour and courage ; truth and goodness constitute respectively its flag-staff and banner; the four horses that drive the chariot are vigour, discrimination, self-control and benevolence; forbearance, compassion and equanimity constitute the triple cords which bind the horses to the chariot." When the external paraphernalia of the chariot have been thus described, Tulsidas gives us the central idea of his poem, namely God-devotion as being the charioteer, who leads the chariot to spiritual victory. The warrior, who sits inside the chariot, must have as his sword and shield dispassion and contentment respectively. Generosity constitutes the axe in his hands, and his intellect is the magical missile – the Shakti of ancient times and the atom-bomb of modern. If the warrior wants to exercise his bow and arrows, science would constitute his bow, a steady and motionless mind would be the quiver, and the Yamas and Niyamas the arrows, that are deposited in the quiver. By Yamas and Niyamas Tulsidas is, of course, referring to the teaching of Patanjali who regards अहिंसासत्यास्तेयब्रह्मचर्यापरिग्रहा: as the Yamas and शौचसन्तोषतप:स्वाध्यायेश्वरप्रणिधानानि as the Niyamas.

These are the arrows that must be deposited in the motionless and steady mind and taken out as necessity requires. One does not know whether one might agree with the sage Manu who tells us on this head that we must practise the Yamas always, but that we may not practise the Niyamas from day to day. We do not think the second opinion is right; in fact, if तपस् and ईश्वरप्रणिधान are not to be practised day after day, how is spiritual victory to be attained ? Finally, we are told by Tulsidas that the worship of the Spiritual Master is the impenetrable armour of the warrior which no arrows can pierce, and which might therefore be called the unimitable equipment in his victorious journey through life : एहि सम विजय उपाय न दूजा।

5. *God-devotion as superior to mere intellect or morality* — We shall now proceed to consider a very important section of the Padas, which deal with the relation of God-love to God-knowledge, in other words, of Bhakti to Jnana. We have here a number of Padas to our credit in the discussion of this subject – two from Tulsidas, two from Surdas, and one again from Tulsidas. In the first two Padas, we shall have again two सांगरूपक्स, involving an incomparable moral imagination, in the first of which Jnana is compared to a lamp of great luminosity, while Bhakti is regarded as a

jewel of great brilliance. The distinction between Jnana and Bhakti according to Tulsidas thus comes to be the distinction between a dazzling light and a brilliant jewel, the first of which kills the insects of passion that come to attack it, and the second dispels them away without killing them. We may say in passing that Jnana could not be credited with the virtue of Ahimsa while Ahimsa becomes the soul of Bhakti. After we have discussed these two great सांगरूपकs from Tulsidas, we shall proceed to two very fine poems from Surdas on the subject of the relation of Jnana to Bhakti, Jnana being exhibited in the advice of Uddhava to the Gopis, and Bhakti in the answer which the Gopis give to Uddhava. After these two antinomies from Tulsidas and Surdas between Jnana and Bhakti, we have a note of almost final reconciliation between the two from the pen of Tulsidas in the fine poem सुनु मुनि तोहि कहउँ सहरोसा, in which it will be shown that Jnana is not antithetical to Bhakti, but that the two could be very well reconciled together. In the last poem which we shall consider in this chapter, we shall come to a discussion of the New nine kinds of Bhakti according to Tulsidas. In this discussion we may say that Tulsidas has almost excelled himself. It is true that he has borrowed his material from the Adhyatma Ramayana and his classification of the nine kinds of Bhakti and their typification in the personality of one single individual, viz. Shabari, who is an embodiment of all the nine kinds, are simply admirable : सोइ अतिसय प्रिय शबरी मोरे, सकल प्रकार भगति दृढ़ तोरे ॥ We may thus conclude that God-devotion is the highest virtue of which man is capable. It will then not be very difficult to prove that the whole catalogue of virtues that may have been discussed in any great moral treatise are merely emanations from, or aspects of, this supreme virtue of God-devotion, and vices merely derelictions of, or aberrations from, that great central virtue.

Let us now proceed to discuss the first great सांगरूपक from Tulsidas on the subject of Jnana as compared to a light of great luminosity. Tulsidas spends a great deal of imaginative moral effort in the enumeration of the different stages in the production of physical light, and their comparison, stage by stage in the moral process, up to the attainment of the bliss of self-illumination. Tulsidas gives us four stages in the process of the production of light. The first stage is the production of butter, the second stage is the making of ghee, the third is the lighting of the lamp, and the fourth the effects of the light. Under these four stages, he discusses how physical and spiritual illumination is to be reached.

Tulsidas begins by telling us how, when a cow feeds on good grass, a high quality of milk is produced. From the milk, by the process of जावनु, curds are produced. From curds, with the help of a मथानी, butter is produced. This makes the First stage.

This butter is to be placed on fire which is to be lit up with suitable wood for liquefaction. When the dross is burnt away, pure ghee is produced. This is the Second stage.

Then a level lamp-stand with suitable projections is to be taken, and in it wicks made of pure cotton are to be placed and they are to be lit up. This makes the Third stage.

When the wicks give out light, darkness is dispelled; insects that come to attack it are destroyed, being burnt up in the flames, and steady white illumination spreads all round. This forms the last stage.

Let us now see the process by which the Spiritual illumination is to be attained.

Here सत्त्व is the cow which feeds on the यमs and नियमs and yields milk in the form of pure धर्म.

From this milk the curd of मुदिता is to be produced with the help of धृतिजावनु, and this to be subjected to the process of churning, which may be called विचार (विवेक), and the result is the production of butter in the form of विराग or वैराग्य. We may well compare here the celebrated discussion on 'विवेकवैराग्य' in the twelfth Chapter of Ramdas's दासबोध (12. 4.).

Now the fire of योग is to lit up for which शुभाशुभ कर्मs serve as fuel. On the fire is to be placed the नवनीत for liquefaction. When the dross of egoism has been burnt away, the result is the production of pure ghee in the shape of Jnana.

Now the level lamp-stand of equanimity is to be taken, in which the ghee is to be poured, and in which are to be placed wicks made of the triple threads of the three qualities and of the three states of consciousness. This will give out light of great luminosity called विज्ञान, which will, on the one hand, destroy all the insects of passions that may come to attack it, and on the other, spread the illumination of self-bliss all round.

The two processes of the production of physical and spiritual illumination may for convenience sake be now set down in a comparative chart as follows:—

Stage I

1	धेनु	सत्त्व
2	तृण	यम, नियम
3	पय	धर्म
4	दहि	मुदिता
5	मथानी	विचार (विवेक)
6	नवनीत	विराग (वैराग्य)

Stage II

7	इंधन	शुभाशुभ कर्म
8	अग्नि	योग
9	घृत	ज्ञान

Stage III

10	दीवट	समता
11	वाती	त्रिगुण
12	दीप	विज्ञान

Stage IV

13	शलभ	मदादि
14	सुप्रकाश	आत्मसुख

It is hoped that these parallel columns may enable the scholars to make a comparative study of the different stages through which the two processes of physical and spiritual illumination pass.

In another great सांगरूपक, Tulsidas tells us in a beautiful manner how the jewel of Bhakti is to be found and utilised. Just as illustrations for the last सांगरूपक were drawn from the Science of Dairying, illustrations in the present सांगरूपक are drawn from the Science of Mining.

The Vedas and the Puranas are the mountains that surround the mining territory, in which the incidents in the life of Rama serve as mines. Good men are the connoisseurs who know how to find out jewels. ज्ञान and विराग constitute the two eyes for their subterranean vision. Piercing intellect constitutes the pick-axe by which to dig from layer to layer. At last, the jewel of Bhakti is found, which sends out continuous illumination day and night. It puts an end to all darkness in the shape of अविद्या. There is no gusty wind of लोभ to extinguish its light. Locusts and insects, in the shape of lower passions like काम, क्रोध and मोह, which come to attack it, dare not approach it and are dispelled by the dazzling luminosity of the jewel. We are told by Tulsidas that this jewel is really everywhere but it cannot be found out except by the grace of the Lord: सो मणि जदपि प्रगट जग अहई, राम कृपा बिनु नहिं कोउ लहई ॥

Is it not a great coincidence that, on the very day on which I wrote the above account, I read a note in the "Times of India" as follows :—

THE TIMES OF INDIA DATED FRIDAY, THE 11TH JULY, 1952.

BIG DIAMOND MINED

Rewa : July, 9— A diamond weighing about 229 carats has been mined by the Panna Diamond Mining Syndicate from its mines in Panna, the Company's officials claimed here today. They said that the diamond which has not yet been cut had a greenish tint which was considered lucky for its wearer. —P. T. I.

Let us hope that we may be lucky enough to get this superb diamond of Bhakti, and wear it.

We have seen above a discussion of the antinomy between Jnana and Bhakti made by the great Tulsidas in his two opposing साङ्गरूपकs, one serving as a thesis and the other as an antithesis. We shall now proceed to consider another antinomy between Jnana and Bhakti in two famous poems of Surdas. It is very unfortunate that the poet-saints of India, to whatever part of it they may belong,— to Uttar Pradesh, Maharashtra, or Karnatak—have all misunderstood Uddhava, and most of them have misunderstood also the relationship of the Gopis to Krishna. In their interpretation of the relationship between the Gopis and Krishna, they have not rightly stressed the mystical aspect of the relationship, which they interpret more or less on sexual lines. It is given to women as also to men to have a vision of God, and that is all that the Gopis aimed at, and did achieve in their relationship with Krishna.

Surdas like other poet Saints misunderstands Uddhava and represents him as a mere Jnani rather than as a Bhakta. On the other hand, those who will take the trouble of reading the most celebrated chapters at the close of the Bhagavata in which Krishna is mentioned as addressing his final words to Uddhava before passing away, will not fail to be impressed by the highly devotional and mystical relationship that existed between Uddhava and Krishna. In fact, the present writer is tempted to believe that Uddhava was perhaps the greatest devotee that ever lived. To put in the mouth of such a great devotee – a realised devotee of God – utterances pertaining to shallow doctrines of mere knowledge is doing injustice to the memory of Uddhava, and to the spirit of realisation as a whole.

People who belong to the ordinary rung of Advaitism are more or less epistemological Advaitins; others are psychological Advaitins; only a few others are mystical. When it is a question as to how to interpret the real meaning of Advaitism itself, it would be absurd to interpret it either from the purely epistemological or from the purely psychological point of view. Jnana means knowledge no doubt, but what knowledge ? This knowledge is really nothing but the intuitive realisation of God. This is not the proper place to discuss the three sides of Advaitism. It would be enough for the present to say that the Advaitism of Uddhava was of a highly devotional and mystical type, instead of a merely intellectual or psychological one. It is from this point of view that we have to assess the value of the so-called intellectual Advaitism which has been put in the mouth of Uddhava by Surdas.

The three celebrated doctrines that have been put by Surdas in the mouth of Uddhava are known to every student of Vedantism. In the first place, the Brahman or the highest reality must be Nirguna, it must transcend all qualities, it must transcend pleasure and pain, it must transcend good and evil. It is such an idea of transcendent Brahman which this epistemological Advaitism aims at.

The second doctrine is the doctrine of appearance. This doctrine cannot be better put than in the words of Surdas himself : " The world is an appearance. The five elements are an appearance. The three qualities are an appearance. All embodied forms which are made up of these are an appearance. Form and contour, names and qualities, family and caste, father, mother and consort, are all appearances. " Students of comparative philosophy know how this doctrine of appearance may compare with another account of apearance which we see, for example, in such an absolutistic philosopher like Bradley. It is again not our concern here to discuss the comparative merits of the two systems of appearance. It would be enough if we just point to the difference between the two systems, the one being based on a spiritual foundation, and the other on an empiristic one.

Lastly, the fundamental platform of the so-called Advaitins is that there is no road to liberation except through knowledge. What knowledge is, they leave entirely undecided. Knowledge does not mean an intellectual conception, or a philosophy of the world. If Jnana be taken to mean intuitional realisation, there is no objection to regard it as responsible for liberation. The Bhagavadgita has so often used the word Jnana in this sense.

(1) न हि ज्ञानेन सदृशं पवित्रमिह विद्यते ।
तत्स्वयं योगसंसिद्धः कालेनात्मनि विन्दति ॥

(2) तेषामेवानुकम्पार्थम् अहमज्ञानजं तमः ।
नाशयाम्यात्मभावस्थो ज्ञानदीपेन भास्वता ॥

It may also be remembered that the Bhagavadgita does not find any contradiction between a Jnani and a Bhakta. On the other hand, it regards a real Jnani as a Bhakta of the highest type :—

तेषां ज्ञानी नित्ययुक्त एकभक्तिर्विशिष्यते ।
प्रियो हि ज्ञानिनोऽत्यर्थम् अहं स च मम प्रियः ॥
उदाराः सर्व एवैते ज्ञानी त्वात्मैव मे मतम् ।
आस्थितः स हि युक्तात्मा मामेवानुत्तमां गतिम् ॥

It is the doctrine of intellectual Advaitism which the Gopis passionately attack. It is unfortunate that they had not learning enough to make a distinction between Jnana and Yoga : ऊधो हमहि न योग सिखै है. Barring this, however, they insist on God-devotion as the supreme way to God, and their devotional approach to God is worthy of our respectful consideration. The first criticism of the doctrine of knowledge which the Gopis make is that the conception of Nirguna only fills them with deep sorrow : निगुण सुनत दुख पैहै. How will it look, they ask, if instead of interlacing their hair with flowers, they kept a crown of dust over their heads : जिहि सिर केस कुसुम भरि गूँदै तेहि किमि भसम चढ़ै है. Secondly, they say, they have nothing to do with the doctrine of liberation as above enunciated : मुक्ति रहै घर बैठि आपने. Their liberation exists elsewhere. Thirdly, they say that knowledge has merely led men to infatuation. It is not merely the theoretical approach that we want. We want, say the Gopis, a practical approach to God. Tell us, Oh Uddhava, they say, how to modulate our lives, and how to regulate them so that we may be able to reach Hari. And what is meant by Hari ? The expression used by Surdas in this connection is आपुन आपु लखै है. This is susceptible of two interpretations. In the first place, the self should reveal himself before us, and secondly, Krishna should reveal himself before us. Criticising as they do the Advaitic doctrine, it will not be correct to interpret that the expression should mean to Gopis that the self should reveal himself before them in a Yogic manner. On the other hand the expression आपुन आपु लखै है may well refer to Krishna himself. It is customary in Hindi as aginst Marathi to use the word आप for " others " to show respect. Here it is the respect for Krishna that is intended. Show us the way, they say to Uddhava, by which Krishna in his own form might reveal himself to us. Their only concern is to know when that enchanting figure, wearing the nine brilliant diadems, might come back to Gokul. Braja is the alpha and the omega of their life, and they would not tolerate the subsistence of Krishna even for a moment anywhere outside Braja.

We have seen hitherto the two antinomies between Jnana and Bhakti in Tulsidas and Surdas respectively. Let us see now how they are reconciled by Tulsidas in his eudeamonistic doctrine, which gives to Jnana the things which belong to Jnana, and to Bhakti the things which belong to Bhakti. " A Bhakta is one, " he says, " who renounces his faith in everything else and places it only in me. The one mark of distinction between the Jnani and the Bhakta is that while the Jnani believes in his own powers, the Bhakta believes in mine, and surrenders himself entirely to me. " Would it be too much to ask our readers to recall to their minds the controversy between the Markata (monkey) school and the Marjar (cat) school in the later development of Ramanujian thought? To return to our discussion, however, Tulsidas tells us that as a consequence of this surrender, it becomes the task of God to save his Bhakta from dangerous situations as a mother saves her child. Let us quote the words of Surdas himself. " I am the constant door-keeper of my devotee, " says the Lord, " I make it a point to save such a one from dangerous situations as a mother saves her child by withdrawing it instantly from a fire or from a serpent " : गह सिसु बच्छ अनल अहि धाई तहँ राखइ जननी अरगाई. While a Bhakta, according to Tulsidas, might be compared to a young child, the Jnani might be compared to a grown-up son. The mother loves them both. But the latter cannot naturally expect to have her former attention. Finally, we are told by Tulsidas that a real Jnani is one whose knowledge is not inconsistent with his devotion. Tulsidas gives almost a pragmatic justification for this reconciliation between Jnana and Bhakti. As both the Jnani and Bhakta are susceptible to temptations, prudence becomes the better part of valour, says Tulsidas, and a Jnani does not renounce his faith in God. It may not be correct to attribute such a merely pragmatic view to a Jnani. The Bhakti, by which he did ascend to the topmost rung of the ladder of Jnana or Illumination, could not be kicked away as soon as he has reached the highest rung. Illumination has sprung from and has grown out of a devoted search after God, and as soon as the basis is taken away, the topmost rung will crumble to the dust.

We finally come to a unique poem in Tulsidas, in which he discusses his new sheme of the Nine kinds of Bhakti. From the times of the Bhagavata downwards, we have known a famous verse which tells us

श्रवणं कीर्तनं विष्णोः स्मरणं पादसेवनम् ।
अर्चनं वन्दनं दास्यं सख्यमात्मनिवेदनम् ॥

There are some points of merit and also some

points of defect in this. We do not want to enter into these here, because our principal business is to consider Tulsidas's conception of Bhakti. There is one point, however, concerning स्मरण and कीर्तन, which we may here discuss. Now, these two words are understood in different ways in the South and in the North. In the South, the Smarana is Namasmarana and Kirtana is a religious sermon or a lecture interspersed with songs. In the North, Smarana means internal recollection through the mind and Kirtana external recollection by word of mouth. Both the views are good in their own way. Tulsidas, however, does not make this nine-fold division of Bhakti as it is usually understood the basis of his scheme.

It has been customary to regard Tulsidas as an Avatara of Valmiki. We do not know whether we should believe in such an idea. Probably we may require great factual evidence before we can prove that one is an Avatara of another. Nevertheless, Tulsidas might well be regarded as a literary Avatara of Valmiki, in as much as he clothes in a Hindi garb most of the ideas and sentiments that are to be found in Valmiki. In this nine-fold scheme of Bhakti,—what he calls Navadha Bhakti,— Tulsidas is very closely following what the Adhyatma Ramayana has said about the same topic. Tulsidas has almost adopted the whole of the scheme of the Adhyatma Ramayana in toto, though there are a point or two of excellence in Tulsidas, and a point or two of excellence in the Adhyatma Ramayana. We shall combine the two schemes, group them in a logical order, and then see the ingredients of what might be called the nine-fold scheme of devotion.

Putting the two schemes together, we might say that there are three strands of development in the nine-fold scheme. These might, for the sake of convenience, be called the "Contributory", the "Essential", and the "Effective". Under the first come a number of moral virtues which are necessary for spiritual realisation. The second consists of three different kinds of Bhakti, pertaining to the service of the saints and of the spiritual teacher. Under the third strand come properly the five kinds of Bhakti which might be exhibited in an effective pursuit of God. So, on the whole, these three strands show one, three, and five different kinds of Bhakti which, together make up the nine-fold scheme. They may, for the sake of ready reference, be exhibited as follows:—

CONTRIBUTORY : MORAL VIRTUES.

1. अमान, विरति, सन्तोष, परदोषादर्शन and so on.

ESSENTIAL : SERVICE OF TEACHER AND SAINTS.

2. गुरुपदपंकज सेवा
3. संतन कर संगा
4. मोते संत अधिक करि लेखा

EFFECTIVE : PURSUIT OF GOD.

5. मम गुण गान (व्याख्यातृत्वं मद्वचसाम्)
6. रति मम कथा प्रसंगा
7. मंत्रजाप
8. मोहिमय जग देखा
9. मम भरोस

Let us go on to a little more detailed discussion of the above scheme.

According to the Adhyatma Ramayana and Tulsidas, the first kind of Bhakti is concerned with moral virtues in general. There are many illustrations of these moral virtues, a proper development of which alone constitutes the first kind of Bhakti. Tulsidas cites these virtues as अमान, विरति, संतोष, परदोषादर्शन and so on; but he is careful to tell us, in Aristotlean spirit, that these virtues cannot be achieved in a single day. He uses the words 'Nirantara' and 'Bahukarma'. We must continuously practise these virtues until they become perfect in us. Aristotle tells us 'ethos is ēthos': character is habit. When we add one instance of a particular virtue to another, day after day, then we can say that that particular virtue becomes established in us.

This, however, raises the question as to which of the different virtues may be regarded as supreme. In the Bhagwad Gita, as we shall see presently, Bhakti or God-devotion is regarded as the supreme virtue. In ancient European ethics, we are conversant with the discussion in Plato as to whether wisdom, temperance, courage or justice might be regarded as the highest virtue. In modern ethics the same discussion applies in the case of benevolence, justice and equity. In Christian times, faith, hope and charity were regarded as great virtues, and of all these charity was regarded as supreme. Everywhere we find there is an attempt in reaching what may be called the central or the supreme virtue. In Tulsidas as well as in the Bhagvadgita devotion to God is regarded as the highest virtue.

In the second strand we have got three different kinds of Bhakti, enumerated both by Tulsidas and the Adhyatma Ramayana. सन्तन कर संगा, the company of the saints, is the first virtue; गुरुपदपङ्कजसेवा, the service of our Spiritual teacher, constitutes the second; मोते संत अधिक करि लेखा, to regard one's Spiritual teacher as higher than even the Godhead, the third.

In the last strand of our spiritual development, we exhibit five different kinds of spiritual virtue, one after another. The first and the second are concerned with the singing of the qualities of God (ममगुण गान) as well as his exploits (रति मम कथा प्रसंगा) and his words or message (व्याख्यातृत्वं मद्वचसाम्). In order that God-devotion might develop in us, we must sing his praise, think of his qualities, narrate his exploits and contemplate on the spiritual words which he might have left for us. The third Bhakti under this head is concerned with the uttering of God's name (मन्त्रजाप). The fourth and the fifth consist in the seeing of God everywhere (मोहिमय जग देखा) and a complete belief in God (मम भरोस), which is also expressed by the great Vedantist, Shri Madhvacharya, in his famous words रक्षिष्यतीति विश्वास: " God is in the heaven and all is right with the world. " This maxim ought to direct the aspirant's progress, and help him in his onward march. According to Tulsidas, therefore, मम भरोस, a complete belief in the beneficence and the power of God, constitutes the highest kind of Bhakti.

We might contrast with this the views expressed by Narada. According to Narada, the highest kind of Bhakti cannot be defined in terms of भरोस. It must be defined in terms of Prema : सा त्वस्मिन परमप्रेमरूपा. Again, one who reads the Narada Bhakti Sutras cannot but be struck by the mystical nature of the Bhakti which he has enunciated : यल्लब्ध्वा पुमान् सिद्धो भवति, अमृतो भवति, तृप्तो भवति ।। यत्प्राप्य न किंचिद् वाञ्छति, न शोचति, न द्वेष्टि, न रमते, नोत्साहीभवति ।। यज्ज्ञात्वा मत्तो भवति, स्तब्धो भवति, आत्मारामो भवति ।।

Narada also gives certain definitions of supreme Bhakti according to Parashara, Garga and Shandilya, but he ultimately stresses his own point of view, namely, that Bhakti may be regarded as परमव्याकुलता about God.

We do not want to enter here into the ticklish question as to whether Bhakti may be regarded to be essentially भरोस or प्रेम, faith or love. Suffice it to say that, according to Tulsidas, राम भरोस is the apex of all virtues. He has already elucidated for us the nine-fold scheme of Bhakti. Supernal Bhakti, according to Tulsidas, is a diamond with nine different facets, each representing God from its own point of view and all together making up what we may call our total devotional attitude towards God. This total devotional attitude, according to Tulsidas, was exhibited by Shabari (सकल प्रकार भगति दृढ़ तोरे) and no person could be regarded as an ideal saint, who does not exhibit all these kinds of devotion.

ETHICS IN THE HINDI SAINTS

A Constructive Survey.

1. Any one, who has closely followed the development of the argument in the present chapter, will be easily able to call to mind the number of virtues in the various poems which the Hindi saints exhort us to cultivate, and the vices which they want us to avoid. This is just the problem of an analytical study of Ethics. The analytical study concerns itself with an enumeration and elucidation of the different virtues and vices, and the synthetical with the building up of a theory of Ethics thereon. It is true that the Hindi saints have not written any formal treatise

on the science of Ethics; but their contribution to this science nevertheless remains truly remarkable from the analytical point of view.

2. We shall presently enumerate the main virtues and vices that have been so exhibited in the various poems of this Chapter. But before we do this, let us call to mind the classifications of virtues which have been made by certain great Western moralists—classifications such as intellectual and moral, civic and philosophic, idio-psychological and hetero-psychological, self-regarding and other-regarding, and so on. As we are not writing a work on Ethics, a detailed discussion of these need not concern us here. Suffice it to say, that the mention of these classifications has been necessary in order to show the background upon which our own classification has been made, namely, individual, social and spiritual.

3. In order to do full justice to the analytical side of Ethics in Hindi saints, we first made a complete inventory of all the virtues and vices that have been mentioned in the present chapter. As this process, however, did not mean more than a bare enumeration of virtues and vices, and that too of very large number of them, we selected the more important of these in order to base a synthetical construction thereon. Thus we selected eight individual virtues, four social virtues, eight spiritual virtues, and six vices.

This might for our purpose constitute a significant inventory of the virtues and vices that have been dealt with by Hindi saints. The inventory might stand as follows:—

INDIVIDUAL VIRTUES :

1.	Activism.	करनी
2.	Non-attachment.	विराग
3.	Discrimination.	विवेक
4.	Self-control.	दम
5.	Courage.	धीरज
6.	Patience.	सबूरी
7.	Sufferance.	गरीबी
8.	Equanimity.	समता

SOCIAL VIRTUES :

1.	Good Company.	" सन्तन्ह कर संगा "
2.	Sympathy.	दया
3.	Benevolence.	परहित
4.	Sacrifice.	त्याग

VICES :

1.	Braggartism.	करनी विन कथनी
2.	Pollution of Mind.	"दिल अपना नहिं राखै साफ"
3.	Greed.	तृस्ना
4.	Hypocrisy.	कपट
5.	Arrogance.	मगरूरी
6.	Voluptuousness.	" अब मैं नाच्यौं "

SPIRITUAL VIRTUES :

1.	Celibacy.	ब्रह्मचर्य
2.	Penance.	तप included in यम and नियम

3.	Introversion.	"बाहर जाता भीतर आनै"
4.	Study of Philosophy.	आतमविद्या
5.	Reverence for Master.	गुरुपदपंकजसेवा
6.	Meditation on God (His Name, Qualities, Exploits, and Words)	मंत्रजाप, ईशगुणगान, मत्कथालाप, व्याख्यातृत्वं, मद्वचसाम्
7.	Divine Optimism.	मम भरोस
8.	Vision of God everywhere.	"मोहिमय जग देखा"

4. It may now be asked, relevantly, which of these virtues might be regarded as the most fundamental according to Hindi Saints. (i) Each age, it has been said, exhibits its own particular virtue. The Greeks, for example, regarded Measure, Order or Harmony as their chief virtue. The Christians regarded Charity as supreme, the Middle Ages insisted upon Chivalry as the greatest virtue. When we come to the 18th century, we find that the virtue of that age is the virtue of Benevolence. In the 19th century stress was laid on Equity. (ii) As with the ages, so with the philosophers. Plato, for example, has been credited with regarding Justice as the highest virtue. Critics of Plato say that Plato was unable to define the nature of justice accurately : to him, it was said, it might be either a fourth virtue or a summation of the other three. On the other hand, we feel that Plato did regard Justice (Dikaiosyuni) as the highest virtue, being the virtue of the philosopher. When we come to

Aristotle, we come to a very great Ethical philosopher. It is true that there is no guiding thread through the list of the virtues he has discussed. That seems to be Aristotle's chief defect. But his insistence upon Magnanimity as the supreme virtue, his doctrine of the Mean, which has been regarded as the life-blood of moral conduct, his dictum that character is habit, thereby giving a practical turn to our cultivation of moral virtues, (compare also the characterization of virtue by Tulsidas as निरन्तर and वहुकर्मा) and his seeing, as through a glass, darkly, that the highest human virtue may be a contemplation of the Divine Theoria, are really great contributions to ethical philosophy. After Plato and Aristotle, the two great names in the history of ethical thought are evidently those of Spinoza and Kant, and one cannot but be struck by the contributions they made to ethical philosophy by introducing their central conceptions of an Intellectual Love of God and the Kingdom of Ends respectively. Finally, coming to the modern period, Sidgwick, in his distinctive doctrine of Philosophic Intuitionism, reconciling the claims of egoism and altruism, and Green with his budding doctrine of Self-realisation, which later on assumed such big proportions both by way of exposition and criticism, cannot but be regarded as the chief lamp-posts of the present-day ethical thought.

5. Reverting to the question posed at the beginning of the last paragraph, we might ask what is the guiding thread through the list of virtues advocated by the Hindi saints, which might enable us to determine the nature of the central virtue, as Kant was able to discover his Unity of Apperception through the labyrinth of the Categories. We can easily find an answer to this question if we go back to the preceding song we have discussed, namely, on the nine-fold scheme of Bhakti. We are not concerned here so much with the different species of Bhakti as with the nature of Bhakti itself. God-love would then be found to be the central virtue in which are focussed all the virtues that have been mentioned in our inventory, and which thus illumines them all. All virtues, to deserve the name, must merely be the expressions, manifestations, or aspects of this central virtue, and all vices only derelictions or aberrations therefrom.

6. The present writer must confess to a sense of inspiration which he received years ago from a study of Augustine, who, true Christian as he was, recognising the three virtues of faith, hope and charity, could succeed in making charity the supreme virtue, and showing others to be merely aspects of it. In addition, he made his idea applicable to the Platonic virtues also. So, Charity or Love, according to Augustine, was the

basal conception upon which the whole superstructure of moral life was to be built. I cannot resist the temptation of quoting succintly the passages which influenced my thought in this direction :—

"*Faith* and *Love* are mutually involved and inseparabble; *Faith* springs from the divinely imparted germ of *Love*, which in its turn, is developed by Faith to its full strength, while from both united springs *Hope*, joyful yearning towards ultimate perfect fruition of the object of love."

These three Augustine regards as the essential pillars of Christian virtue; along with these, indeed, he recognises the old four-fold Platonic scheme of virtues, namely, of Temperance, Fortitude, Justice and Prudence, which he also explains as being equally the expressions of the central Christian virtue of Love :

"*Temperance* is love keeping itself uncontaminated for its object, *Fortitude* is love readily enduring all for the beloved's sake, *Justice* is love serving only the beloved and, therefore, rightly governing, *Prudence* is love sagaciously choosing the things that help her and rejecting the things that hinder."

7. When, with this torch in my hand, I began to survey the contribution of the

Bhagavadgita to ethical philosophy, I found that the same idea was very powerfully expressed in the 12th chapter of the Bhagavadgita also: not simply love, but God-love which is the टेक, the पल्ल or the ध्रुपद of the spiritual song that the author sings at the close of the 12th chapter. One who will take the trouble of reading the passage from अद्वेष्टा सर्वभूतानाम् to the end of the chapter will not fail to be struck by the insistence upon God-love which is the burden of the entire song.

यो मद्भक्तः स मे प्रियः
भक्तिमान् यः स मे प्रियः
भक्तास्तेऽतीव मे प्रियाः

and so on. So, the eight chief virtues which the Author enumerates in that passage may all be regarded, according to him, as the manifestations of the one central virtue of God-love: (i) मैत्री; (ii) करुणा; (iii) समता; (iv) संतोष; (v) यम; (vi) शौच; (vii) असङ्ग and (viii) श्रद्धा.

8. This tempted me to find out whether we might not make the same principle of God-love applicable to the virtues embodied in the literature of the Hindi saints. This is the synthetical or the constructive side of the ethics of Hindi saints. Let us, for example, select four out of the individual virtues, two out of the social, and four again from the spiritual virtues from the inventory we have made at the beginning of our

discussion, and see how they are all expressions of God-love. The virtues we select are :—

INDIVDUAL VIRTUES.

1. Non-attachment. 3. Self-control.
2. Discrimination. 4. Patience.

SPIRITUAL VIRTUES-

1. Study of Philosophy. 3. Meditation on God.
2. Reverential Service to the Spiritual Teacher. 4. Divine Optimism.

SOCIAL VIRTUES.

1. Sympathy. 2. Benevolence.

10. Beginning with the individual virtues, we may say that God-love is so absorbing that it does not suffer any other claimant to the throne; thence arises the necessity of dispassionateness (विराग) for everything except God. Discrimination (विवेक) and God-love may be related to each other like a lame and a blind man : God-love would not become effective unless it has the direction of Discrimination. How, again, would it be possible for us to love God unless we have controlled all our sense-organs and mind ? Hence self-control (दम) becomes an essential propaedeutic to God-love. The vision of God is not a matter of child-play; it requires long and patient toil (सबूरी), almost to the point of exhaustion or even dis-belief.

11. Let us now take the social virtues. If God is in all men, God-love must manifest itself through sympathy (दया) to all human beings. Sympathy thus becomes the source of Dharma. Tulsidas himself has said elsewhere,

> दया धर्म का मूल है, पापमूल अभिमान ।
> तुलसी दया न छाँड़िए, जब लग घटमें प्रान ॥

Then, again, sympathy and benevolence are related to each other as the negative and positive poles of the spiritual battery. Where sympathy or compassion (दया) would stop with inspiring high ideals in individuals, benevolence (परहित) would move out and show itself in positive acts of beneficence to humanity. परहित is just the Tulsidasian spiritual equivalent of the Benthamite ultilitarian conception of Benevolence.

12. Coming to the spiritual virtues, the study of philosophy for oneself and for others (आतमविद्या) becomes a cardinal requisite for the determination of the nature of God, and consequently for our attachment to Him. Even if we may not agree with Tulsidas in his doctrine मोते संत अधिक करि लेखा or that of वाल्मीकि 'मद्भक्तेष्वधिकापूजा', we could at least grant that, without rendering the highest reverential service to our Teacher (गुरुपदपंकजसेवा), the double lock of God-love and God-vision would not open out to us. Martineau has spoken of Reverence as the highest in the scheme of ethical virtues ;

with far greater force is this applicable to the reverence which we bear towards God or our Spiritual Teacher. Meditation on the Name (मंत्रजाप) and Qualities (गुणगान) of God are related to God-love in terms of reciprocal causation. Unless we have मंत्रजाप and गुणगान, God-love cannot be created in us and unless the germ of God-love is in us we may not be tempted to, and certainly not succeed in carrying on our मंत्रजाप and गुणगान. Finally, of what value would our God-love be to us unless it sees in every happening in History and in Nature the beck and call of God, and unless it sees the fruition of the logical law of Sufficient Reason in the mystical realisation of a God-centered Optimism (मम भरोस) ?

CHAPTER III

The Relation of God to Saints.

The subject-matter of our present chapter is God in relation to the Saints in Hindi Mystical literature. The problem of God is always an interesting and difficult one, and when we try to find its bearing on mystical literature, it becomes all the more difficult, because mysticism transcends philosophy, and cares only for the intuitive apprehension of God.

In our present chapter, we shall first speak about the Problem of God as it appears in some major Saints of Hindi literature. Here, we shall come across the philosophico-mystical argument of Ramanand, the description of God as Niranjana by Kabir, and the conception of Tulsidas that the Niranjana God assumes the form of Saguna. After this, we shall have two intercalary views of Tulsidas bearing on the subject, namely, the inscrutability of the reasons for the incarnation of God, and God as inspiring different emotions in different men. We shall next proceed to consider the theistic-pantheistic utterances of Mirabai, the highly poetic analogies of Raidas about the relation between Saint and God and Nanak's doctrine of the unity of the internal and the external perception of God. We shall then pass on to the second part of our problem, namely, the prayers which the Hindi saints have offered to God. These prayers fall under two heads, first the Philosophical prayers, and second the Lyrical prayers. In the Philosophical prayers, man's mind is equanimous with the Real. In the Lyrical prayers, it goes out of itself to reach the highest Ideal. We have examples of the first in the ethico-philosophical poem of Dadu, Raidas's poem with its strong emphasis on the necessity of mutual perception by Saints and God and, lastly, a poem in imitation of Tulsidas on the parity between Saint and God — the Saint being an oarsman through the river of life and God an oarsman through the ocean of existence. The lyrical prayers may be illustrated firstly from Surdas's two poems, which give us the instances of a bird on a tree caught between the hawk and the hunter, and of a sparrow on the high seas, which has no other place to perch on, except the mast of God. Then again, we have a lyrical poem in Surdasian style on a blind man praying to God to make him reach the topmost part of the hill through tortuous and dark ascents. After this, we shall come to two more poems, giving us desperate utterances of a female and a male devotee respectively, on the fulfilment of their aspirations towards God.

Finally, at the end of the chapter we shall discuss a very remarkable poem by Bahiro which, after reviewing the various kinds of liberation, comes to regard resignation to God as the highest consummation for man.

1. *God in Ramanand and Kabir, Tulsidas and Mirabai, Raidas and Nanak* : (*i*) *Ramanand*— We shall begin the first part of our discussion with the view of Ramanand about the nature of God. Now, Ramanand is a big name. He was supposed to be a resident of Banaras and to have belonged to Ramanuja's school. He became the teacher of Kabir by being obliged reflexly to utter the words "Rama, Rama." He was also the spiritual teacher of Raidas. He did not make any distinction between a Brahmin, or a Mohammedan or an Untouchable. It is for that reason, probably, that his views were not much liked in his time by the orthodox people. Ramanand is supposed to be also a teacher of Vitthalpant, the father of Nivrittinatha and Jnanadeva. How this squares with his being the teacher of Kabir is a question which historians have to tackle. If, however, this be taken as a fact, then the line of Jnanadeva might also, in one sense, be regarded as being connected with Ramanand, though his proper teacher belonged to the Gorakhanath school. Ramanand has written one very fine poem. He

has no other poem than this to his credit, and it comes to us from the Granthasaheb of Guru Nanak. It is a brilliant poem. It would do credit to any one who might write treatises on mystical subjects.

We might see from the song of Ramanand that it has got more Kabirism about it than Tulasism. One does not know how many changes may have been effected in it before it went into the Granthasaheb. But, discussing the poem as it is before us, it is a wonderful poem both philosophically and mystically. "Where shall I go out?" asks Ramanand: कत जाइए रे, घर लाग्यो रंगु. "My whole house has been filled with colour, and with different kinds of colour". We have preferred this interpretation on account of the parallel conception of चंदन चोआ down below; but रंग may also mean अनुरक्ति or devotion. Ramanand goes on to say: "My intellect has become stationary and my mind refuses to move. Where shall I go out? You ask me to go out to search God and to worship Him. It is not necessary for me to go anywhere. Wherever I may go, I shall find merely stones and water": जहँ जाइए तहँ जल पखान. It is not necessary for one to go out. God is inside us. God is here, there, and everywhere: ....जेथें तेथें धोंडापाणी। उगाच वणवण हिंडोनि। काय होतें॥ says Ramadas. So, on the whole, we may see Ramanand teaches the doctrine of the universal pervasiveness of God—pervasiveness, in Green's terminology, in nature as in man. He is present in the whole universe and, at the same time, he is present in the mind of man.

" Once upon a time the idea occured to me," says Ramanand, " that I might make a very fragrant mixture of sandal and other perfumes, and then go out to worship God. But my teacher showed my God within myself to whom I could make all my offerings " :

एक दिवस, मन उठी उमँग
घसि चंदन, चोआ बहु सुगंध ।
पूजन चले ब्रह्म ठाईं,
सो ब्रह्म बतायो गुरु, मनहिं माहीं ।।

That raises a very important question. Ramanand's house was full of colour, and his mind was full of fragrance. Now, those who are students of mysticism know that Ramanand is speaking here about certain peculiar experiences which are not to be found generally among other mystics. People speak about light and sound, more or less, but they rarely speak about colour and fragrance; for example Mirabai speaks about colour :

उड़त गुलाल लाल भयो अंबर । बरसत रंग अपार रे ।।

Mirabai's experience is distinguished by the phenomenon of colour, and Nivrittinath's experience by the phenomenon of fragrance: चंदन परिमळु. Colour and fragrance as manifestations of spiritual energy are some-what rare, and these Ramanand experienced inside himself. So, it was not necessary for him to go outside at all.

Then, he says that his entire delusion in its extent and intent had come to an end by the vision of God: जिन सकल निकल भरम काटे मोर. It is significant to remember that Ramanand here makes the vision of God the cause of which the termination of all delusion is the effect. This is just the point of controversy between the path of Knowledge and the path of Devotion, between Philosophy and Mysticism. According to the one, there would be no vision of God unless there is a prior termination of all delusion. According to the other, it is only when there is a prior vision of God that all delusion terminates. Ramanand chooses the latter alternative.

On the whole, therefore, we may say that, in this short poem, Ramanand contributes three very significant ideas to mystical thought, namely, (1) the universal immanence of God, (2) colour and fragrance as forms of spiritual energy, and (3) the termination of all delusion by the vision of God; and it is no wonder that he became the founder of the school of mysticism in Northern India.

(*ii*) *Kabir*—Another famous idea of God in Hindi mystical literature is the idea of God in Kabir. Of course, the subject is a big one, and we cannot hope to do full justice to it in a part of a chapter like this. We shall, however, take one central and fundamental point in Kabir's idea of God, namely, his doctrine of God as Niranjana. As the present writer has been studying Kabir's poems, he finds that Kabir's thought is focussed on the central conception of the collyrium-less entity, which is the God Niranjana. Kabir says

देव निरंजन और न दूजा ॥
परम पुरिख तहँ देव अनन्ता ॥

and he identifies the Niranjana God with the Parama Purusha. Also, the Niranjana or the Parama Purusha, the Highest Being, is expressed in terms of the spiritual Sound and the spiritual Light, which are usual ways in which Kabir tries to express the nature of God.

' सबद धुनि घंटा . . . .
परम प्रकाश सकल उजियारा. '

In these expressions he tells us how ' Niranjana ' is the ' Parama Purusha '. That seems to be the central thought of Kabir so far as the nature of God is concerned. Kabir, here, has an analogue to the doctrine of the Upanishad which speaks of

निरञ्जन : परमं साम्यमुपैति

or else to the lullaby of Madalasa when she addresses her child as

शुद्धोऽसि बुद्धोऽसि निरंजनोऽसि.

It seems, therefore, very natural that the word ' Niranjana ' should mean the God without collyrium, the spotless or immaculate God, the Highest Being full of 'Light and Sound'. This is the primary meaning of the 'Niranjana' of Kabir.

But, later on, as Kabirite theology developed, and as the word 'Niranjana' came to have a cosmological significance, 'Niranjana' became responsible for the creation of 'Swarga' and 'Patala', even of Brahma, Vishnu and Mahesha. And here it was that Kabir himself was obliged to separate the concept of 'Niranjana' from the concept of 'Saheb'. He says :

'जिन साहब से भये निरंजन सो पुरुष है न्यारा।'

So it seems that in such a passage, Kabir is giving us, in the relation of 'Saheb' and 'Niranjana', an analogue of the way in which the 'Vedanta' talks of 'Brahman' and 'Ishwara'. This point was made much of, by the followers of Kabir, and all the evils of creation were later attributed to this 'Niranjana', so that critics came to say, that instead of being an 'Ishwara', he was almost the equivalent of the evil principle 'Saitan' in creation.

One of the arguments adduced for this concept of the Evil Principle is the way in which he is described both as the son of his mother as well as the husband of his mother. Now, this is simply an उलटबांसि or an allegory to represent a fundamental thought in a seemingly paradoxical fashion.

What Kabir meant was that this 'Ishwara' was born from 'Brahman' with the help of 'Maya', so 'Maya' was his mother; and with the help of 'Maya' he created the whole universe, so 'Maya' was his wife. Not understanding this allegorical conception about 'Niranjana', people have regarded this doctrine of 'Niranjana' in later Kabirism as the doctrine of 'Saitan' which is an absolute misunderstanding of the allegorical meaning underlying the conception of 'Niranjana'.

Those of us who have studied the 'Rigveda' know that in a famous passage 'Pūshan' is described as the husband of his mother and the paramour of his sister.

मातुर्दिधिषुमब्रवं स्वसुर्जारः शृणोतु नः

Now, the allegorical interpretation of this passage as the students of Vedic culture know is that 'Pūshan' or the Sun-God is the husband of the night who is his mother, because he proceeds from her. He is also the paramour or lover of his sister, the Dawn, whom he closely follows. So, these natural phenomena of the night, the dawn and the Sun have been allegorically metamorphosed into the conception of the mother, the sister and the husband. Similar, it may be supposed, was the case with the Kabirite Doctrine of 'Niranjana'.

Lastly, in regard to that doctrine it may be pointed out that Kabir was quite aware of the meaning of 'anjana' as collyrium or evil—physical, moral and metaphysical; and he says —

'अंजन आये अंजन जाये'

(collyrium comes and collyrium goes, but 'Niranjana' remains as he is.)

'कहै कबीर भरम से मन भागा
एक निरंजन सों मन लागा ।'

His mind was taken away from illusion, and was now fixed on the conception of 'Niranjana'—the one Absolute and Immaculate God. This then seems to be the central point in Kabir's conception of 'Niranjana'.

(*iii*) *Tulsidasa*—We have seen above what Kabir's idea of the Niranjana God was. Tulsidas's idea of God is mainly that of 'Saguna'; but he does not fight shy of the concept of 'Nirguna'. In a very famous passage in Tulsi-Ramayana, beginning with 'सोइ सच्चिदानन्दघनरामा', Tulsidasa deliberately uses the word 'Niranjana' in his description of God :

अगुन अदभ्र गिरा-गोऽतीता । सब दरसी अनवद्य अतीता ॥
निर्मल निराकार निर्मोहा । नित्य निरंजन सुख संदोहा ॥

Thus, while in Tulsidasa Rama is the highest God, Rama is at the same time an expression of this 'Niranjana'. In fact Tulsidasa, in the lines above referred to, puts together the positive and the negative attributes of God, as is done in certain passages of the Upanishads, for example,

कामामयोऽकाममयः क्रोधमयोऽक्रोधमयः
तेजोमयोऽतेजोमयः इदंमयोऽदोमयः ।

In fact, in this passage, God is described as being capable of contradictory attributes, because he surpasses them all. In this way, Tulsidasa puts together the positive and the negative attributes of God in his description of Rama.

Ultimately, however, if the balance be struck between Nirguna and Saguna in Tulsidasa, Saguna would appear to be superior to Nirguna. Tulsidasa says—

'निर्गुन रूप सुलभ अति, सगुन न जानहिं कोइ.'

It is possible for people to understand Nirguna, but it is not possible for anybody to understand Saguna. What is the reason ? Tulsidasa answers that the exploits of the Saguna God so much transcend the imagination of the reader and the hearer, that these are befooled in concentrating their minds on God as Saguna ; that even the great Sages come to their wits' end in hearing the exploits of the Saguna God.

In regard to the nature of Saguna and Nirguna in Tulsidasa, we shall have occasion to speak often in our later discussions. At present it is enough to say that in Tulsidasa the Saguna may not be regarded as contradictory of Nirguna, though Saguna is superior to Nirguna, and the highest form in which the Saguna expresses itself is his favourite deity Rama.

Next, we go to Tulsidasa's doctrine of incarnation. If we were to ask Tulsidasa whether Rama was the only incarnation of God, probably he would have no hesitation in saying 'yes', even though he regards other deities also as worthy of deityhood. Tulsidasa's Bhakti was of an intimate and concentrated—we might even say of a jealous—type. He had no other object for his worship than the one single deity Rama. What the meaning of this Rama is, we shall see later on. Now the question arises, if God incarnates himself in the form of Rama, what are the reasons for his incarnation ? Here Tulsidasa gives a very original concept for the incarnation of God. He says—

" हरिअवतार हेतु जस होई ।
इदमित्थं कहि जाइ न सोई ॥ "

Look at his acute Sanskrit learning ! Nobody is able to say what the ultimate nature (इदम्) of this God is, and in what manner (इत्थम्) he incarnates himself. " I am at my wit's end ", says Tulsidasa, " in finding an explanation for how God appears in the shape of Rama ".

If Tulsidasa had been accosted as to whether he was contradicting the doctrine of old —

यदा यदा हि धर्मस्य ग्लानिर्भवति भारत ।
अभ्युत्थानमधर्मस्य तदाऽऽत्मानं सृजाम्यहम् ॥

then he would have answered, " I quite see the point; I am not against it. "

संत मुनि वेद पुराना ... ...

All these have talked of the veritable appearance of God in the form of Rama. So says Tulsidasa also :

" असुर मारि थापहिं सुरन्ह, राखहिं निजस्रुति सेतु ।
जग बिस्तारहिं बिशद जस, राम जनम कर हेतु ॥ "

This is exactly on the lines of the Bhagvadgita and other ancient scriptures. Whenever evil spreads in this world, whenever religion is threatened, whenever good people suffer and evil men prosper, then it behoves God to incarnate Himself in the form of an Avatāra.

" This is true ", says Tulsidāsa, " but most of us stop here at a mere doctrinaire explanation of the nature of Incarnation. " Really, the nature of the Incarnation is beyond our reason and imagination.

" राम अतर्क्य बुद्धि मन बानी ।
मत हमार अस सुनहु सयानी ॥ "

Tulsidasa also makes a further point in his doctrine of Incarnation :—

" राम जनम कै हेतु अनेका ।
परम विचित्र एक ते एका ॥ "

There are hundreds of reasons why God might

incarnate. Who are we to set a limit to the reasons why God should incarnate? Hence Tulsidasa takes resort to his doctrine of Vichitravāda:

'परम विचित्र एक ते एका'

This is the same doctrine which Badarayana had preached in his 'Vedanta Sutra: आत्मनि चैवं विचित्राश्च हि. The present writer may expound it later in another connection, but it is enough at present to say that Tulsidasa's doctrine of Vichitravāda is exactly on the mystical pattern of Badarayana.

We have seen hitherto, how Tulsidasa tries to connect the idea of 'Niranjana with a Saguna God, and then, how he shows that the ways in which this God appears in the form of a 'Saguna' Avatara, are inscrutable. We now pass on to a very original way in which Tulsidasa exhibits an array of emotions in his discussion of a new scheme of nine Rasas. We say 'new' as contrasted with the old scheme of Rasas, namely from Shringara to Shanta as in the following scheme :—

शृंगारहास्यकरुणरौद्रवीरभयानकाः।
बीभत्साद्भुतसंज्ञौ चेत्यष्टौ नाटये रसाः स्मृताः॥
निर्वेदस्थायिभावोऽस्ति ....
.... शांतोऽपि नवमो रसः॥

If we examine the account which Tulsidasa gives of how at the time of the Svayamvara of Sita in the Court of King Janaka, Rama appeared to various persons in various shapes as they looked at him, we can see how Tulsidasa had a new nine-fold scheme of Rasas in his mind. He talks, in the first place, of the triplet of Rasas, namely, Vira, Bhayānaka, and Raudra. The heroic kings, who were assembled in Janaka's court, were filled with 'Vira Rasa', saw Rama as worthy of their steel, or they found him to be an embodiment, the highest embodiment, of 'Vira Rasa' himself. Those who were cowards were filled with terror when they looked at the form of Rama (भयानक रस). In regard to the relationship of 'Bhayānaka' and 'Raudra', Raudra may be said to be the objective aspect of Bhayānaka. What is 'Raudra' from one point of view, is 'Bhayanaka' from the other. Tulsidasa says, "Besides the heroic kings and the cowardly kings, there were Demons also, who were present in the court of Janaka, and who manifested the 'Raudra Rasa, for they saw Rama as being an embodiment of 'Raudra'."

Let us now proceed to take into consideration other kinds of Rasas, namely, Shringara and Vātsalya. The ladies, who had assembled in the Court of Janaka, each looking at Rama in her own way, were filled with 'Shringara'; Janaka and his wives were filled to the brim with 'Vātsalya', as they looked upon the youthful Rama as the future husband of their daughter Sita. Then there were Philosophers in the Court of Janaka, whose minds were filled with 'Adbhuta Rasa': 'प्रभु विराटमय देखा'. This 'Adbhuta Rasa' is very well expressed in a famous passage, we may say it is a 'Vedic' passage, where the 'Virata Rupa' is described as —

> विश्वतश्चक्षुरुत विश्वतोमुखो
> विश्वतोबाहुरुत विश्वतस्पात् ।

In that way, Rama appeared in a 'Virata' form to the Philosophers in Janaka's Conrt.

The Yogis who looked at Rama were filled with 'Shanta Rasa', the perfection of equanimity or tranquillity.

And, finally, the 'Bhaktas', the devotees of God, who had assembled in the Court of Janaka, were filled with 'Ananda' or 'Bhakti Rasa'. There was, of course, no question of Bibhatsa, Karuna, or Hasya of the ordinary rhetorical scheme in the case of Rama.

Beyond these eight Rasas which we have enumerated, there was, says Tulsidasa, an inexpressible 'Rasa' which Sita experienced while she looked at Rama. We shall call it the "*Akatha Rasa*". Tulsidasa says :—

> 'उर अनुभवति न कहि सक सोऊ ।
> कवन प्रकार कहहि कवि कोऊ ॥'

The emotion Sita experienced at heart was 'Akatha'. It could not be expressed in words.

The present writer thinks this 'Akatha Rasa' might be regarded as Tulsidas's great contribution to the nine-fold scheme of 'Rasas'.

Rama in himself was more than a combination of these 'Rasas'. Our modern Gestalt Psychology tells us that the whole is the sum of its parts, but Tulsidasa says that the whole is *more* than the sum of its parts, that the whole is a unity which transcends the mere aspects or facets. It is this transcendent unity which Rama was, while all the Rasas were merely expressions of that unity:

(iv) *Mirabai*— After this account of the original way in which Tulsidasa has treated the nine Rasas, let us pass on to another song this time from Mirabai. A famous song of Mirabai tells us how a Gopi who had gone out to sell her butter exclaims :

'कोई स्याम मनोहर ल्योरी'

To put it in philosophical language, the "theos" of the Gopi became a "pantheos"; her devotion, a cosmic experience. The 'Gwalin' went to Mathura to sell her milk products, but instead of saying "butter or curds", she began to ask people to purchase *Shama* or *Krishna*. The reason was, says Mirabai :

'कृष्ण–रूप छाकी है ग्वालिनि'

The Gopi was filled with the enjoyment of the

form of Krishna. It was on account of this that the joy of her experience produced a delirious chatter in her. We are reminded that this experience of the theos being a pantheos has been elsewhere represented in two other fashions; first, in 'Bihari' when he speaks of an 'Alikhita Patra' (अलिखित पत्र), a letter which was never written at all, by a lady to her lover, and the answer also was another 'Alikhita Patra' (अलिखित पत्र). It was a mute language; the emotions could not be expressed. The present writer has also been given to understand that in one place, Radha, while writing a letter to Krishna, wrote a letter as if Krishna was writing a letter to her, and she began to write 'My dear Radha'. She was so much engrossed in Krishna-Rupa, she was so identified with Krishna, that she entirely forgot her own personality. It is in this way, we see how out of a theistic we really pass on to a pantheistic experience in Mirabai. It is, what may be called in Mirabai, an expression of 'Sāmanjasyavada' a non-contradictional compatibility between the personal and the impersonal.

(v) *Raidas*—After Mirabai we come to Raidasa, who is held in very great esteem for the brilliance of his intellect, his high poetic capacity, as well as for his devotion to God. In one song he tells us how God could be looked at from various points of view. In the first place he says :

'प्रभुजी तुम चन्दन हम पानी'

"Every cell of my body has been filled by Thy presence as every particle of water may be filled by the scent of Chandana." So God is an immanent cause.

Secondly, the devotee dances like a wild peacock before a dense cloud. God is thus a teleological cause. Thirdly, Raidas speaks of God as being a 'Deepaka', and of himself as a 'Bāti' or a wick. This wick is kindled by the light of God. In this way, God is the instrumental cause.

Next he speaks of God as the purificatory cause:

'जैसे सोनहिं मिलत सुहागा'

"Thou art, O God, ammonium chloride, and I am impure gold. It is only by Thy mixture with me that I can become purified."

Finally, there is a very important point which Raidasa stresses, namely, what we might call 'Inverted Immanence'. What is Inverted Immanence? In the Bhagvadgita we are familiar with the famous verse

'मयि सर्वमिदं प्रोतं सूत्रे मणिगणा इव.'

God, there, is the 'Sutra', round which the pearls of the devotees are woven. Raidas inverts the description. He says that God is the pearl, while he himself is the thread, so that God is as valuable as a pearl, and himself as valueless as a thread.

There is, however, a great 'Vyanjanā' here. The pearl-connoisseurs know that the pearl would have no value whatsoever, unless a thread is made to pass through it. Hence unless Raidas was there as a 'Bhakta', and unless his thread went through the pearl of God, God himself would have no value whatsoever. "It is the devotee who gives value to God, and it is thus", says Raidas "I am giving you value". This is what we may call the conception of inverted immanence in Raidas.

(vi) *Nanaka*—Finally, in the discussion of the doctrine of God, we come to a very famous utterance from Nānaka. In Nānaka also we begin with a certain universal immanence, for, he says that God is like fragrance in a flower or image in a mirror. In fact, He pervades all existence. Secondly, he tells us that this experience must be had both internally as well as externally, in mind as in nature, as Green would put it.

'बाहर भीतर एकहि जानो
यह गुरु ज्ञान बताई'

says Nanaka. In other words, according to Nanaka, 'Jnana' means the vision of God both internally and externally.

Now, those who are the followers of the path of God know how difficult it is to see the same form both inside and outside. It must not be imagination; it must not be hallucination; it must be a veritable perception of God. It is only when this experience, namely, '*Bahar Bhitar Ekahi Jano*' is attained, that the mind can be said to have realised the spiritual existence of God. And then finally, Nanaka tells us, that this universally immanent God must be identified with one's self:

'कह नानक बिनु आपहि चीन्हे'.

God must be identified with one's self. This is as much as to say that we must have the experience of 'Tattvamasi' or 'Soham'. Unless this takes place

'मिटै न भ्रम की काई।

the moss of delusion will not disappear; infatuation will not come to an end.

So, on the whole, we may say that Nanaka expresses these points: first, God must be seen both internally and externally; further, God must be identified with one's own self; and finally, it is only when this experience is attained that illusion may disappear.

After having discussed the nature of God according to Hindi saints, we now pass on to two other analogous considerations, namely, the Philosophical or Intellectual Prayers, and the Lyrical or Emotional Prayers, both of which are to be found in Hindi Mystical literature.

As we said at the beginning of this chapter, the 'Philosophical Prayers' are equanimous, they keep the mind on a level. Compare, for example, the Philosophical prayers in Sanskrit literature—

भज गोविन्दं भज गोविन्दं ।

and याचेऽहं करुणासिंधो ।

of Shankara and Madhva respectively. The Emotional or Lyrical Prayers take the mind out of itself, and lift it to divinity. Compare, for example,

सदा माझे डोळां जडो तुझी मूर्ती

and इदे समय हरिये

of Tukaram and Vijaya Dasa respectively. Both these kinds of prayers are to be found in the great Hindi saints.

2. *Philosophical prayers as in Dadu, Raidas and Tulsidas : (i) Dadu:*— Let us begin with Dadu. In the poem तौ निबहै जन सेवक तेरा, we have a great ethical or didactic prayer. Let us see the main points in this prayer. In the first place, Dadu prays to God to keep him ever on the right path. Secondly, if he breaks any thread asunder, let God join the ends together. In this connection, it is necessary to remember that Dadu was a great spinner and weaver. Compare, for example, his great poem कोरी साल न छांडे रे which we shall notice later on.

The reference is to the idea that while weaving a thread, it may break into two parts and thus spoil the garment. Let God help him by joining the two parts together. Then, there is the question of the manipulation of events in such a way, that he may never forget the greatness and goodness of God.

हम विसरें त्यों तू न विसारै ।

Then, again, God is implored by Dadu to prevent infatuation and sin. "I may try to separate myself from you, O God, " says Dadu, "but you must not allow me to do so. You must clasp me to your heart." He also says he possesses no virtues whatsoever which may please God. He, therefore, earnestly calls upon God to give him his "darshana" out of His great benevolence and compassion. This is a great didactic or ethical prayer.

Let us see a few points of philosophical importance in this prayer of Dadu. In the first place, Dadu seems to rely fully on the omnipotence of God. Whatever man may do, God has the power either to extend its goodness or destroy its badness. The question arises as to what is the relationship between self-effort and Grace. Man may make his own effort, and yet it remains with God to crown that effort with success by His Grace. So, whatever faults Dadu might commit, it behoves God to help him out of these. A second point in this connection is the way in which in another similar situation in Pandavagita, Duryodhana had attacked Krishna for having, through him, committed so much mischief and evil. " It is not I ", he says, "who is responsible for the evil actions. It is you, O Krishna, who with your seat in my heart have made me commit them "

केनापि देवेन हृदि स्थितेन।
यथा नियुक्तोऽस्मि तथा करोमि ॥

Dadu does not go to that length. He acknowledges his faults, and he calls on God to help him out of them, by His goodness and omnipotence.

Lastly, in this connection we might quote another example, namely, from James's " Will to Believe ". James says, " Whatever move a novice may make in a game at chess, the expert has the ability always to make such a move as to defeat all the moves of the novice. We in this world are novices. We are making our own moves. If we pray to God, it rests with him in His benevolent omniscience to make such a move as to destroy our moves in their badness, and lead them on to good ". It is in this way probably that Dadu prays to God to help him out of his faults, to make him a holy man, and ultimately to grant His Darshan to him.

(ii) *Raidas*— Next we go to a philosophical prayer from Raidas :

नरहरि चंचल है मति मोरी.

There are certain important points which Raidas makes. The most important of these is, as he says, that "Mutual love is possible only after mutual perception and inspection" :

तू मोहि देखे हौं तोहि देखूं
प्रीति परस्पर होई ।

"I shall love you, O God", says Raidas, "only if I am able to see you as you are able to see me. That you are able to see me, everybody knows; but unless you endow me with the power of seeing you, there can be really no love between us." Then again says Raidas, "Thou art a repository of virtues, as I am a repository of vices :

गुन सब तोर मोर सब अवगुन.

Ungratefulness is writ large on every inch of me":

कृत उपकार न माना.

I and thou, thine and mine, have rent a wedge in human existence. It is only when this duality ceases, that one could cross the sea of life by the grace of God :

मैं तैं तोरि मोरि असमझि सौं
कैसे करि निस्तारा ।

Hence Raidas implores God to give him His 'Darshana'. Unless God shows Himself to him, says Raidas, he will never be able to love Him. Real love of God, in fact, depends on the actual perception of God.

(iii) *Tulsidasa*—The third prayer we may consider is —

मैं मझधारा का माँझि हूँ.

We all know that when Rama wanted to cross the river Ganga at Ramchaura Ghata, the 'Mallah', who was in mid-river, would not go near the shore for fear, as Tulsidasa expresses it elsewhere, that his boat might be turned into a damsel by the pollen of Rama's feet. If his boat was turned into a damsel, he would lose his only means of subsistence. Hence, as Tulsidasa expresses it, the Mallah requested Rama that he might be allowed to take away the 'raja' or pollen from of his 'Padakamala', as there was an uncanny power of personification (मानुषीकरण) in that 'raja'

तरनिउँ मुनिघरनी होइ जाई.

The same idea has been expressed by Tulsidasa in his 'Kavitavali' also: the people in 'Panchavati' were afraid lest, due to the presence of Rama in Panchavati, all the stones in Panchavati might be turned into damsels.

We have to notice a further point in the story. In reply to a query by Rama as to what were his charges for carrying him across the river, the Mallah answers, "No charges! Two of the same trade do not charge each other. A doctor does not charge any fees on a doctor, nor a barber on a barber. I am a Mallah, you are a Mallah. I carry you beyond the river Ganges, you carry me beyond the ocean of existence." So the Mallah insists on an absolute parity between himself and God. But this is a sort of a parity in which one side is loaded very heavily against the other. Crossing the river and crossing the ocean could not be compared to one another, and hence in reality the argument of parity does not hold. On the other hand, when the Mallah asked Rama to sit in his boat, he was not sure whether he would be able to carry the boat to the other shore by his own individual effort. So unless God conferred His Grace on him, it would not be possible for him, he says, to carry Rama Himself to the other shore.

So, we may say that the parity insisted on by the Mallah is a parity only by sufferance.

3. *Lyrical prayers as in Surdas and Bahiro*—
(i) *Surdas*— When we talk of lyrical prayers in Hindi Literature, we cannot have any other idea in our mind except that of Surdas, who is the greatest Hindi lyrical poet. In one very famous poem—

अबकी राखि लेहु भगवान,

Surdas gives us a Saint's prayer to God to guard him from evils coming from opposite sides. He takes the illustration of a sparrow on a tree being shot hy a huntsman from below, and pounced upon by a hawk from above :

दोउ भाँति दुख भयो कृपानिधि

In such a pathetic situation, the sparrow lifts herself emotionally towards God and prays to Him to protect her from the opposing evils. In a Marathi poem also there is a good reference to this story :

पिपीलिकारूपें हरि प्रगटला
अवचित डंखला पारध्यासी
बाण पारध्याचा लागे ससाण्यासी
... ...
बाण लागताचि गतप्राण झाला
रक्षितो भक्ताला येणें परी

Now, in this poem, the author brings in only a 'Pipīlika' or an ant, which is capable of stinging the huntsman and making him shoot off the mark, but not capable of killing him. Surdas has thought better. He has brought in a serpent. The serpent stings the huntsman, and the arrow, which was originally aimed at the sparrow, hits the hawk. And so the huntsman dies on account of the serpent's bite, and the hawk dies on account of the huntsman's arrow. So both these opposite evils destroy each other by the Grace of God.

In this connection, the present writer is reminded of a famous Sanskrit verse which runs thus :—

कान्तं वक्ति कपोतिकाऽऽकुलतया नाथान्तकालोऽधुना
व्याधोऽधो धृतचापसज्जितशरः श्येनः परिभ्राम्यति ।

इत्थं सत्यहिना स दष्ट इषुणा श्येनोऽप्यधः पातितः
तूर्णं तौ हि यमालयं प्रति गतौ दैवी विचित्रा गतिः ॥

Here also the author brings in a serpent. Surdas has followed him, and it was due to the Grace and protection of God that the sparrow was saved from both the huntsman and the hawk. In this way, whenever we find ourselves in a critical situation we should lift our minds towards God, throw ourselves upon His mercy, and pray to Him to protect us from opposing evils.

The present writer is reminded of the position in which India was in the year 1942 during the last Great War. On the one side the Japanese had already bombed Calcutta and other Indian stations, on the other side the Germans and the Italians, with their conquests in Egypt and near the Caucasus, were intending to descend into India. India was caught between the devil and the deep sea, the Japanese on one side and the Germans and Italians on the other. But the cry of the devotees of India was heard by God, and India like the sparrow was saved from an intensely critical situation by the Grace of God.

Let us now take another lyric from Surdas, which has been very much in vogue as sung to the accompaniment of the lyre. Though there is not much of metaphysical thought in it, still there is very intense devotion. The poem in question, namely,

मेरो मन अनत कहां सुख पावै

is an illustration of 'Aikāntika Bhakti'.

A sparrow on a barge in mid-ocean, when the tempest is raging high and the night is falling, and when there is no other place to go to, addresses the ship thus: "Thou art my sole resort, O my Barge". Even so the devotee regards God as his only Barge, on whom he is to rely and in whom he is to rest. There is no other place to go to. Where could the sparrow go in the midst of the ocean? Wherever she casts her eye, she finds only high seas and mountainous billows. Similarly, in the tempestuous sea of life, the only resort for us is God. Surdas further says, following his usual method of analogies and similies, the One God to whom we should send our heart-felt prayer is far above all other petty deities, just as the Ganga is above all rivers, or the lotus above all brambles. There is no use milking a she-goat when we have a wish-cow; similarly, why should we dissipate our energies for nothing? Let us concentrate our mind on the one omnipotent God, who is capable of taking away all our evils under all circumstances.

Then, there is a further prayer-song in the Surdasian manner, in which the use of words is fully worthy of the thoughts it contains:—

नैनहीन को राह दिखा प्रभु.

The situation is like this: Surdas is a typically blind man, who very often talks about the experiences of blind men. A blind man is described in this poem as climbing a very difficult hill. 'डगरिया' in Hindi literally means a road; probably, the Marathi composer of the Hindi song in the Surdas film might have had a hill-top in his mind. The blind man has to climb to this hill-top in pitchy darkness. There are deep ravines below, and one false step would mean instant annihilation. The blind man has to rise to the city of God, which, in the manner of Bunyan, is situated on the top of a hill. He implores God to help him and lead him on the upward path by taking him by the hand, so that the light inside him might be ignited. By that light, he may be able to traverse the darkness and ascend to the city of God.

The significance of the initial song in Sursāgar is great—

आँधे को सब कछु दरसाई.

It is God's great omnipotence which has made a blind man see things, which are not accessible to the vision of ordinary men. What things a blind man could spiritually see, we shall discuss later on. It was said about Homer and Milton, that they wrote poems about heaven when they could not see things even on earth, both being blind men. Even so Surdas. He was physically blind, but from the inside, he had the vision of a great seer. Hence there was nothing very impossible for him by way of the apprehension of God.

After these prayers, which contain the essence of the lyrical devotion of Surdas, let us pass on to two other prayers, one from a female devotee and the other from a male devotee, both in the pure Braja style. As might be seen by the contrast between the two poems, the female devotee sings in devotional and pathetic terms and is prepared to leave away everything for the sake of God, while the male devotee speaks in bold and self-respectful terms and is prepared even to die for God.

Let us see, in the first place, what the female devotee says. We shall here give a free translation of the poem. "I shall leave the house and leave the forest. I shall leave cities and citizens. I shall even leave the parapet near the famous 'Banshibat' (वंशीवट). I shall be afraid of nobody. I shall be prepared to leave my body. But tell me, how would it be possible for me to leave my love? I shall duly discharge my regal duties with full ceremony. People have lost their sense, and accuse me of having lost mine. I shall prevent nobody from calling me a fool if he likes. I shall bid good-bye to all talkers and listeners. I shall leave my father and my brother; and, forsooth, my very mother. But how will it be possible for me to leave Lord Krishna ?" This is her 'Aikantika Bhakti' towards God.

Let us see what the male devotee says. He is prepared to brave all dangers for the sake of God. In a famous song—

तौक पहिरावौ, पाँव बेडी लै भरावौ

the devotee says, "Put an iron ring round my neck, or imprison me in heavy chains. Fasten strong ropes round my body, or flay me alive if you please. Administer poison to me, and then pierce a dagger in my heart. Drown me in mid-stream under a heavy load of stones. Make me sleep on a bed of scorpions, or burn me alive by setting fire to my garments. Throw me down from a precipice, or make a dark cobra inject its poison into me. You may do all these things; but you cannot take away my love towards Girdhari,—the darling of Nand."

(ii) *Bahiro*—We now come to the final verse of our chapter. This verse is an embodiment of complete resignation to the will of God :

इतनी कृपा हो स्वामी जब प्राण तन से निकले.

The devotee throws himself altogether into the hands of God. "Make me, or mar me as you please", he says. The song is composed by a poet not much known to fame; but the ideas it contains are very well worthy of our consideration. Bahiro is imagining here what ought to be his prayer to God when he is leaving his body. He says there are five alternatives possible. "In the first place, I want a sort of रटनमुक्ति, " he says—

श्रीकृष्ण कृष्ण कह कर, मेरी जान तन से निकले.

"Let me say Krishna, Krishna, and die in God." This is what we have called रटनमुक्ति, which belongs to a Bhakta of the type of Narada, and is analogous to what we might call स्मरणमुक्ति.

ओमित्येकाक्षरं ब्रह्म व्याहरन्मामनुस्मरन् ।
यः प्रयाति त्यजन् देहं स याति परमां गतिम् ॥

says the Bhagvadgita. The second type of liberation may be called निकटमुक्ति.

जब साँवरो निकट हो
तब प्राण तन से निकले ।

says Bahiro. "To be in the proximity of God, to be in His presence while dying constitutes the second kind of absolution. This is somewhat like Madhvācharya's doctrine of liberation, namely सामीप्य. Proximity in one sense means proximity before death, and proximity in the other, means proximity after death. Then another kind of alternative he suggests is that of अन्तर्भावमुक्ति

चित्त में जो तू अड़ा हो
तब प्राण तन से निकले ।

"Let me die," says Bahiro, "when Thou art absolutely caught up inside my mind." We know how Ramanuja laid great stress on the conception of अंतर्यामिन्, and his doctrine of liberation was that of सारूप्य. To be like God, not to be simply in His presence or to be near Him, but to be exactly like Him, was what Ramanuja demanded.

'निरञ्जनः परमं साम्यमुपैति'

says the Upanishad. After this we come to the fourth type, namely, आत्मदर्शनमुक्ति. Says Bahiro, "Let God give me His vision (आपहि दरस दिखावे) with the ringing of His anklets (नूपुर की धुन सुनाना), and let me die in that vision and audition, being fully absorbed in God so that there might be no distinction between myself and God." This is like the सायुज्यमुक्ति of Shankaracharya. "यथा नद्यः स्यन्दमानाः समुद्रेऽस्तं गच्छन्ति नामरूपे विहाय," says the Upanishad. This kind of मुक्ति could also well be seen in the Bhagavadgita which says यत्र चैवात्मनात्मानं पश्यन्नात्मनि तुष्यति, or in Patanjali, when he says तदा द्रष्टुः स्वरूपेऽवस्थानम्. So, uttering the name of God, feeling His presence near himself, experiencing His immanence in the mind, or realising his identity with God, the seeker goes on to the last Mukti, namely, शरणगमनमुक्ति.

जब हो तुम्हारी मर्जी
तब प्राण तनसे निकले ।

says Bahiro. This is the Mukti which Krishna taught to Arjuna in the Eighteenth chapter of the Bhagavadgita, सर्वधर्मान् परित्यज्य मामेकं शरणं व्रज ।

We have to "surrender" ourselves to God. Self-surrender, according to the author of the poem is the highest type of Mukti. In modern times, we know Shri Aurobindo Ghosh made "surrender" the chief plank of his Integral Yogic Philosophy. In ancient times, specially in Christ, we find that there is an unmistakable evidence of this type of liberation. Let us carry our minds back to the books of Matthew, Mark, Luke and John, and we shall find how, on the night previous to the day of his crucifixion, in the garden of Gethsemane, when he was experiencing great agony of soul, Jesus Christ prayed " Father, if thou be willing, remove this cup from me; nevertheless, not my will, but Thine, be done"; also how, when, on the next day, he was experiencing great agony on the Cross, he exclaimed in Hebrew, 'Eli, Eli, lama sabachthani.' "My Lord, My Lord, why hast Thou forsaken me"? "I desire," he says, "that my life be spared for spreading Thy gospel; but if it be Thy will that I should pass away, let Thy will be done". This is the great Christian doctrine of liberation through surrender. Ramanuja's Prapatti is also a good Sanskritic counterpart of the same doctrine. The poet Bahiro has given us the quintessence of the doctrines of the great Theistic and Vedantic philosophers, such as the रटनमुक्ति, the निकटमुक्ति, the अन्तर्भावमुक्ति, and the आत्मदर्शनमुक्ति, rounding them off with his own doctrine of शरणगमनमुक्ति, which involves an absolute self-surrender of devotee to God.

CHAPTER IV

The Beginnings of the Pilgrimage

In the last chapter we have taken a panoramic view of the different ideas held by the Hindi Saints about the nature of God and the prayers which they have offered to Him. In the present chapter we shall proceed to a description of the actual path of their pilgrimage, as well as the conditions which are necessary for taking them to their desired goal. In the first place, the aspirants must feel the necessity of a spiritual teacher who will guide them through the moral and the physical turmoils of life. In that matter, we shall consider the characteristics, both moral and spiritual, which are necessary for the spiritual teacher. In this respect the description given by Kabir in regard to these qualities of the Spiritual Teacher can never be excelled. We shall then proceed to discuss the means by which the meditation on God is to be accomplished, namely, the Name of God, as also the relation which Tulsidas tries to establish between the Name and the Form of God. After this comes the methodology of meditation which is described here in five stages. One of the chief contributions which Kabir makes to the process of meditation is what he calls internal meditation : विनहि मुखके जप करो, नहीं जीभ डुलावो. What this means we shall presently see. After this comes the requirement of intensive concentration which is the very life-blood of the meditational process. After concentration come three other requirements, namely, those that have been mentioned in Patanjali as दीर्घकाल, नैरंतर्य and सत्कार. A man must continue his meditation to the end of his life. He must utilise every breath of his life in its service, and, finally, all this must be accomplished in a spirit of devotion. After dealing with these different stages of the meditational process, we shall come to discuss the place which Yoga and Absolutism occupy in the sphere of meditation. Ultimately, we shall find that the meditational process rises superior to both these elements. After this we shall proceed to consider two different types of aspirants with their two different attitudes – the militant and the submissive. The one might be called the tough-minded type, and the other the tender-minded. Kabir, peculiarly enough, illustrates both these, while the tender-minded type finds its superb illustrations in Surdas and Mirabai. In reference to these latter Saints, we shall consider the phenomenon of the so-called Dark Night and the Dawn.

1. *The Guru and His moral and spiritual characteristics* :— Let us begin by considering

Kabir's famous description of the river of life with its tremendous difficulties through which a spiritual guide alone can carry us across. The river of life has been described in an allegorical way by many poets and saints. Some have talked about the flood of the river as submerging the ship of a man's life; others have spoken about the whirlpool in the river; some others have talked about alligators that strike the ship with their tail and destroy it; others again have spoken about the rudderless condition of the ship, which can make it certainly go astray, and possibly to ruin. Kabir, in the present song, गुरु बिन कौन बतावे बाट, gives us other analogies to describe the troubles in which the ship of a man's life might find itself. He first tells us that there is a vast mountainous region in this river of life, and a towering pillar against which the ship might strike and break itself at any moment. Then there are two projecting rocks, the Scylla and the Charybdis, through which it is very difficult for the ship to pass unscathed. Then again Kabir tells us that a sharp shower might overtake the course of the ship, and a tempestuous storm might submerge it at any moment. Finally, even if the ship of man's life escapes all these dangers, there is a gang of robbers which may overtake it, plunder it, and denude it.

This is a great allegory, and a continued allegory for that matter, which supplies Kabir with a number of illustrations, through which he brings out the dangers, which beset the moral and spiritual progress of man. The so-called mountainous region is the region of delusion, which is both extensive and threatening at the same time. Egoism shoots up like a towering pillar (लाट), against which the ship might strike at any moment. Sex and rage constitute the two cruel rocks, through the narrow straits of which it is difficult for the ship to pass; envy is the sharp shower which may at any time throw the ship in a state of confusion, and illusion is the tempestuous storm through which the only destiny of the ship is to suffer a wreckage. Finally, if a man succeeds in escaping all these dangers, he might find himself surrounded by a gang of robbers like avarice and greed, which might destroy his moral and spiritual worth and render him helpless and hopeless. Who can direct the ship of a man's life, asks Kabir, except a spiritual guide, who knows the danger spots and situations, and possesses the power to carry the ship successfully to the other shore of existence?

The two songs in which Kabir celebrates the greatness of the Spiritual Teacher stand unexcelled. The two songs are :—

(1) साधो सो सद्गुरु मोहि भावै

(2) कोई सतगुरु संत कहावै।

The two songs are full of "bon mots", which

express aphoristically what Kabir exactly means by the different qualifications that he attributes to a Sadguru. If we put the two songs together, we shall find that there are four chief groups of characteristics which Kabir assigns to the spiritual teacher. First, there are the moral characteristics of a Sadguru; then there are certain physiological characteristics which demarcate the real Sadguru from a false one; thirdly, there are certain mystical characteristics which belong to a Sadguru proper, and fourthly, there are the social characteristics by which he uplifts all humanity. His success in the spiritual upliftment of humanity marks him out as a real teacher from other so-called teachers. Finally, we shall come to two points in which Kabir summarises the description of a Spiritual Teacher.

To begin with the moral characteristics, we might say that joy is the first characteristic of a Sadguru according to Kabir: सदा विलास त्रास नहि मन में. Lascitude, weariness, neglect and dissatisfaction do not find a place in his being. भोग में जोग जगावै is the typical way in which Kabir speaks of the Saint as keeping the fire of Yoga aflame in the midst of enjoyment. The second moral characteristic of a Sadguru, according to Kabir, is that he maintains full actionlessness in the midst of action: करम करै निहकरम रहै जो. This, in fact, is the essence of the ethical teaching of the

Bhagavadgita. Kabir might or might not have studied the Bhagvadgita, but he must have imbibed the doctrine of actionlessness from the Bhagvadgita. A man who devotes all his actions to God really remains actionless. The third characteristic of a Sadguru is that he enters the region of the fearless (निरभय पद सरसावे,) thus enhancing the first characteristic, namely joy, of which we have spoken above. We may say that fearlessness and joy are related to each other in reciprocal causation. Fearlessness produces joy as joy produces fearlessness, as the Upanishads have put it, आनंदं ब्रह्मणो विद्वान् न बिभेति कदाचन, न बिभेति कुतश्चन ।

Coming to the physiological characteristics, here again we have three chief points to note. A real spiritual teacher, says Kabir, dose not shut the doorways of sense, nor does he feel any necessity for controlling his breath : द्वार न रूंधै पवन न रोकै. His spiritual joy enables him to control his motor and sensory organs automatically, without his playing any active part in the process. Nodding, he does not move, says Kabir, speaking or walking he remains concentred : डोलत डिगै न बोलत बिसरै. A remove local, in the words of Bacon, dose not bring about in him a remove internal. All the while, he is in the consciousness of the spiritual realisation to which he has attained. He remains always self-poised in the midst of all his activities. The second physiological characteristic of a

Sadguru, says Kabir, is that he always enjoys the state of Sahaja Samadhi. This expression means that he has merely to look out to see God. Such a state of Sahaja Samadhi can easily be differentiated from another in which there is प्राण निरोध— प्रान पूज्य किरिया ते न्यारा, सहज समाधि सिखावै. On the whole we may say that there are three such types of Sahaja Samadhi, one the physiological, the second the absolutistic, and the third the mystical. The physiological Samadhi is attained in a full control of the breath in a state of Kumbhaka; the absolutistic and the mystical we shall explain later on, when we come to the song साधो सहज समाधि भली in the fifth chapter of this work. The last physiological characteristic, which Kabir, in his peculiar mannerism, attributes to such a spiritual teacher is that he erects a bottomless cottage between the heaven and the earth : धरती त्यागि अकासहुँ त्यागै, अधर मडैया छावै. The present writer has explained elsewhere the real meaning of this expression. The sum and substance of what Kabir tells us is that between the navel, which constitutes the earth, and the सहस्रार, which constitutes the heaven, such a Sage establishes in the thorax a bottomless cottage in the form of Kevala Kumbhaka. This Kumbhaka is, of course, different from the other two kinds of Kumbhaka, viz., अध: and ऊर्ध्व. Shankaracharya characterises the Kevala Kumbhaka in the following manner :

सहस्त्रशः सन्तु हठेषु कुम्भाः संभाव्यते केवलकुंभ एव. It is a sort of Kumbhaka in which no attempt at Kumbhaka is made. It is a state of breath or breathlessness, automatically induced, which in turn brings about a perfect equanimity of mind and body.

Then again, there are three mystical characteristics of such a Sadguru. The first such characteristic of a Sadguru is that the spiritual teacher is able to make his self-consciousness enter Shabda : ' शब्द में सुरत समावै. What that means only a mystic would be able to understand. A second characteristic is that, wherever the eye is cast, such a Sadguru is able to see only God and nothing else : यह मन जाय जहाँ जग जवही, परमातम दरसावै. In between all the things and himself is God who prevents the vision of the other things. A third mystical characteristic, according to Kabir, is that the Sadguru is able to see outside exactly what he sees inside. There is in such a realiser a perfect parity between internal and external perception :

भीतर रहा सो बाहिर देखै ।
बाहर रहा सो भीतर देखै । दूजा दृष्टि न आवै ॥

This point is note-worthy, in as much as Kabir tells us that when a teacher has seen any mystical form inside, he is able to see it exactly outside. The internal and external perception of God must be alike. If there is internal perception to which nothing external corresponds, it may be a case of imagination, hallucination or illusion. If, on the other hand, there is something external to which nothing internal corresponds, then it cannot be evidently a case of supersensuous experience and may be ultimately unreal.

As regards the spiritual upliftment of his disciples, we may say that according to the law of Spiritual Gravitation, the experience of a worthy Spiritual Teacher must automatically descend to his disciples. As water at a higher level must descend to a lower level, so the experience of a spiritual teacher must descend automatically to those who are walking on the path which he has trodden. Kabir tells us that such a spiritual teacher not only drinks the juice of God's name but also makes others drink it : आप पिए मोहि प्यावै. The ambrosial experience which a teacher gains is thus automatically transferred to the disciples. A second such characteristic is that if the teacher is able to fasten his mind on the अलक्ष, the disciples also are able to see the unseen form of God : नैनन अलख लखावै. He lifts up the curtain of darkness, and makes them visualise the Paramatman : परदा दूर करै आँखिनका परमातम दरसावै. Also, if he is an expert in amalgamating himself with spiritual sound, his disciples also automatically find themselves experiencing the Shabda and coming into unison with it. There is, however, one point to be noted. Kabir tells us that such a teacher does not entangle his disciples in the Shabda: नहि अनुहत अरुझावे. If, by Anahat, Kabir means the sound that comes from the digestive process, as an Upanishad expresses it, and if he may have in his mind any distinction between the Anahat and Shabda, his advice that a disciple must not get himself entangled in Anahat is understandable. If, on the other hand, there is no distinction between Anahat and Shabda, the more one gets himself entangled in Anahat, the more fortunate he must regard himself to be. We may warn the readers, however, that the false sounds which a man hears from the digestive process should not be confounded with the unstruck sound which a mystic is fortunate to hear. Sound and form are both expressions of God, and it matters little in what way God manifests Himself to the aspiring disciple.

Finally, Kabir tells us that the great characteristic of a spiritual teacher is that he enables his disciple to abide in God. To him, according to Kabir, there should be no distinction between हंस: and सोऽहं and no return to the mundane world: कहत कबीर बसावे हंसा, आवागमन मिटावे. To see such a person, says Kabir, is to see God: जाके दरसन साहब दरसै. Such a spiritual teacher is really God, and whatever emotions or feelings, conceptions or aspirations, we might entertain about God, might as well be entertained about such a spiritual teacher, who is His replica upon earth. Ramdas tells us in the same strain जैसा देव तैसा गुरु । शास्त्रीं बोलिला हा विचारु । म्हणौन सख्यत्वाचा प्रकारु । सद्‌गुरुसी असावा ॥ (दासबोध) IV. 8. 32.

2. *The Name and its relation to Form*— The second group of songs in our present chapter concerns itself with the part which the Name of God plays in the meditational scheme and the relation it bears to Form. There are two very classical songs on this head from Tulsidas which we shall notice presently. We shall, however, begin the discussion by stressing the importance which Kabir himself assigns to God's Name, thus showing the ultimate identity of the teachings of Kabir and Tulsidas on this head, though Kabir inclines more or less to the Impersonal and Yogic scheme, and Tulsidas to the Personal and the Devotional. In a fine song अपने घट दियना बारु रे, Kabir tells us that the Name of God is the oil in which the wick of the self is to be drenched, and then ignited by the fire of God. This is how Kabir brings together the Name, the Self, and God. The Name is the material cause, and God the instrumental cause, for bringing to fruition the qualities of the Self. Then Kabir gives us two rules of conduct, one the negative and the other the positive. Negatively, he tells us that we should habituate ourselves to forget the world from time

to time, considering its entire ephemerality. Positively, Kabir advises us to keep the goal we have in view fixedly before our mind and to pursue it relentlessly. When this is done, says Kabir, then जग-मग जोत निहार मन्दिर मे, the aspirant would be able to see the glittering light of God inside the tabernacle of his heart. This is an indication of God's presence and grace, and a sure harbinger of future progress. When this light of God is seen inside our heart, says Kabir, we should offer our body and mind and possessions as oblations on the Divine Altar. It is the Name, therefore, says Kabir, which thus brings together the Self and God.

We shall now proceed to two songs of Tulsidas on the method of meditation to which we have referred, and which have deservedly made the name of Tulsidas immortal. Tulsidas insists upon the Name of God equally with Kabir. We shall first give an account of the famous passage from Tulsi Ramayan नाम रूप दुइ ईस उपाधी, which regards Nama and Rupa as the two attributes of God. This is a very great philosophical poem from the pen of Tulsidas. It is not a mere literary interpretation of it that matters; but it has a great philosophical import. When in our first chapter we spoke about the poem from Vinaya Patrika 'केशव कहि न जाय का कहिये', we pointed out that Tulsidas wanted to go beyond reality, unreality and real unreality. Here also we have a very great philosophical poem from the Ramayana of Tulsidas. We are told in this poem that Nama and Rupa are the two "attributes" of God—exactly the word which Spinoza has used concerning his Substance. Thought and extension are the two attributes of Substance but do not constitute the Substance. Similarly, Nama and Rupa do not constitute God, but they are the attributes of God. There has been a great deal of discussion as to what Spinoza means by his attributes. Some people have taken his theory of attributes to be a parallelistic theory, and others a double-aspect theory. Even so, we can take Nama and Rupa either in a parallelistic sense, or as the two aspects of the same Substance, namely God. In order to understand the full significance of the expression 'attributes', we have to study Spinoza. Attributes, says Spinoza, are what the intellect perceives as constituting the essence of Substance. In addition to attributes, there are modes in Spinoza's philosophy as there are झांकियां in Hindi literature. These are of course unreal. The double-aspect theory implies that Nama and Rupa are the obverse and the reverse sides of the same coin, or the two different facets of the same diamond, namely God.

A second point in Tulsidas is that if we enquire which of them is greater, whether Nama or Rupa, Tulsidas gives a cautious though an intelligent answer. It is impossible for us to say which is greater, says Tulsidas. To say either Nama or Rupa is greater is committing a sin: को वड़ छोट कहत अपराधू सुनि गुन भेद समुझिहहीं साधू. But the philosopher knows in his heart, says Tulsidas, which is greater, and sits silent.

Tulsidas makes a further point. We are told that he who contemplates on God's Name without thinking about His Form, without thinking as to whether his meditation by means of the Name would ever result in his vision of the Form, is superior to the man who meditates on the form of God, because his meditation is Nishkāma. To meditate on God conceiving His Form in our mind is Sakāma and to meditate on God without conceiving His Form is Nishkāma. God comes with greater love, says Tulsidas, to the man who meditates on His Name without thinking about His Form: सुमिरिय नाम रूप विन देखे । आवत हृदय सनेह बिसेखे. So, this is another point in Tulsidas's discussion.

There is a fourth important point in the song of Tulsidas which we are considering, namely, the conflict between Saguna and Nirguna as being resolved by Nama. What does this mean? Now those who have studied Kant's philosophy and especially that most difficult chapter on Schematism would understand exactly what Tulsidas means. According to Kant, perception and understanding will not meet without the help of an intermediate imagination. Similarly, conflicts of Saguna and Nirguna, says Tulsidas, cannot be resolved without the office of an intermediary, namely, the Name. Name is उभयप्रबोधक the illuminator, सुसाखी the witness, and दुभाखी the interpreter between सगुण and निर्गुण. It teaches Saguna to respect Nirguna, and Nirguna to respect Saguna. The great function of schematism in bringing together the opposite irreconciliables is the function here performed by Nama according to Tulsidas.

Let us now consider another important point in which there is a great insistence on Nama as the symbol of ultimate reality. Now consider into how many difficult and most important provinces of Philosophy this conception of Nama leads us. What is the doctrine of Sphota in Indian philosophy ? When the present writer came to his newly built bungalow at Allahabad, he saw a fruit called फूट which is something like a Tarabuja. But the peculiar quality of it is that as soon as it ripens, it breaks out into many parts simultaneously. It develops lines of cleavage. According to some great Indian Systems of philosophy, it is from the Sphota as the ultimate realily that all the existences in the universe spring. The Vaiyakaranas say that the ultimate reality is Sphota, while the Mimansakas and the Alankarikas also say that Sphota is the Ultimate reality. The very opening lines of Panini's Ashtādhyayi tells us how everything came from the Damaru of Shankara supported by the famous verse from the Kāśikā नृत्तावसाने नटराजराजो । ननाद ढक्कां नवपञ्चवारम्. Similarly this Nama plays the part of a Damaru, develops lines of cleavage, and ramifies into different existences. It is the ultimate reality, the Noumenon as it might be called in Kantian terminology. It also performs the same function which the Logos does in Christian philosophy, or "Buddhi" in Samkhya philosophy. What does the Logos do? 'In the beginning was the word, and the word was with God, and the word was God' is an utterance from St. John of which everybody is aware. So the word or Logos is intermediate between man and God. Similarly in Samkhya philosophy, the reconciler between Prakriti and Purusha is Buddhi. It interpretes Prakriti to Purusha, and Purusha to Prakriti. Similarly here, it is the Nama which interpretes Saguna to Nirguna, and Nirguna to Saguna. Look at these three great philosophic conceptions in this poem, namely, the conception of attributes, the conception of schematism, and the conception of Sphota. All these are implicit in the poem. What the present writer has done is only to express them in the language of modern thought.

We shall next proceed to discuss the second song of Tulsidas in this connection— काहे न रसना

रामहि गावहि. "In the case of myself and in the case of people like myself, says Tulsidas, " the tongue has only brought shame to the temple of the mouth." " That mouth in which God should have taken his seat, my tongue has defiled and has brought shame upon it. " In that, it has an accomplice, namely the ears. It is engaged in परापवाद, परनिन्दा and कामकथा and has a peculiar taste for fruitless discussion (वादविवाद स्वाद). The ears are helping it by a contemplation of sexual and erotic matters, which serve as the moonlight for the blossoming of " dispute ". So what is the way out ? Tulsidas says " Engage thyself in the utterance of God's Name, so that thou might take away the sins of the ears ". This is the first point which Tulsidas makes.

How is this going to be done,— the tongue uttering the Name of God and the ears being deprived of their evil propensities and made pure ? The rhetoricians' trick of explaining such a phenomenon with the help of either विभावना which is कारणाभावे कार्योत्पत्तिः or असंगति which is भिन्नदेशकालत्वेऽपि कार्यकारणभावोत्पत्तिः would not help us here. As Kant would say, it is the unity of apperception alone which would bring the tongue and the ears together. Whatever the tongue does would be reported to the central telephone exchange, namely the Self which Kant calls the ' unity of apperception ', and through that also the ears would be exonerated from their sins. So, it is the self or the unity of apperception that is here the schematiser between the Rasana and the Shravanas. Other possible physiological explanations would be those of restitution, exchange, or transfer. Those who would like to take merely a physiological view of things would explain the phenomenon by such laws as those of Restitution, Transfer, or Exchange.

Incidentally, we may refer to Bergson's observations in this connection. Bergson made capital out of a particular experience which he saw in the first Great War. Some soldiers developed aphasia because their speech centre on the left side of the brain, namely Broca's area, was pierced by a bullet shot. But later on, after a year or two, there was a sort of a restitution of the function of speech on the other side of the brain, so that the right side began to work. We know that the centre of speech in the brain for the right-handed man is on the left, and the centre of speech in the brain for the left-handed man is on the right side. Processes of restitution or transfer or exchange which might be made use of for the explanation of this phenomenon themselves rest upon the "unity of apperception" whose physiological expressions they are.

In the case under discussion the tongue could not be expected to wash off the sins of the ears merely by the laws of restitution, exchange or transfer. The unity of apperception would alone serve the purpose of the telephone exchange for inter-communication, as well as of the clearance-house for the washing of sins. The Self must intervene before the tongue could wash off the sins of the ears.

Then there is another very important physiological statement which Tulsidas makes. There is the Ravi in us and there is the Shashi, the Ida and the Pingala, the two parallel chords of the sympathetic nervous system. Now Tulsidas says that the flavour-centre in the brain lies near the Shashi (शशीसमीप रहि), and away from the Ravi. Shashi gives nectar, and Ravi produces mirage. Thou livest, Oh Tongue, says Tulsidas, near the Shashi; then, why not partake of the nectar produced by Shashi, instead of following the mirage produced by Ravi ? Do not follow Ravi, follow Shashi. As a matter of fact, the symmetry of the body-system would require that the flavour centre be situated absolutely equidistant from both the Ida and the Pingala, and, therefore, there should be no partiality for one in favour of the other. Why is it then that Tulsidas advises the flavour-centre to co-operate with the Shashi which, he says, is nearer it, and keep the Ravi at a distance ? It is evident that Tulsidas does this for merely poetical reasons, and there need be no physiological sanction for it. Tulsidas, however, simply wants to encourage the tongue to partake of the nectar of God's name, and we do not want to deny that privilege to the tongue.

Lastly, in this poem, Tulsidas asks us why not make a combination of Mati and Kriya, why not make reason the mate of action जातरूपमति युक्ति रुचिर मनि, रचि रचि हार बनावहि. Let the golden thread of thought pass through the jewels of actions and produce a beautiful necklace. Do good things, and think of good things, and adorn the neck of Rama by this beautiful necklace. " In that way," says Tulsidas to the tongue, Thou wilt not merely have taken away the sins of my ears because they have heard bad things, but Thou wilt get eternal renown for having saved Tulsidas from the evil life and led him Godward." All this comes out of the Rasanā making the utterance of the Name of God its sole funetion. This is the great doctrine of Tulsidas on the value of the utteranee of the Name of God. We shall see in the next Pada from Kabir that follows what he has to say about it :—

अजर अमर इक नाम है.

3, *Five points in the methodology of meditation:* (i) *Internal Meditation*—The distinction between Tulsidas and Kabir is the distinction between the tongue and the breath. You have, according to Kabir, to meditate entirely within yourself by the help of the breath, and one of the characteristics of the success of your meditation would be that the Name would reveal itself before you: सुमिरन जो आवै So, that Name which will reveal itself before you in meditation automatically, unconsciously, even without your thinking about it, is the only Name which is Ajara and Amara. So it is exactly antithetical to what Tulsidas says, and yet both are right. If Kabir is right in insisting that the Name must reveal itself before you in meditation, Tulsidas is right in insisting that we should not discuss whether Nama or Rupa is superior. Then Kabir tells us to direct our attention upwards and open the window of the lateral ventricle: खिडकी खुलवावो. Shri Aurobindo Ghose lately said that one of the chief endeavours of the Sadhaka should be to direct one's consciousness upwards. What that is or what physiological process it involves only the Sadhakas might know. But even if one is successful in directing one's consciousness upwards, that does not enable him to open the window. This is also the idea which is familiar in a Kanarese poet. "When I opened the door," he says, "I found the glory of God everywhere. हरिकरुणवेंबुव कीलिकं दोरेयितु । गुरु करुणवेंबंथ शवितयिंद । ओत्तागि हिडिकोंडु द्वारवनु पोगलु । एत्त नोडिदरत्त शृंगार सदना ॥" It is, however, to be remembered that it is not merely by the effort of the Self that the window of the lateral ventricle would be opened. It is only by the

Grace of God that it will open—not by any effort of man. Then says Kabir, let the self of such a Sadhaka take a bath at the confluence. What is this confluence ? Those who have studied Kabir's Philosophy know that the confluence is where Ida, Pingala and Sushumna meet, where the so-called Ganga, Yamuna and Saraswati meet. All these three nerves meet in the lateral ventricle. So let the consciousness of the aspirant take a bath there, and swim like a fish in that lake, and when it will be able to do so, one miracle will happen, namely, that it will be able to see an inexpressible form upon which it should medidate – ताहि विच इक रूप है । वोहि ध्यान लगावो. So unless our consciousness is directed upwards, unless it bathes in the lake of the lateral ventricle, unless it enters the territory called Ajara, and unless it is able to see that inexpressible Form of God, he shall not be entitled to have satisfied himself with saying that he has entered the path of God. Such a one alone, says Kabir, deserves the name of a Sadhaka.

The following exposition of अजर अमर इक नाम है is a variant on the exposition that has preceded. The exposition that has gone by was made in a lecture on the "Culmination of Spiritual Experience" in the Rashtrapati Bhavan at New Delhi, and the exposition that is to follow was made in the Radio Lecture on Kabir on the first Kabir Jayanti Day at Allahabad.

Let us proceed to discuss the stress which Kabir lays on the Name of God. Kabir tells us like other great Saints of Hindustan as well as of South India that it is the 'Name' (नाम) which matters. अजर अमर इकनाम है. Now what Name is Ajara and Amara ? Kabir gives an answer which rarely any person has given : अजर अमर इकनाम है, सुमिरन जो आवै, not one which offers of itself to our mind, but that which reveals itself to us supersensuously in the process of meditation. There is a vast difference between these two conceptions. It is not the Name which we of our own accord take for ourselves that constitutes the Ajara and Amara Name. 'While we are meditating', says Kabir, 'there is a celestial Name which unfolds itself to our auditory sense at the height of meditation'. That Name is 'Ajara and Amara'. So when a man comes into possession of this Name, his path Godward becomes clear.

The second point in Kabir's methodology of spiritual experience is that he insists always upon internal meditation –

बिन ही मुख के जप करो, नहिं जीभ डुलावो —

'Do not move your lips, do not move your tongue and yet utter the Name of God.' How is this to be done ? Students of Vedantic Psychology have known that there are four kinds of speech – परा, पश्यन्ती, मध्यमा and वैखरी. Watson, the great Behaviourist of modern times, has said that every idea is accompanied by a certain throat-throbbing. The Name is also attended by a certain throat-throbbing. We must go beyond this throat-throbbing. How this is to be done, only the aspirants know.

A third point of Kabir's spiritual methodology is that he says that we should direct our Self upwards in the process of meditation – उलटि सुरत ऊपर करो. Open the window, which in medical psychology is called the lateral ventricle,— open that ventricle : खिरकी खुलवावो. Let the Hansa or swan-like self go by the western path; let it go up; जाय हंस पच्छिम दिसा, and let it take a bath in the Triveni Sangam (त्रिवेणी संगम). What is the Triveni Sangam? It is the confluence of Ida, Pingala and Sushumna. In this confluence, let the ascending self take a bath. After purifying himself by this bath, he will find that he is face to face with an indescribable Form of God.—ताही बिच इक रूप है—upon which he should concentrate his attention. That Form is indescribable. Here the Form is not to be conjured up by the imagination, nor is it an object of hallucination. It is what veritably reveals itself to you in the process of meditation, as the Name had revealed itself earlier. When these things are attained, says Kabir, we may regard ourselves as definitely on the path to God.

(ii) *Concentration*— We next proceed to another verse

या विधि मन को लगावै

which tells us that the spiritual aspirant must be full of concentration. Concentration, says Kabir, should be so intense that as soon as you begin to concentrate, the form of God should appear before you—मन के लगाए प्रभु पावै. Kabir gives us three illustrations.

The first is the illustration of an acrobat. What does an acrobat do ? He climbs on a bamboo to the beat of his attendant's drum, then he begins to walk on the rope, taking a very heavy load on his head. If he falls down, he may die instantly. He is so concentrated, that, in spite of the heavy load on his head, he is able to walk on the rope in a balanced posture. In the same way, says Kabir, an aspirant should walk in a balanced manner on the rope of the meditational process, though the weight he carries may be very heavy indeed.

Secondly, Kabir gives us the illustration of a serpent. It is a popular tradition in the mythology of Hindustan that the serpent who lives merely upon air (पवनाशी) comes sometimes to lick the dew-drops in a jungle. In this process, the serpent is supposed to put its jewel aside in front of itself, and keep an intent eye on it, while partaking of the dew drops : ओस चाटने आवै, मनि तजि प्रान गंवावै. Even so, says Kabir, the aspirant should rather lose his life than lose the jewel of Atman which is the *telos* of his life, and on which therefore the active seeker must intensely concentrate in the midst of all his actions.

Thirdly, the aspirant of Kabir must have that intensity of devotion which characterises a 'Sati'. What does she do? Her husband is burning on the pyre. Her father and mother have gathered round about her, and her relatives are looking intently at her. She is unconscious of the presence or even the existence of the persons that are gathered round her. Her whole attention is concentrated on her dead husband. Possessed by dutiful love, she throws herself upon the funeral pyre, to be burnt along with her dead husband. Such a fury of devotion the aspirant must have before he is locked in an eternal union with God. He must offer himself as a sacrifice before the altar of God by waving the Arati of his life in the midst of lights and sounds and perfumes.

In the opening paragraph of the present chapter we have seen how there are five chief characteristics of the meditational process of which two have been hitherto discussed, namely 'internal meditation' and 'concentration' in the two songs अजर अमर इक नाम है and या विधि मनको लगावै respectively. We shall now proceed to discuss the remaining three characteristics, namely, दीर्घकाल, नैरन्तर्य and सत्कार, as mentioned by Patanjali in his famous Sutra. स तु दीर्घकालनैरन्तर्यसत्कारासेवितो दृढभूमिः. Patanjali advises us in this Sutra to pursue the path of God (1) to the very end of our life (2) without losing a single moment and (3) with a fully devotional attitude. Let us now discuss these three points in the three songs that follow. दीर्घकाल will be discussed in the first song with reference to चेतना है तो चेत ले; नैरन्तर्य will be discussed in the second song with reference to यहि जुग करले, giving importance to the here and the now; and सत्कार will be discussed in the 3rd song with reference to साईं को मन भावै, where we are told that every action of the aspirant should be intended to propitiate the Lord.

(iii) दीर्घकाल— In the song चेतना है तो चेत ले निशिदिन मे प्रानी, Nanak advises us to continue our spiritual meditation to the very end of our life. This is exactly in the spirit of Bādarāyaṇa who tells us आ प्रायणात्तत्रापि हि दृष्टम्. We should continue our meditation till the last breath leaves us. Nanak tells us that moments are passing away from our life, as drops of water from a pitcher with a hole— फूटे घट ज्यों पानी. This reminds us of a very famous song of Purandardas– नेरे छिद्रद कुंभद नीरिनंते नाना देशगळल्लि नाना कालगळल्ली– in which Purandardas gives us the same analogy, saying that moments are passing away from our life as drops of water from a pitcher with a hole. He, therefore, advises us to look at the different places, and times, and conditions through which our life has passed. He says this will fill us with the idea of giving a good account of ourselves during the remaining part of our life. Nanak further tells us that it is never too late to mend. This idea has been echoed by a poet in recent times when he says अब भी नही बिगड़ा है कुछ, थोडा समय बाकी रहा, कस कमर मन बसमे कर, देखो खुदाई आगई. We are further told by Nanak that we are following vain mirages in our life and are not cognisant of Reality : झूठे लालच लागिके, नाहीं मर्म पिछाना. We follow vain pursuits, and thereby miss the chief aim of our life. Finally, Nanak tells us that it is only when we contemplate on God that we enter the region of the fearless.

(iv) नैरंतर्य— Turning to good account every moment that we pass through in our life is stressed nowhere better than in Kabir's song भूले मन समझ के लाद लदनिया. "How much burden are you placing upon the ass of your body ?" asks Kabir. "Where are you leading the crowd of your nomadic followers ? Ahead there is a foreign land. There is neither market, nor any merchant. If you want to buy or sell, you should do it here and now." Kabir is here referring to the proper discharge of our spiritual functions without letting a single moment to pass unutilised. If you want to drink water, he says, drink the water of this well. The water is jewel-like and crystal-clear. This is the advice which Kabir offers to those who are desirous of pursuing the path of Nirvaṇa.

It was by a great coincidence that this song came to hand at the time just before the Police Action at Hyderabad began a few years ago. All the aspirants that had gathered at the Ashram at Nimbal were wonderstruck to see what great similarity there was between the teaching of Kabir in this Pada and the things that were being enacted at that very moment at or near Nimbal. Just a few miles away, there was danger of an imminent attack from Razakars, across the Bhima in the Bijapur District, and a few incidents had already taken place. Those who have visited the Ashram at Nimbal know that there is already a Tanda of Lamanis there, and many people of that tribe come with a view to buy and sell. Kabir's advice was almost prophetically addressed to these nomads, who were directed to buy and sell where they got down from the train or their carts, without entertaining the idea of going further. Ahead, there was a Foreign land and they might lose their property, possessions and even their life if they went further. The water at Nimbal Ashram was absolutely jewel-like and crystal-clear, having come out of an artesian well. Kabir's song was almost a description of the place and conditions in which the Nimbal Ashram existed at that time. The sum and substance of Kabir's advice to such people that had gathered at Nimbal was to engage themselves in their spiritual pursuit there and then, without postponing them for a single moment, or going to a foreign place which was full of danger.

(v) सत्कार— Let us now go to the final song under the methodology of meditation—the song of the spiritual Charkha, the sole function of the plying of which is the propitiation of God. Our true intent, says Shakespeare, is all for your delight. Similarly here, it may be said, that the true intent of the plying of the Spiritual Charkha is all for the propitiation of the Lord : साईं को मन भावै. There are three famous songs on this head :

(1) कोरी साल न छांड़ै रे from Dadu.

(2) झीनी झीनी बीनी चदरिया from Kabir.

(3) आर गोडविन्नेनु मगळे from Sharifsaheb, a Canarese Saint.

Somehow, all these spinners and weavers were Mahomedans—Dadu, Kabir and Sharifsaheb – and they all agree in teaching us the supreme value of the Spiritual Charkha. Let us now put all these three songs together, and see what these mystical weavers and spinners mean by the Spiritual Charkha, by means of which the process of meditation might be consummated.

In the first place, says Sharifsaheb, we must take the cotton of our mind and take away all the dross and the dust out of it – कसरने कळेदु कळेगळ तेगेदु, all the evil propensities and all the evil passions – and then a sliver might be produced.

The holes and protuberances, says Dadu, should be taken away before the final product becomes ready. These should not be allowed to remain.

Then, according to Sharifsaheb, our Āsana, the posture upon which we sit for meditation, is to constitute the pedestal of the Charkha. Our two sympathetic cords, the Ravi and the Shashi, Ida and Pingala as we said sometime back, should constitute the two poles of the Charkha. Now the spokes of the wheel are held in position by the ten Vayus (दश वायुगळेंब नूलिगळ विगिदु), and the Charkha is to be set in motion. Of course, these are additions to what Dadu and Kabir have said.

Coming to the subject proper, these Mahomedan spinners and weavers agree in saying that there should be concentrated attention in the plying of the Charkha : एक–मना इस आरम्भ लागा. Sharifsaheb gives the illustration of a lady who is spinning, and advises her only to look to the act of spinning. "Do not look here and there," says Sharifsaheb : दारिकाररु निन्न मारिय नोडलु । मारि एत्ति नोडवेडम्मा. "Passers-by may come and cast a glance at you. But do not return their look. That is not your job. Your job is merely to spin. Do that." Such a one-pointed and concentrated attention is what is wanted by this spiritual spinner.

Then there is a further important idea in Kabir. Other people talk of only one Chakra. Kabir talks of eight chakras : अष्ट कमलदल चरखा डोलै.

He tells us that all the eight chakras, namely the मूलाधार, स्वाधिष्ठान, मणिपूर, अनुहत, विशुद्धि, आज्ञा, ललाट and सहस्रार, should be simultaneously set in motion. It is not merely one chakra which is inside us. There are eight such chakras or plexuses. The setting in motion of the eight chakras simultaneously is a wonderful phenomenon, and constitutes the majestic progress of the aspirant towards God. There has been a certain amount of discussion and a little difference of opinion as to what we should mean by the expression अष्टकंवलदल चरखा. Some people say that we ought to regard it as a sort of an अष्टदल कमल, which is not correct, because there are no अष्टदलऽ at all in a Kamal. There are two, four, six, ten, twelve, sixteen, but not eight petals in Kabirite physiology. So, in the expression अष्ट कमलदल, Dala must mean a Samūha. That entire galaxy of the eight chakras should be set in motion, and this is done by means of our concentrated spiritual meditation. It is not merely by the control of our breath (प्राणनिरोध) nor even by shutting the senses (इन्द्रियनिग्रह) that the spiritual energy inside us can be set in motion. So, it is a very wounderful idea, namely that of the setting in motion of the eight physiological chakras through concentrated attention.

Then further, प्रेम प्राण लगाइ धागै, says Dadu. Our Prema and Prana should constitute the Tana and the Bana. Prema means devotion to God, and

Prana means physiological breath. Our physiological breath must be made the vehicle of our love to God, says Dadu. In a similar vein, Kabir has said that the Anahat Shabda should be made the horse on which the Self should ride : सबद तुरय असवार व्है । दीजै सुरत पठाय. So Prema and Prana must go together. In the process of uttering the name of God through our breath, there ought to be also devotion to God. It is not merely a mechanical utterance of the name of God, but a remembering of the Name of God through devotion. A famous Saint in South India, the Saint of Umadi, used to explain the famous line from Ramadas प्रेम प्रीतीनें बांधावें in this manner. Our breath, he used to say, should be tied to our devotion to God. The two must go together. Kabir and Dadu make these the Tana and the Bana ; but they also make a further important addition, implied in the expression अंतर्गतिरंगराता. Inner spiritual emotions spring inside us, they say, in the process of our spiritual contemplation. Those purple or multi-coloured emotions that spring inside us would constitute the coloured threads in the piece that we are weaving. So, अंतर्गतिरंगराता is a very important expression. We must have that spiritual concentration and that devotion to God, which should result in multi-coloured experience.

Then Dadu says that we must be very careful lest any one thread might break, because those who are spinners and weavers know that, if we miss even a single thread, there will be a misconnection, resulting in a broken end or a gap in the cloth woven. Let us therefore take care that our 21,600 breaths, which constitute the threads, might be woven into a beautiful and continuous cloth. It is evident that this number is arrived at by multiplying 24 hours by 60 minutes, and the product by 15 breaths per minute. Not a single breath should be lost, says Dadu, for fear that there might be a gap in the spiritual cloth woven.

Now great people, says Dadu, are humble workers. It is a very important conception. The greater you are, the more humble you are. So, the more concentrated you will be in God, the more of a devout worker you would be. That constitutes the real criterion of a spiritual spinner and weaver. He might be the Head of all, even the President of the Union, and yet unmindful of his dignity, he would spin like a common worker: सकलशिरोमणि बुनै विचारा.

Ultimately, what is to be the product of this devout labour of spinning and weaving ? It is to be a good garment, a beautiful and a durable garment. Sharifsaheb calls it a Pitambar; Dadu calls it a Gahar Gajina; and Kabir calls it a Chadar. Whatever the name one may give to it, in all humility we should offer it to God as our supreme dedication. Kabir says about this

Chadar "Sages and Saints and Gods have made this Chadar dirty. I have worn it well about myself, and kept it pure and clean" : सो चादर सुर नर मुनि ओढ़ी । ओढ़ि कै मैली कीनी चदरिया. "Now in my last hour," says Kabir, "I offer it to you in the original condition in which you gave it to me," reminding us of the utterance in a similar condition of a great Kanarese Saint, who might be regarded as his spiritual ectype :

अप्पा गुरुराया निदु निनगे ओप्पितु,

"My master, I have only dedicated to you what was already yours." If our spinning and weaving in this spiritual process results in the ultimate dedication of our life and actions to God, what higher consummation could we ever hope to achieve?

4. *The place of Yoga and Absolutism in the meditational process*— After a discussion of the methodology of meditation, let us now proceed to consider the place of Yoga and Absolutism in mystical experience. We have two famous songs – one of Matsyendra and the other of Mansur, one dealing with the place of Yoga and the other with the place of Absolutism so far as mystical experience is concerned. In Maharashtra, the poem तो भी कच्चा वे कच्चा is supposed to be a conversation between Matsyendra and Gorakha. Very peculiarly, the same poem has been found in Pandit Sukhdev

Bihari Misra's posthumous manuscript as attributed to Jnaneshwar and Nivritti. It seems, therefore, that while Maharashtra assigns it to Matsyendra and Gorakh, Uttar Pradesh assigns it to Nivritti and Jnaneshwar. In any case, the poem speaks about the half-ripe condition of mystical experience to which a Yogin attains. The Yogin might be expert in performing any Asanas he pleases, or in exhibiting any Mudras he likes. He may reduce his body to a mere skeleton by famishing himself, or he might besmear his body all over with ashes, wet or dry. He might make the Kundalini enter the Brahma Randhra and yet he may not attain to any mystical experience. He may come in possession of miraculous powers by means of his Yoga. He might at pleasure extract his Soul from his body, and make it enter into any desired body he pleases. This is a phenomenon which in Yogic terminology is called परकायाप्रवेश. Shri Shankaracharya, in reply to a query of Mandan Mishra's wife, had to take resort to this परकायाप्रवेश, in order to answer questions whose solution was demanded by that lady. The Yogin might disappear at the place where he is seen, and may re-appear at distant places like Gokul, Mathura, and Kashi. He may be able to walk on the surface of the waters, and whatever he might speak by word of mouth may come out true; and yet a mere possession of such miraculous powers may not enable him to attain to mystical experience. The attainment of high intellectual powers may not also demarcate a man as a mystic : शास्त्रों में कुच रहा न वाकी, पूरा ज्ञान कमाया; nor will a mere possession of high moral qualities help him much : धन कामिनि को नजर न लावे, जोग कमाया भारी. Matsyendra tells Gorakh (or alternatively Nivritti tells Jnaneshwar) that, until a man is able to see his own Form by the Grace of his spiritual teacher, he may not be regarded as having attained to the highest mystical experience.

In a celebrated song अगर है शौक मिलनेका we understand from Mansur what an absolutistic meditation might be. His, it seems, is a sort of an intellective contemplation, in which the identity of the Self and God is the fundamental conception. Mansur tells us to reject all ceremonial religion whatsoever. He advises us to leave away the prayer carpet and rosary and asks us not to bend our knees in prayer. He recommends us to throw the sacred books in the running stream. There is no use, he says, in keeping day-long fasts. So far about the rejection of ceremonial religion. As to the attainment of success in absolutistic contemplation, he advises first that one should destroy one's self-consciousness (जला कर खुद-नुमाई को), take up the hand of the Apostles of God, and regard oneself as their bondsman : पकड़ दस्त तू. फरिश्तोंका, गुलाम उनका कहाता जा. He advises us further, like Kabir and other great Saints, to utilise every breath for the contemplation of Reality : हरदम लौ लगाता जा. He further says that the Prince of Beggars asks you to repeat "अनलहक़, I am none but Reality. I am God" :

हुकुम है शाह कलन्दर का, अनलहक़ तू कहाता जा.

The expression अनलहक़ is susceptible of a two-fold interpretation. It might either mean that one should regard oneself as identical with God or, to vary the phrase, to regard oneself as nothing but the Truth, the Reality, or the Absolute. Now all these latter expressions, Truth, Reality, and the Absolute are the fundamental platforms of Present-day philosophers. To Mansur, likewise, God seems to be an absolutistic conception. A mere repetition of अनलहक़, however, will not land us anywhere. अहं ब्रम्हास्मि, तत्त्वमसि, are good pieces of advice, no doubt, but a repetition of them Mantra-wise, with or without the rosary, would be of no avail. महावाक्याचा उपदेश भला। परी त्याचा जप नाहीं बोलिला, says Ramdas. What matters is the experience of the identity of Self and God, not a mere assertion of the Identity. Finally, Mansur gives us an insight into his own personal experience. He tells us that he had realised the Absolute in his heart : हक़ मैंने दिल में पहचाना. This would be an arrogant statement to a man who is not a philosopher; but to one, who has given his life to a contemplation of the Absolute, this would look like a truism. This

Absolute, says Mansur, is the restaurant of the intoxicated, and he advises his followers to be its continued members : वही मस्तों का मैखाना, उसी के बीच आता जा. Mansur, therefore, is not satisfied merely with drinking the spiritual wine himself, but he calls upon his followers also to join him in partaking of those spirituous draughts.

5. *The two attitudes : the militant and the submissive*— After a discussion of the place of Yoga and Absolutism in the scheme of spiritual realisation, we come to a very significant point, namely, the difference between the two attitudes, the militant and the submissive, which such seekers show in their pursuit of the spiritual goal. These attitudes might also be called the optimistic and the pessimistic, the attitudes of determination and resignation, of power and impotence. Milton's L'Allegro and Il Penseroso very beautifully bring out the distinction between these two attitudes. Generally, Saints belong to one of these two types, but there might possibly be a saint here or there who might belong to both. We shall see a little later how Kabir illustrates a combination of both the tough-minded and the tender-minded attitudes.

If we examine the militant attitude, we shall find that it exhibits itself at three different levels, at the level of seeking the spiritual initiation from a teacher, at the level of the pilgrimage on the path, and at the level of the conquest of the spirinal fort. We shall illustrate all these levcls by quoting first a passage in Kabir where he accosts his spiritual teacher with an audacious question, then a song which tells us what great intrepidity is required in the pursuit of the spiritual path, and finally a passage from Kabir himself where he speaks of the conquest of the spiritual fort, the सोऽहं गढ़. Peculiarly, this सोऽहंगढ़ of Kabir sounds very much like the सिंहगड of Maratha history and the last few lines of the poem clearly bring out to the mind a picture of the courageous travail experienced by the Marathas who went to attack it, how they climbed up the fort by means of ropes attached to the backs of wild alligators and how ultimately they succeeded in capturing the invincible fort of सिंहगड. To this we shall come presently.

Let us begin by considering the audacious attitude with which Kabir first approached his spiritual teacher. If the song, which is quoted below, can be regarded as an authentic song of Kabir, it is wonderful how he approached Ramananda with a firm courage and determination to seek out a proper spiritual teacher. "Guru Ramanandji" he accosts his teacher, "you should be very careful in choosing a disciple for yourself. If you want to take my hand, you should take it up after mature consideration. I am not like one of those little children who are satisfied with tinkering toys (झुनझुनिया). If you want to catch hold of my hand, you should hold it firmly and in such a manner that you will never lose its grip. I am not a seeker of stone-deities; my worship is of the Eternal and Imperishable God. I am not one of those 1484 disciples who fall prostrate at your feet. In the flat ship of my life, there has been no oarsman, and mountainous waves are rising to submerge it in a fierce storm. If you, therefore, decide to take me up as your disciple, you should do it after mature consideration of your powers." We cannot do better than quote the song in the original in order to give our readers an idea of its power :

गुरु रामानन्दजी समझ गहो मेरी वैयाँ ॥ टे ॥
जो बालक झुनझुनियां खेले, उनमें का मैं नहीं हूँ ।
म्हारे तो एक सत की पूजा, पत्थर पूजा नहीं है ।
वैयाँ पकड़ो तो गेहे के पकड़ो, फिर छूटण के नहीं ।
चौदासे चौरासी चेला, उनमें का मैं नहीं हूँ ।
थारे नांव में खेवटिया नाहीं, लहर उठे बिकराला ।
कहे कबीर सुनो हो रामानन्दजी, जान बूझ करना चेला ॥

We have in the Gujarathi poet Preetam an excellent description of the invincible courage required for the pursuit of the spiritual path. He gives us two significant illustrations to show the courage required in treading the path. It is only the man who rushes to the bottom of the sea with indomitable courage, says Preetam, that can come out with his hands full of pearls; on the other hand, he who stands simply looking on on the shore will be rewarded with mere oyster-shells. Then again, says the poet, when a man throws himself in the midst of a conflagration, he can be rewarded with beatific joy; on the other hand, if he simply stands looking on, he will be tormented by burning fire. Such an intrepidity, says the poet, is required for the treading of the spiritual path. Here also we cannot do better than quote Preetam in the original :

हरिनो मारग छे शूरानो, नहि कायरनुं काम जोने ।
सिंधुमध्ये मोती लेवा, मांही पडचा मरजीवा जोने ।
मरण आंगळे ते भरि मूठी, दिलनी दुग्धा वामे जोने ।
तीरे ऊभो जुए तमासो ते कोडी नव पामे जोने ।
प्रेमपंथ पावकनी ज्वाळा भाळी पाछा भागे जोने ।
मांही पडचा ते महासुख माणे, देखनारा दाझे जोने ।
राम-अमलमां राता माता, पूरा प्रेमी परखे जोने ।
प्रीतमना स्वामीनी लीला, ते रजनीदिन नरखे जोने ।

In this connection, we cannot but be reminded of the 'audacious courage' shown by our present Prime Minister in the many incidents of his life, particularly in the intrepidity which he showed in rushing to the thick of the mêlée, during the Allahabad and Delhi riots in the years 1939 and 1947, when, without caring for his life, he rushed in to rescue those, who, but for his help, would have been literally cut to pieces.

We shall now proceed to Kabir's description of the necessity of an undaunted spirit in the region of the spiritual conquest. There are three stages of this conquest. First, we have to march to the fort of सोऽहंगढ़, then to ascend it, and finally to conquer it. Kabir tells us in his famous song नौकरी शरियत से करना that we have to do all these three things. In the first stage, we should take orders from our spiritual commanders and follow them implicitly. Then we should control the horse of the mind by the reins of reason, and not allow it to go helter-skelter. We will be reminded in this connection of an Upanishadic passage which tells us दुष्टाश्वयुक्तमिव वाहमेनं मनो विद्वान् धारयेताप्रमत्तः, or of Plato's Phaedrus, where we are told how the Charioteer controls the unruly horse by the help of its ruly compeer. Then, says Kabir, after a full control of our mind, we should march stage after stage to the place of the confluence, in the present case the confluence of the Ida, Pingala, and Sushumna. There we should offer our worship to God in order that we might come out victorious in the contest.

The second stage consists in shooting at the target with concentrated attention, so that we may not miss our mark. The ancient era was an era of arrows, the modern era is an era of bombs. In any case, accuracy of aim and intrepidity of shooting is the primal necessity : अखी लगाकर मार निशानी पीछे मन हटना, says Kabir. We should not turn our back when once we have set our hand to our task. It is not improbable that Kabir might have taken this metaphor of shooting by means of the arrow from the famous Upanishadic passage प्रणवो धनुः शरो ह्यात्मा ब्रह्म तल्लक्ष्यमुच्यते । अप्रमत्तेन वेद्धव्यं शरवत्तन्मयो भवेत् ॥. It will not be difficult to find parallels for this in other provincial literatures also. One such occurs to our mind at the moment from Kanarese literature in the famous poem, गुरिया ओगदेनो ब्रह्मके, in which the same metaphor has been employed, and Brahman has been regarded as the target at which to aim.

When we come to the third stage of the spiritual conquest, we are reminded irresistibly of the way in which the सिंहगड was conquered in Maratha history, and the सोऽहंगढ़ of Kabir even onomatopoeically puts us in mind of it. Tanaji Malusare climbed to the peak of the mountain by means of ropes attached to the waists of the wild alligators, and the whole army went up by means of the ropes. Similarly, Kabir asks us here to ascend the सोऽहंगढ़ by the rope of breath. When we go up, as did Suryaji to the top of the सिंहगड, we may be fortunate to experience the beautiful climate of the "Ajara Desh" and take a bath in the "Amara Kunda." Incidentally, Kabir brings in his occult conception of the Ajara and the Amara in his description of the conquest. The parallel from Maratha history tells us that the very fine climate we experience at the top of the सिंहगड as well as the pond (देवटाकें) with its extremely limpid waters which lies at the top, might be taken to be almost the physical replicas of the spiritual experience of the Ajara Desh and the Amara Kund of Kabir. After we have taken a bath in this Amara Kunda, the pond of immortality, we should then unfurl our saffron flag as a mark of our conquest of the fort. It matters little whether in this process Tanaji died or Suryaji lived, but Maratha history became firm after this memorable conquest of Sinhagadh. Even so our spiritual conquest of सोऽहंगड will take us definitely to the throne of spiritual power. Kabir advises us not to miss the opportunity provided by this life. Let us remember, he says, that we may not be born upon the earth from time to time. An opportunity missed is an opportunity lost!

It is surprising that such an intrepid seeker and realiser like Kabir should have felt the necessity of an attitude of submission, which is almost antithetical to the militant attitude which we have described above. This attitude of submission is carried to an extreme in the so-called विरहावस्था, the pangs of separation of the lover from the beloved. It is most surprising that both in Kabir and Jnaneshwar, who are stalwart mystics, we should find this inconsistent attitude of विरहावस्था, when their very names fill us with ideas of great spiritual courage and philosophic insight. Jnaneshwar also speaks of a bodice of sandal and a bed of flowers as burning the body with fire :

चंदनाची चोळी माझें सर्व अंग पोळी......
सुमनाची सेज सीतळ .... पोळे आगीसारखी......

It is wonderful how such mystics should try to mimic the Gopis in point of their expression of love towards God. Would not an attitude of mere submission do ? Or must it degenerate into the so-ealled विरहावस्था ? On the other hand, if we consider cases like those of Surdas and Mirabai in Uttar Pradesh, and Namdeva and Tukaram in Maharashtra, we shall not be surprised that they seek an attitude of submission, inasmuch as they are not particularly distinguished by their intrepidity of aspiration, except on rare occasions, as in the case of Tukaram, towards the end of his life. If Mirabai expresses her love towards Krishna in particular terms, her expression might be condoned. But why on earth should Surdas express it in like manner ? Jyayasi inverts the relation, and speaks of God as a bride instead of a bridegroom. This is, in fact, as bad as regarding God a veritable bridegroom. On the other hand, we find that Tulsidas's relation towards God is of an equanimous devotion and Ramdas's of activism, mingled at most with करुणरस but never with विरह. From this point of view, therefore, that we should find an attitude of विरहावस्थ: in Kabir in many of his songs is most surprising.

In the song under discussion प्रीति लगी तुव नामकी, Kabir tells us how his mind is panting for God like a fish out of waters, how his very eyes are feeling 'thirsty' (नैना तरसे दरसको), imitating in that manner another song which speaks of नयन को लगी प्यास अब तो साहेब देखना, and suggesting the possibility or the reality of transfer of functions between the throat and the eye. Kabir tells us that his eye-lashes ceased to close, meaning thereby that he was always wakeful. Now this eternal wakefulness might mean one of two things—it might mean insomnia, or it might mean unison. We might not probably attribute the first to Kabir, while the second might be justified by his long efforts for self-realisation. Finally, Kabir tells us that he would be never separated from his Lord, if once he was able to find Him. This is the promise which a devotee always makes to God in the beginning, but always breaks at the end. A great Kanarese saint has said मोदल भक्तिगे बदलवागदे, meaning thereby that our devotion to God should never change the aspect it bore at the beginning of the search; on the other hand, it should deepen in intensity as it proceeds. Jnaneshwar has also told us that those persons alone deserve the title of Mahatmā who worship God with an ever-inereasing devotion from day to day :

मग वाढतेनी प्रेमें । माते भजती ते महात्मे ॥

6. *The Dark Night and the Dawn*—In a poet like Surdas, however, as we have already pointed out, the attitude of submission is understandable, in as much as he was a tender-minded, in contrast to a tough-minded Saint like Kabir. We read in the histories of mystical experience, how almost in every Saint's life the darkest hour is nearest the dawn. Bunyan and St. John can be our illustrations on this head. The phenomenon is not restricted to any particular religion, race or community, and may be found in seekers after God all over the world and at all times. 'The Ever-lasting No' seems the necessary preliminary to the 'Ever-lasting Yea.' The sick soul and the psychology of surrender are expressions with which are familiar everywhere. In the history of Indian thought, Ramanuja shows a true attitude of surrender in his doctrine of प्रपत्ति. Dr. R. G. Bhandarkar going a length further used to say that he was not even a प्रपन्न, but only a प्रपित्सु, not one who succeeded in surrendering himself, but one who was only desirous of surrender. Aurobindo Ghosh in modern times, as we have had occasion to see, has revitalised the doctrine of self-surrender.

This is the kind of self-surrender of which Surdas is speaking in the poem सुना रे मैंने निर्बलके बल राम. Unless we realise our absolute impotence before the majestic power of God, it may not be possible for God's Grace to descend upon us. When the great elephant, Gajendra, was full of arrogance and power, and when he was on the point of being killed by the great alligator, he found that his own efforts were of no avail, and as soon as he began to utter the name of God with full devotion, God came to his help when he had uttered the single syllable रा, before even he had uttered the full name राम. This is a sort of a Samadhi Alankara in which a totality of conditions is not required for the production of an effect, but even a fraction of it might suffice. So did it happen in the case of Gajendra. Similarly, we are told elsewhere by Surdas in his famous lines 'दुःशासन चीर खस्यो । सभा बीच कृष्ण कृष्ण द्रौपदी पुकारी ', that God came to the help of Draupadi and protected her against the wicked assaults of दुःशासन on her sacred honour. Surdas, therefore, goes on to speak of four kinds of power that a man possesses, आत्मबल, तपोबल, बाहुबल, धनबल. It is not necessary for this scheme of Surdas to be taken serially; in fact, it might be exactly the reverse धन, बाहु, तप, आत्म°. In fact, these so-called sources of strength of which Surdas speaks have an analogue in the teaching of Chaṇakya, which itself is based on the Ramayana of Valmiki, which talks of साम, दान, भेद and दण्ड as the chief sources of power, in the famous poem which he puts into the mouth of Hanuman—

न साम रक्षःसु गुणाय कल्पते
न दानमर्थोपचितेषु युज्यते।
न भेदसाध्या बलदर्पिता जनाः
पराक्रमस्त्वेव ममेह रोचते ॥,

implying thereby that Hanuman ultimately had to rest upon his own बाहुबल. A devotee like Surdas does not think of any of these poetical or political sources of strength. To him, as compared to any of the above sources of strength, a new one, namely, कृपाबल, alone stands as the highest. It is the Grace of God which supersedes any other sources of strength which man may fondly cling to in his heart : सूर किसोर कृपा ते सब बल.

We have hitherto discussed two typical examples, from Kabir and Surdas, with reference to the submissive attitude. We shall now consider the third specimen under that head, namely, Mirabai, with reference to two of her famous songs. In the first तुम पलक उघारो दीनानाथ, Mirabai, as we have already seen, who was troubled with the buffets of misfortune and the maltreatment of her relatives, is imploring God to send down his Grace upon her. "Those who were well-intentioned towards me," she says, "have now become my enemies. I have been an eye-sore to everybody. I am being dried up while standing day and night. What burden of Mira could there be on Thee, On Lord of the 'Universe'? It is like an ounce added to a hundred pounds of weight. (It is mythologically customary to regard the शेष or Atlas as taking the burden of the world upon their head.) Thou hast taken the burden of the whole universe, physical moral and spiritual, upon Thyself. Open Thy eye-lashes, therefore, and look at me with Thy Gracious vision." While we have seen in the former song Kabir speaking about his own eye-lashes which do not close, Mirabai requests God in this song to open His. As to whether the opening of the eye-lashes is to be understood as a physical or a mystical fact, we leave our readers to judge.

Mirabai is conscious of the fact that her Guru was a perfected Saint who had reached the acme of spiritual experience (गुरु रैदास मिले मोहि पूरे). Hence it was that she compliments herself upon having been the recipient of his spiritual benediction. Having received this, she says, her head shone as if it was adorned with a lotus (धुरसे कमल भिडी). As Raidas, her Teacher, belonged to the Kabirite school, it would also not seem impossible that by कमल she might have meant the सहस्रार, and the meaning of the expression धुरसे कमल भिडी might then be that she regarded herself as fortunate that her thousand-petalled lotus had come into contact with God. On the other hand, if we understand the reading as कलम instead of कमल, as is sometimes done, that would also give a very good interpretation. According to this interpretation, Mirabai thought herself fortunate that the spiritual instruction of her Teacher was ever grafted on her. Her own tree, which was of an inferior variety, was, by the infusion, made capable of yielding a rich and delicious harvest. The inferior tree, in which the branch of a superior one is grafted, yields thereby richer and more plentiful fruit. So did it happen in the case of Mirabai.

Lastly, in this song, Mirabai gives expression to an utterance of great mystical value. She says "When Raidas, my spiritual teacher, came and gave me a sign, my light was merged in the Divine Light." Now what is this sign? In the spiritual literature of Maharashtra and Karnatak it is customary to understand this 'sign' either as a happy ensign, or even as a prognostication. More often than not, it is understood in the latter sense. In the present case, however, by the word सैन we might understand a happy ensign, which her spiritual Teacher gave her and by which her further spiritual progress became assured. There are many such signs spoken of in mystical literature. What are these signs? They are the forms of spiritual experience, which reveal themselves before the advancing mystic. Such ensigns we may find mentioned, for instance, in a famous passage in the श्वेताश्वतर Upanishad, namely, नीहारधूमार्कानिलानिलानां खद्योतविद्युत्स्फटिकशशिनाम् ।, or in the celebrated Abhanga of Jnaneshwar which tells us कापसाचे गोळे फिरती पोकळी । मोतियांची जाळी विखुरती ॥ गरुडाच्या भरारी जाती

दृष्टीपुढें । शेपाचें वेटाळें गुंडाळती ॥ वज्राचिया चुरा शुभ्रवत् दिसे । तया माजी वस्तु शोभतसे ॥. These signs carry us gradually to higher and higher levels, until the way is opened for us, as Mirabai expresses it, for a union with God.

We finally come to a poem of very remarkable value from Mirabai, in which there is an extraordinary mixture of music, rhetoric and mysticism. Almost any person, who is interested in musical performances, knows what great importance is attached to the song जोगी मत जा मत जा. The poem is exceedingly popular. Not merely does it contain music of the highest order, not only does it express mystical experience which is absolutely 'sui generis', but from the point of view of rhetorical science also, it might be taken to be one of the best specimens of poetical compositions— a fact which has not been hitherto noticed.

Mirabai makes five requests to her Lord. She addresses him as a Jogi. Whether by Jogi she means her spiritual teacher Raidas, or Lord Krishna himself, it is not an easy matter to settle. It has been supposed that Krishna had appeared once in the form of a Yogin to the Gopis. Whatever this might be, Mirabai implores the Lord, in the first place, not to depart from her. Whether this refers to physical vision of the Lord or a mystical vision, we have no grounds to determine. In any case, she pathetically implores her Lord not to depart : जोगी मत जा, मत जा, मत जा. This is Mirabai's first request. In the second place, she says, that, as the path of God-devotion stands in a category apart it may not be possible for an insignificant creature like herself to be able to tread that royal path. She would, therefore, request her Lord to take her by the hand to a by-lane which will lead to it : 'हमको गैल लगा जा'. We may notice here the great difference between the two readings गैल वता जा and गैल लगा जा, which latter is infinitely more valuable, as we shall see later, so far as वस्तुध्वनि is concerned. Thirdly, if that may not be possible, she says, she may ascend a funeral sandal-wood pyre, and she requests her Lord to set fire to it by his own hand, and then go. Fourthly, when her body would be reduced to ashes in the funeral pyre, let her Lord come and besmear his body with her ashes ; that also would be a cause of great satisfaction to her. Finally, as the culminating act of the process, she would regard herself as most fortunate if the Lord deigns to merge her light in the Divine : 'जोत में जोत मिला जा'.

We shall see by a consideration of all these five alternatives that Mirabai requests her Lord to be in constant contact with her in some form or other. It will be easily seen that there is a gradation in the different alternatives which she proposes. Physical presence of the Lord, taking her by the hand to lead her to a by-path, setting fire to her funeral pyre, besmearing his body with her ashes, and finally the mergence of her light with the Divine light may easily be seen to be the ascending rungs in the ladder of spiritual communion with the Divine. This is an excellent illustration of what we might call उत्कर्षालंकार. The word सार, as used by rhetoricians, does not come up to the level which उत्कर्ष reaches. The present song might thus be taken to be an extraordinary specimen of उत्कर्षालङ्कार.

It is customary among rhetoricians to speak of three kinds of ध्वनि—अलङ्कारध्वनि, वस्तुध्वनि and रसध्वनि. So far as the first is concerned, we have in the poem, as we have seen above, a very remarkable illustration of अलङ्कारध्वनि in the form of उत्कर्ष. Secondly, as her spiritual Teacher is the single focus of Mirabai's attention throughout all her demands, as he is in fact the very alpha and omega of her existence, this might be taken to be a superb specimen of वस्तुध्वनि. Finally, we find in the poem a very notable illustration of करुणरस. Mirabai is weeping, she offers to ascend the funeral pyre, is prepared to have her body reduced to ashes provided her Lord besmears his body with them—all these are full of the highest kind of करुणरस or pathos. There could be no better example of the combination of अलङ्कारध्वनि, वस्तुध्वनि and रसध्वनि than this sublime poem of Mirabai.

CHAPTER V

The Highest Ascent

We now pass on to the final chapter of our present part, namely, on the Culmination of Spiritual Experience, in the Pada literature of the Hindi Saints. The chapter will be devoted to the discussion of this spiritual experience under nine different heads, each containing a group of songs in an ascending order of spiritual experience. Group 1 will contain a description of the varieties of mystical experience attained by the various Hindi Saints. Under this head we shall consider, in order the spiritual utterances, in the first place, of Mirabai, the Mystic-Princess, then of the two great Hindi saints, Surdas and Tulsidas, then of that group of spiritual realisers revelling in their description of mystical experience, such as Gorakhanath, Dharamadas and Yari, and finally, of the two great Maratha saints, who contributed to mystical literature in Hindi, Ekanath and Mahipati, the first because he was a citizen of Paithan in the Deccan, which was under Mahomedan influence, as well as because he later lived at Benares for some time in the maturity of his spiritual experience, and the second because he settled and died at Gwalior. After the description of the varieties of mystical experience by the above great Saints, we shall pass on to group 2, which contains the famous description by Charandas of the psychological and moral effects of God-realisation. After this, we shall proceed to group 3, wherein we shall find Kabir describing the sublimity and ineffability of mystical experience in language which cannot be excelled. Kabir is not satisfied with a mere description of spiritual experience in the ordinary terminology of the mystic, but goes on, as we shall see in group 4, to rejoice in his description of what the present writer has called "flavourism", in which Dadu also joins him. Closely allied to the description of flavourism, we have in group 5 Kabir's inebriated description of God-intoxication, which reconciles the madness of intoxication both with equanimity and freedom. As a result of this God-intoxication, we have in the next group the description by Kabir of the lifting of the cosmic deceit. As the former group contains a Sufistic description of mystical experience by Kabir, the present one contains his account of mystical experience in a Vedantic vein. After this, we proceed to probably the most important group of poems in the present chapter, namely, on the nature of ecstacy and its contribution to the sustenance of the world. In the group that follows we have the post-ecstatic ejaculations of Gulal, Narharinath and Raidas, Gulal the Bhojpuri musician-poet, Narharinath, the spiritual teacher of Mahipati whom we have already mentioned, and Raidas, one of the greatest of the Untouchable saints of India. Finally, we have from Kabir, in an autobiographical manner, a description of apostleship and prophethood, which may be regarded as the very cope-stone of mystical life to be ever reached by man.

1. *Varieties of super-sensuous experience :* (i) *Mirabai*— First, we shall consider the contribution which Mirabai has made to mystical experience in three of her songs :

(1) पायो जी मैंने राम रतन धन

(2) फागुन के दिन चार रे।

(3) साधु की संगत पाई रे।

In the first song, Mirabai speaks of God as an अमोलिक वस्तु, and as a रतन धन, which has been bestowed upon her in his graciousness by her spiritual teacher. She also speaks of this jewel of God as not capable of being stolen away by anybody. Now, these words of Mirabai put us in mind of a famous Abhanga of Jnaneshwar, who lived about three centuries before her, and who was the founder of the school of Mysticism in Maharashtra. Jnaneshwar tells us in a famous Abhanga :

अमोलिक रत्न जोडलें रे तुज।

कां रे ब्रह्मबीज नोळखिसी।

न बुडे न कळे न भिये चोरा ।
ते वस्तु चतुरा सेविजे तूं ॥,

which Abhang was later regarded as an auspicious sign and command at the time of the foundation of the Inchgeri Math by its great spiritual founder. It is remarkable how both Mirabai and Jnaneshwar speak equally of God as अमोलिक, as a रत्न, and as a वस्तु, the invaluable jewel of Reality. They speak equally of the impossibility of its being stolen away, or pilferred by anybody. In a similar vein, we are told by the great Karnatak saint Mahalingrang in his famous verse : रत्न वंददे नोडिरो । कळ्ळर भयविल्लवो आ रत्नक्के, how God may be regarded as a most precious jewel, which also expresses the same sentiment as that of Mirabai and Jnaneshwar. We may also compare with this the utterance of another great Kanarese saint, Bhavatāraka, who tells us that God is like a great spiritual treasure, which can never become exhausted, nor can be stolen away by any body. We thus see how the song of Mirabai is reminiscent of like utterances of great saints of other provinces of India such as ths Maharashtra and the Karnatak.

Secondly, we may see how the song of Mirabai under review is an exemplification of सामंजस्यवाद which reconciles the Saguna and Nirguna philosophies. She not only puts us in mind of the two great Hindi saints, Kabir and Tulsidas, but also reconciles them. If, for example, we take the line of Mirabai सतकी नाव केवटिया सतगुरु, we will notice that the doctrine, enunciated by her in the expression सतकी नाव, is exactly that of Kabir in his famous line — सत नाम का भरभर प्याला आपु पिये मोहि प्यावै ।

We may also incidentally note what great emphasis was laid upon the सतनाम by the founder of the Sikh Faith, namely, गुरु नानक. Also in regard to the spiritual teacher being regarded as a great oarsman in the ocean of life, as described by Mirabai in the line केवटिया सतगुरु भवसागर तरि आयो, we have the analogous description of Tulsidas— मैं मझधारा का माँझी हूँ । तुम भवसागर के केवट हो, which describes God as a great oarsman who carries us beyond the ocean of life. In this way, the song of Mirabai is reminiscent of both Kabir and Tulsidas, as it was reminiscent of Jnaneshwar, Bhavatarak and Mahalingrang, as we have seen above.

Finally, Mirabai tells us that a spiritual experience once attained becomes the capital which by its use gives us compound interest, and goes on increasing day after day : दिन दिन बढ़त सवायो. It is in fact a geometrical progression in spiritual experience about which Mirabai is speaking. To add a cubit to our spiritual stature, we know, involves infinite labour. Geo-physicists talk of the Himalayas as adding to their stature by two feet per year. Not less difficult is the process of adding to our spiritual stature except by continuous labour and infinite pains. While a mere climber can attain to the heights only through a long process of tortuous ascents, it is devotion alone which can carry us aloft at once like an aeroplane, the rate of speed being determined by the quality of the heart.

In the second song of Mirabai फागुन के दिन चार रे, it seems we are treated to a discussion of the Holi festival, but this is not so. The poem is a fine example of Mirabai's mystic experience both of sound and colour. In the first place, she tells us we have to live here in this life only for a few days : फागुन के दिन चार रे. The Holi holidays last only for four days. Allegorically, this signifies that our human life here below is a very short-dated one, and that, therefore, we must turn it to the best account possible. 'Vita brevis; ars longa,' says the Latin proverb; अनन्तपारं किल शब्दशास्त्रं । स्वल्पं तथायुर्बह्वश्च विघ्नाः ॥ says a Sanskrit Subhashita. Every moment that is given to us in this life we must turn to the best spiritual account. When we come to the description of spiritual sound by Mirabai, we are told that the mystical aspirant hears the sound of musical instruments like a drum unbeaten by the hands : विनि करताल पखावज बाजै. In fact it seems that all the musical sounds are intertwined and intertimed by the beats of the Anahat. Mirabai, however, makes particular mention of the mystic being able to hear all the 36 Ragas without a vocal sound. This is a very significant contribution of Mirabai to ordinary mystical experience, so far as the Ragas are concerned. We are also told by Mirabai that the spiritual aspirant enjoys the experience of colours wherever the eye is cast. Both the 'Ambars' become deeply saturated, as it were, with colour, says Mirabai, the human garment, as well as the celestial sky. Further, Mirabai tells us that exquisite colours seem to shoot, as it were, from every pore of the human body. As we shall see later, the pores of the human body are regarded by other mystics as outlets of sound, light and joy. Mirabai also tries to explain this phenomenon allegorically by combining together moral and mystical experience. Character or virtue, she tells us, constitutes the colour, and devotion or love the syringe. We have to throw colour by combining the two, namely, virtue and devotion. Mirabai tells us that by this throwing of colour, she welcomed her Lord who had come back to the home after playing the Holi. The curtains of sense should now be lifted, says Mirabai, and we must welcome the Lord after losing all sense of shame. This utterance might be taken to mean merely an utterance of शृंगार. But this is not so. We have here only apparent शृंगार through which shines Mirabai's inner devotion. In the case of Jayadeva, on the other hand, we have an apparent devotion, through which comes out the real शृंगार. We leave it to our readers to choose whether they would prefer to have the garb of शृंगार and the substance of devotion, or the garb of devotion and the substance of शृंगार.

In the song of Mirabai साधु कि संगत पाई रे, which we shall next consider, we come across two very significant points. In the first place, Mirabai tells us that spiritual life cannot be nurtured without the company of the spiritual teacher, and the saints. The spiritual teacher and the saints perform the functions respectively of the mother and the nurse, or to vary the metaphor, of the sower and the gardener. It is only in the company of the good that our virtuous life flowers, and when we come across those who have reached the highest state of realisation, it fructifies. I was fortunate, says Mirabai, to come into the company of the great saints who had attained the highest spiritual perfection : जाकी पूर्ण कमाई रे. Of these, she mentions Namdeva, Kabir and Muktabai. It is significant to remember that Mirabai mentions Muktabai as her compeer lady-devotee, and forgets to mention the latter's great brother Jnaneshwar, who was reponsible for the spiritual life both of Muktabai and of Namdeva. In any case Mirabai tells us that these had mingled their light with the light of God : जोत में जोत मिलाई रे, which is as much as to say, as Washington Irving has put it, 'Deep had called unto Deep', or as Green has said 'Spirit had called unto Spirit', the Spirit within being immersed in the Spirit without, the immanent and the transcendent having become one.

The second important point which Mirabai stresses is the doctrine of progressive realisation. A famous saint of the Karnatak, Narasappa, who died at the age of 105 near Nimbal, and whom the present writer had the fortune to see, used to utter a message of his spiritual Teacher, which was evidently a replica of the teachings of Mirabai in the present song, in his old broken Hindi बन्नत बन्नत बन आई रे, which implies that it may not be given to man to reach the very highest limit all at once, and yet a man can always keep going nearer and nearer to the peak. Jnaneshwar has told us that there is just that difference between a perfected mystic and God, as there is between the fourteenth–day moon and the full moon, or between pieces of 23–carat gold and 24–carat gold. The present writer has chosen to call it the doctrine of Approximation or Asymptotism. It is this perpetual progressive realisation, or attainment to the highest acme possible for man here below, which may be reached by humanity without a tint of arrogance or self-complacency. We only mention the doctrine here without making its application to different spheres of human thought such as morality, epistemology, mysticism, and metaphysics. That is a problem which will be reserved for a later occasion, but it is important to remember that Plato had the same doctrine in his mind when he spoke of the Idea of the Good as the highest attainable peak of Reality, to which all the other ideas make continuous approximation by grades, or when Bradley spoke of the degrees of truth and reality, thus insisting upon the doctrine of approximation both in epistemology and in metaphysics.

(ii) *Surdas and Tulsidas*— Let us now pass on to the next group of our spiritual songs, namely, those of Surdas and Tulsidas, and see what contribution to mystical experience they have made. Surdas opens his great work, the Sursagar, with a poem बन्दउँ श्रीहरि-पद सुखदाई, which may be regarded as a classic both of music and mysticism. In this poem, we are told by Surdas first about the supersensory effects of a meditation on God. He tells us that by the grace of God, a blind man may be able to see all things अन्धे कूं सब कछु दरसाई. In fact, Surdas was himself a blind man when he wrote this poem. We know of great poets like Homer and Milton who were blind, and yet, as has been well said, they could see things in paradise. This is, however, a metaphorical way of putting things. In the case of Surdas, however, it seems there was an internal mystical vision opened to him for the attainment of God. Then he tells us that by the Grace of God, a deaf man would be able to hear, and a dumb man to speak. The classical sanskrit line in this behalf is famous: मूकं करोतिवाचालं..... यत्कृपा तमहं वन्दे. In fact, by proper meditation on God and by His Grace, a supersensous perception in various forms becomes possible. Mahatma Gandhi most probably had in mind some such conception when he had before himself statuettes of three monkeys—one a dumb monkey, second a deaf monkey, and third a blind monkey. Probably this might have been the outcome of the advice which his Guru, the late Mr. G. K. Gokhale, gave him after his return from South Africa 'to shut his mouth and to keep his ears and eyes open;' but Mahatma Gandhi went still further than what Mr. Gokhale had advised him. He insisted upon even being deaf and blind to all things in which ordinary humanity took keen interest. This seems to be the inner meaning of the three statuettes which he used to keep before himself. A similar communication, we understand, was made to a spiritual aspirant, who was on the way to spiritual progress in the year 1920, when he was advised to keep his sensory organs—vision, mouth and the ears absolutely closed, and to direct his mind only to the meditation on God: कण्णु मुच्चु, किवि मुच्चु, बायि मुच्चु, सुम्म नामस्मरणि माडु. It is not without reason that Patanjali speaks in a famous

Sutra to us that supersensuous avenues open out to an aspiring mystic in various shapes and forms: ततः प्रातिभश्रावणवेदनाऽऽदर्शास्वादवार्ता जायन्ते. When we shut all the sense organs to outer perceptions, then probably by proper meditation on God, and by His Grace, internal senses open, and we are able to perceive, hear and speak things which it would be ordinarily impossible for human beings to do. After these sensory experiences, Surdas tells us about the motor experiences of a mystic. पंगुं लंघयते गिरिम is a famous Sanskrit maxim, which we might note in this connection. Surdas likewise tells us—जाकी कृपा पंगु गिरि लंघै. Things which are impossible to achieve without the help of God become easily possible by His Grace. Even a lame man might thus be able to cross the Himalayas. Then, we are told by Surdas about the worldly effects of God-realisation. It does not behove God to keep His devotee in poverty and consequent humiliation. He thus enables His devotee in abject poverty to move on with a 'Royal Umbrella' unfurled over his head : रंक चलै शिर छत्र धराई. What cannot the Grace of God do ? Surdas tells us that we must make an humble obeisance at the feet of God after having attained to their vision : बार बार बन्दउं तिहि पाई. Tukaram continues the idea when he tells us that after having made an obeisanceat the feet of the Lord, let us look at His face. The expression in Surdas 'after having attained to their vision' must be noted. Tukaram has told us जोडोनिया कर मुख पहा सादर। पायावरी शिर ठेवोनिया, which means that it is a very difficult job for a man to have a vision of God from the head to the very feet. It is probably from this point of view that Surdas spoke of continual obeisance at the feet of God. Finally, for the attainment of all these things, Surdas tells us that the Grace of God is an absolute necessity. करुणामय is the title which he gives to God. Another reading has been करुणाकर. We may note that both these might well apply to God, remembering that the only difference between करुणामय and करुणाकर is the difference between Shankara and Ramanuja.

We next pass on to another famous song by Surdas अब तो प्रगट भई जगजानी. This song, however, is open to two interpretations: one personalistic, and the other mystical. While the idea in the line वा मोहन से प्रीति निरंतर क्यों हि रहेगी छानी may support the personalistic interpretation, the idea in the line कहा करूँ सुन्दर मूरति रोमरोम उरझानी would support the mystical. According to the latter interpretation, we might understand Surdas to mean "The form of God (मूरत), which is known to the whole world, has now appeared to my vision. How can my devotion for God be now hidden?" According to the former interpretation, we might understand Surdas to imply "My love to God is now known to the whole world. Why should I be ashamed of it ?" This latter interpretation, however, is in Gopistic fashion. On the other hand, we understand from Surdas that God had been caught up in every hair-cell of his body, as well as inside the organs of his vision, and thus it had been impossible for him to extricate Him with all his effort : निकसत नाहिं वहुत पचि हारी. "How would it be possible for him", he asks, "to describe the unison ? As you cannot separate water from milk, so can you not separate the form of God from myself." It is important to remember in this connection that Surdas's description of God, as having been caught up in the hair-cells of his body (रोम रोम उरझानी), is absolutely on a par with descriptions of God by other mystics, who have told us that every hair-cell of the body of a mystic becomes the source of Divine Light, or Sound, or Colour, or Joy : रोम रोम दीपक भया and रोम रोम सुर उटत है says Kabir ; रोम रोम रंग सार रे says Mirabai, and रोम रोम आनंद उपज करि says Charandas. In any case, it is important to remember that the infusion of God in the mind of man leads to all these supersensuous experiences to which the world is entirely blind.

In Tulsidas we find a celebrated passage विनु पग चलै in which he gives us a metaphysico-mystical description of God-vision, though his other descriptions are tinged with personalism and moralism. In a fine passage we are told how all supersensuous powers might be attributed to God. It is impossible for us, says Tulsidas, either to understand or describe the transcendent powers of God : अस सब भाँति अलौकिक करणी, महिमा तासु जाइ नहि बरणी. Mystic experience, on the other hand, would consist just in knowing at first hand the supersensuous powers of God. We are told by Tulsidas that God is able to walk without feet, and perform manifold actions without hands. He is able to see without eyes, and hear without ears. He is able to smell without a nose, and touch without a body. He can enjoy flavours without a tongue, and utter mighty words without a voice. This description of Tulsidas of the supersensuous powers of God puts us in mind of that celebrated verse in the Upanishad, which tells us : अपाणिपादो जवनो ग्रहीता । पश्यत्यचक्षुः स शृणोत्यकर्णः ॥ It is important to remember that the difference between the descriptions of supersensuous powers in Tulsidas and Surdas is that while Surdas, in a preceding verse, tells us about the supersensuous powers of a mystic, Tulsidas, in the present one, tells us about the supersensuous powers of God. While Tulsidas is giving us an objective and metaphysical treatment of transcendence, Surdas is giving us its subjective and personalistic interpretation.

(iii) *Gorakhanath, Dharmadas and Yari*— After the treatment of Surdas and Tulsidas, who express their mystical experience in a restrained personalistic and moralistic manner, we go on to the riot of mystical experience in such saints as Gorakhanath, Dharamadas, Yari, Charandas and others. Gorakhanath is one of the greatest founders of Yogic mysticism in India, and it is no wonder that he should speak of physiological plexuses and positions in a manner worthy of a Hatha-yogin. Nevertheless, the fact remains that in spite of his Hatha Yoga, Gorakhanath and his compeers had reached a very high level of spiritual experience. In the song शून्य शिखर में सुरत लगाय देखो, we have first the assertion of Gorakhanath, anticipating much modern physiological psychology, that the lateral ventricle must be regarded as the seat of the Unseen Lord, अलख. Secondly, coming to other physiological considerations, the Ida and the Pingala, the left and the right nerves of the sympathetic system, are described by him as waving Chowris on the two sides of the invisible God. Then Surya and Chandra, the Sun and the Moon, are regarded as the brilliant lights illuminating the contour of His residence. It may be remembered that the words Surya and Chandra are used here in their original sense of great brilliant lights and not in the Yogic sense, where they mean the left and the right Nadis respectively, in which case they become identical with the Ida and the Pingala, which are described above as waving Chowris. Further, we are told by Gorakhanath that musical instruments such as drums, flutes, cymbals and trumpets are being sounded in honour of the great Unseen Lord : ताल मृदंग पवपवली बजत है। हरदम पर नौबत झडती. In such a riot of light and sound the Lord of the seven Seas, which expression is to be taken as equivalent to the Self, is described as taking a bath at the confluence of the two great Nadis. The Sushumna is, of course, not mentioned here, but that is the Nadi which is responsible for the lake in the lateral ventricle, where also the two Nadis, the Ida and the Pingala, meet. What the author means by the expression सप्तसागर, which has been referred to above, it is difficult to understand, unless we regard the expression as meaning seven such lakes inside the brain region. Further, we are told by Gorakhanath that the Unseen Lord is taking a bath under a shower of pearls, which is also a great morphic experience : मोतियन की बरषा झड़ती. It is interesting to see that Gorakhanath is describing here the spiritual bath of the Self in the lateral ventricle, which conception was later adopted by Dharamadas in the case of the Saint. Finally, we are told by Gorakhanath that rarely a saint can reach such a haven, not to speak of a निगुरा or a मनमुख. He who follows his own whim has to pay the price of it, and can never be admitted in the transcendent region of spirit.

Dharamadas, in his poem झरि लागै महलिया, continues the language of the spiritual bath which we have come across in Gorakhanath. He takes the conception of the spiritual bath only and makes it applicabe to the Saint. As Gorakhanath describes the spiritual bath of the Self in the lateral ventricle, Dharamadas describes the spiritual bath of the Saint under a shower of ambrosial rain. Nevertheless, it is important to remember that Dharamadas, like Gorakhanath, does make mention of all the three kinds of experiences, namely, those of sound, light and mellifluous juice. Dharamadas begins by saying that before the spiritual bath of the saint takes place, there is first the rumbling of the cloud in the ventricle. Afterwards, there are glitters of lightning. It is interesting to remember that this conception of the rumbling of the cloud first and the glittering of the lightning next occurs only in the case of the spiritual mystic, who hears the sound of the cloud first and sees the flashof the lightning next. Scientifically, however, the glitter of the lightning precedes the rumbling of the cloud. In the region of spirit, however, it may be noted that we cannot determine which of them is earlier and which later — either sound or light may precede the other experience, or the two might even synchronise. It is probably such a kind of experience to which Dharamadas is giving expression. Next Dharamadas goes on to tell us that there is an indescribable wave of rapture, as produced by the wind upon the cloud, which sends down the ambrosial rain. We shall see later that this ambrosial rain is spoken of as "Amirasa" by Kabir and other Saints. Under this shower of ambrosial rain, says Dharamadas, the saint takes a spiritual bath. It is important to remember that the rain falls from the void palace : सुन्न महल. Even the body of the saint seems to shine with luminosity as the rain falls on him. This is of course to the external observer. Internally, however, after the shower of rain in the void palace when the Saint has enjoyed his spiritual bath, the door of the lateral ventricle opens and darkness comes to an end : खुली केवरिया मिटी अन्धेरिया, and there is illumination everywhere.

We next come to the photic, phonic, and morphic experiences of the Mohamedan saint, Yari. It is significant that this saint joins the other Hindu saints in his description of manifold spiritual experience. Yari tells us, in the first place, that the saint experiences an all-pervading light, नूर जहूर सदा भरपूरा, and then begins to hear various kinds of Anahat sound. Yari also makes mention of भृंगनाद: भँवर गुंजार गगन चढ़ि गाजै, which, he says, reaches to the top of the sky. It is true that many authors of books on mysticism have regarded भृंगनाद as the culmination of Anahat experience. However, this is not so. Who can set a limit to the order or the acme of spiritual experience? People vainly suppose that they have not reached a high level of Anahat experience, if they have not heard the भृंगनाद. It is not necessary that the भृंगनाद should be the last to be experienced. The same mistake is made by many aspirants, when they try to interpret the line in श्वेताश्वतर उपनिषद् "नीहार-धूमार्कानिलानिलानाम् । खद्योतविद्युत्स्फटिकशशिनाम् ॥". It is interesting to remember that the Arka or the Sun is here mentioned first, and then the fire, the firefly, and the moon. Experience in some cases may prove just the opposite. The point with which the author of this Upanishad was concerned was simply to make a catalogue, and not to give the order, of the photic experiences which the seeker initially experiences on his spiritual journey. Even so about भृंगनाद. Finally, we are told by Yari, as by Dharamadas and Gorkhanath, that the mystic necessarily experiences a shower of pearls, whether externally or internally: रिमझिम रिमझिम बरसे मोती. On the whole, therefore, according to Yari, the three onomatopoetic words झिलमिल झिलमिल, रुनझुन रुनझुन, and रिमझिम रिमझिम express the photic, phonic, and morphic experiences which fall to the lot of the spiritual aspirant. Even here, it is not necessary that there should be any order between photic, phonic, and morphic experiences. These experiences may cross or anticipate one another, and all these put together may make a riot of spiritual experience. It is interesting to remember that even this great Mohamedan saint Yari stresses the importance of Nāma in the realisation of such an experience : निर्मल निर्मल निर्मल नामा । कह यारी तहँ लियो विस्रामा. We thus see how the immaculate Nāma plays an important part in the experience of saints of all races and nationalities, whether Hindus, Muslims or Christians.

We have considered hitherto experiences such as the spiritual bath, and photic, phonic and morphic experiences in saints like Gorakhanath, Dharamadas, and Yari. Let us now consider what Charandas has to say in regard to his peculiar spiritual experience. "My experience of God", he says, "is different from the experience of people worshipping in ordinary temples. In temples, we have a hazy and blind worship, where the deity does not appear to the vision" : और देवल जहं धुन्धली पूजा, देवत दृष्टि न आवै. "In my case, however", says Charandas, "the deity appears distinctly to my vision." Charandas further goes on to say, "My God eats with me, speaks with me, and walks with me." Now this is a very peculiar kind of experience which has not been stressed by many mystical writers. It is said, however, that Namadev, the great Maratha saint had that experience when God used to eat with him, speak with him. The experience of God as walking with oneself is stressed by mystics of other provinces also, such as

Purandardas, Sarvajna, Jagannathadas, and Tukaram. As to whether God can speak with us, eat with us, or walk with us is a question which, we think, we had better leave to be decided between the Saint and God. It is only they who can speak about the veracity of the experience and other persons have got nothing to do with it. The Saint, however, must remember that he may not be charged with hallucination or illusion, and must beware that he does not introduce poetry in the account of his realisation. There is one point, however, for which one must give high credit to Charandas, as we shall presently see, namely, his conception of a ' virtuous life ' as constituting the worship of God. Charandas here gives an account of his moral worship. He says the true method of worship by which God can be propitiated is to bathe him with honour, to anoint him with love, to place flowers of sweet and humble words on his forehead, and to make him a continuous oblation of one's self. Moral worship is what appeals to humanity, and they may join Charandas in regarding the virtuous and dedicated life as the only true mode of worshipping God.

(iv) *Ekanath and Mahipati*— We now pass on to two Maratha saints, Ekanath and Mahipati, who have composed poems also in Hindi which are of a high calibre. Ekanath lived in Banaras to complete his wouk on the Eleventh Skandha of the Bhāgavata and there, as well as in his own native place, Paithan, he must have acquired proficiency in the Hindi language. Mahipati, a disciple of Narharinath, hailed from Paithan and came and settled at Gwalior *via* Indore. Mahipati has compossed excellent poems both in the Hindi and Marathi languages, which could be seen in manuscript form in the Dhole-Buwa-Math at Gwalior. Ekanath wrote excellent works in Marathi, and is also responsible for some good Hindi poems, of which we select one as pertaining to our present discussion. In his poem गुरु कृपांजन पायो रे भाई, Ekanath tells us that he was fortunate to get the collyrium of God's Grace for his spiritual vision. It was this collyrium which enabled him to visualise things which could not be seen by the ordinary human eye. It was customary to suppose that a proper collyrium or ointment, put into the eye, enabled one to see a sub-terranean hidden treasure. Even so, the collyrium or ointment of God's Grace, says Ekanath, enabled him to see hidden things which were not perceptible to the ordinary human vision. This collyrium enabled him to see God both internally and externally : अन्दर राम बाहर राम. Also, wherever his eye was cast he could see the form of God : जहँ देखे तहँ राम हि राम. Now this idiomatic expression राम हि राम is not familiar to students of Marathi. In Marathi they speak of राम च राम. The present writer came to know about this Hindi idiom only after he had come to Allahabad, when, a Mahomedan Fakir used to pass by his door in the early hours of the morning, reciting the invocation अल्ला हि अल्ला है. Then he could well understand what राम हि राम meant. The Fakir certainly meant that the world was full of अल्ला. Similarly, Ekanath meant by the expression राम हि राम that the world was full of Rama.

The specific contribution, however, which Ekanath makes to the theory of mystical experience is that he regards God as capable of being seen in any state of consciousness : जागत राम सोवत राम सपन में देखूं आतमराम, or, in the terminology of a modern Yogic scholar, in जागृतियोग, सुषुप्तियोग as well as स्वप्नयोग. It is evident that the waking state of consciousness gives us the reality of perception, provided our perceiving organs are sound. One could well imagine that Ekanath may have had a vision in the waking state or in the state of dream, but to have seen Rama in the state of deep sleep (सुषुप्ति) seems to be almost a contradiction in terms. सुषुप्ति involves loss of consciousness, and vision involves a full play of consciousness; hence it is that the state of सुषुप्ति has been compared to the dull condition of a stone, or of an inanimate entity. Possibly, the experience of God in सुषुप्ति may not be too unlike the consciousness of the unconscious. On the other hand, Ekanath should have mentioned the तुर्या state also, which rises beyond सुषुप्ति. जागृति and तुर्या are analogous in the sense that they give absolute reality of perception in consciousness or super-consciousness, the only difference being that while जागृति involves normal consciousness, तुर्या involves super-consciousness. On the whole, therefore, we may say that to get the perception of God in the स्वप्नयोग is difficult, though not impossible; in the सुषुप्तियोग, it becomes a contradiction in terms; and in the जागृतियोग and तुर्या, it is analogous and real. Finally, in the poem we are considering, Ekanath tells us जहँ देखे वहँ राम सरीका, which might be interpreted in the spirit of the verse of Gita यत्र चैवात्मनात्मानं पश्यन्नात्मनि तुष्यति, or the Yoga Sutra तदा द्रष्टुः स्वरूपेऽवस्थानम्. Ekanath was able to see the form of God in his own image, or else, following the Marathi idiom, as Ekanath was himself a Maratha writer, we might understand that he was able to see God continuously, corresponding to the Hindi expression लगातार.

Mahipati's poem साई अलख पलख में झलके might veritably be regarded as a perfect epitome of the growth of mystical experience. We are told by Mahipati, in the first place, about the nature of the spiritual path, then about the lamp-posts on the way which an aspirant encounters on the spiritual journey, and then finally about the consummation of spiritual experience in beatific self-satisfaction.

As regards the Spiritual Path, Mahipati gives

us five points. In the first place, the disciple has to seek a Guru who may initiate him by placing his hand over his head. This only implies that the Guru may tell him the proper method of spiritual meditation. There is no meaning in the passage of the magnetic influence from one to the other. Hence it is not the physical hand but the spiritual hand about which Mahipati is speaking. Then the spiritual teacher imparts to him a two-syllabled Mantra : दो अच्छर बीज पढाया, which is the root-source of all spiritual experience. Thirdly, the spiritual teacher tells him that in the process of meditation, he should drive away all ideas that may saunter up in his mind. Unless the mind is cleared of the weeds of ideas, the Name of God would not take root in it. The driving of ideas should properly be accomplished in the psycho-ethical manner. If this is not possible, then the disciple might invert and revert his breath, and concentrate on it, or else make his mind travel between the मूलाधार and सहस्रार. Thus, when the mind is caught up either in the name of God, or in the breath, or in the passage from मूलाधार to सहस्रार, other ideas will cease, and the idea of God will be regnant in the mind of the aspirant, who will thus be enabled to reach the "Unmani" state. The eye-lashes will now cease to function, and the unmoving eyes will remain focussed on an unmoving spiritual form of God.

As a result of his mystical contemplation,

Mahipati tells us, the aspirant will be able to visualise the following spiritual forms. He may either have an experience of pearl-like forms, which will represent Brahmā, or stars, which will represent Vishnu, or circles of light, which will represent Shiva. In the process, says Mahipati, an unseen form may, by God's Grace, present itself before the mystic. We also understand from Mahipati that an advancing mystic may be able to visualise glitters of lightning, golden sparks, or multi-coloured peacock–feathers. Mahipati thus tells us that light-experience, form-experience and colour-experience will reveal themselves before the mystic, and make his journey smooth. It is interesting to note that Mahipati does not make mention of any forms of Anāhata.

Finally the cumulative result of these experiences will be that the advancing mystic will begin to give thanks to the teacher, to the pathway and to God Himself. " Blessed be my Spiritual Teacher who has conferred his Grace on me. Blessed be the Pathway by which I have travelled. Blessed be the Lord who enabled me to visualise His form ". It may well be said about such a mystic, as was said by a great Karnatak mystic, होदु होदु आगि होगुत्तदे. The mystic becomes absolutely convinced about the reality of his experience which led him from the bottom of the ladder to the peak of spiritual experience. He now congratulates himself that his wanderings in the cycle of existences have ceased, that the rope of birth and death, by which he was hitherto tied, has been reduced to bits, and finally that the Karmic prison-house, in which he was shut up, has been broken to pieces and he has been admitted into the light of day. Well might he now exclaim, as a mystic exclaimed once, "There is no limit to my joy."

2. *Physiological, Psychological, and Moral effects of God-realisation: Charandas* — We now go on to the next group of Padas, namely, those which deal with the physiological, psychological, and moral effects of God-realisation. We shall soon come to a song of Charandas which explains with extraordinary acumen the effects of the realisation of God. Before we tackle this song, however, we shall give the spiritual experiences of Charandas himself, which are on a par with the experiences which we have discussed in our former group of songs. In the song ऐसा देस दिवाना रे लोगो, Charandas is describing the strange spiritual territory, a mere entry into which is sufficient to madden the seeker. In this territory, people whirl round and round without a wine draught by God-intoxication and put an end to all processes of birth and death. Charandas gives us the usual experiences of form, light and sound with which we are already familiar. "In this territory", he says, "we meet with priceless pearls without oyster-shells, and flashes without

lightning." He also makes a very complete list of the different kinds of Anahat Nada which a mystic experiences as marks of spiritual realisation. Thus he tells us that the Anahat is experienced like the humming of a bee, like a conch, like cymbals, like a bell, like a flute, like a kettle-drum, and like the terrible rumbling of a cloud. So far so good. But Charandas also goes on to further experiences in which it would be difficult to understand how much there is of poetry, and how much of realisation. "In such a territory", he says, "flowers blossom without season, and fruits are laden with ambrosial juice." Further, he tells us that "the so-called eight Siddhis produce a solemn peal by the jingling of their ankle-bells and celestial damsels keep musical time by dancing without feet." This is an experience which is not impossible, but the veracity of it must be tested, as we have said before, between the aspirant and God himself. Finally, we are told that these experiences do not fall to the lot of the ordinary seeker. "It was only when my great spiritual teacher Sukadeva conferred his grace upon me", says Charandas, "that I was able to see such a territory."

So far about the spiritual experiences of Charandas. He however seems to be particularly an audile mystic, stressing the sonorousness and the power of the Anahat Sound. Charandas gives us a very complete account of the physiological, moral, and metaphysical effects of hearing such an Anahat sound. In a wonderful poem, जब ते अनहत घोर सुनी, he tells us that when the terror-striking Anahat sound was heard, in the first place, the senses became palsied and the mind remained quiescent, and further, every pore of the body became an outlet as it were of emerging joy, which put an end to all sloth and idleness. This is as much as to say that the joy, produced by hearing the Anahat sound, infused a great spiritual energy in the body-system, driving away all sloth and inaction. In this process of the driving away of sloth by spiritual joy, we are reminded of a similar utterance of Empedocles about Love and Hate. When Hate enters the sphere, he says, Love is driven out, and when Love enters, Hate is driven away. Similarly, Says Charandas, when sloth enters the mind, there is an end to all joy, and when joy enters, sloth and inaction are dispelled altogether. Charandas further goes on to tell us that, in the state of intoxication every particle of the mind becomes drenched as it were in mellifluous juice—a statement which we shall consider later at length when we come to Kabir's description of Amirasa. So far about the physiological and psychological effects of God-realisation.

What does Charandas tell us about the moral effects ? " All of our desires come to an end," he says, " and desirelessness, which is the highest watermark of Stoic aud Epicurean philosophy, becomes fixed in the system. Then, again, Charandas says that as a result of God-realisation, " passion for worldly enjoyment and enhancement cease altogether : लोक भोग सुधि रही न कोई. No enjoyment can now draw away the mind of such a man when it is entirely drawn up by God. The final moral effect of God-realisation, we are told by Charandas, is that the shackles of action and delusion in such a man are broken : करम भरम के बंधन छूटै, and he remains actionless in the midst of activity, and God-centered in the midst of work.

As regards the metaphysical effects of God-realization, Charandas tells us that all sense of duality comes to an end in such a man : दुविधा विपति हनी. " When he has lost himself," says Charandas, " it is superfluous to add that he loses the consciousness of the world, not to speak of the consciousness of quintuple complexes, such as the elements, sense-organs, and breaths."

Finally, as the Yogic effect of God-realization, Charandas adds a personal note in the advice which his spiritual teacher, Sukadeva, had given to him. " Meditate in such a manner, O Charandas, that, by great fortune, you may reach the supreme one-pointed pinnacle in the process of meditation." The reference here is evidently to the peak of the lateral ventricle in which all spiritual experience must ultimately be centered, and enjoyed. We have a similar statement in a Kanarese mystic which tells us कोलु कोलु एन्निरो गुरुविन कोलु मेलेन्निरो, which means that this pinnacle is like the beautiful inverted golden pot which crowns the topmost and one-pointed "pole" of spiritual experience. On the whole, therefore, we see what a wonderful poem Charandas has to his credit in his description of the physiological, moral, metaphysical, and yogic effects of God-realisation.

3. *Sublimity and ineffability of mystical experience: Kabir*— After an account of the physiological, psychological, and moral effects of mystical experience in Charandas, let us now see what Kabir has to say about these matters. While we shall be discussing these, we cannot fail to be struck by the sublimity and ineffability of the mystical experience about which Kabir is speaking. What are the characteristics of this experience according to Kabir? "Only he who has penetrated to the heart of Reality, says Kabir, "can understand the nature of our territory": महरम होय सो जानै साधो ऐसा देस हमारा. The spiritual territory is altogether different from whatever we have seen, or heard. The Veda and the Quran

have not been able to encompass it : वेद किताब पार नहिं पावत । कहन सुननसे न्यारा. The meaning of this statement is that, according to Kabir, new experiences might occur which have not been described either by books or men. Kabir next goes on to give us his further experiences. In the first place, he says, in the void palace are heard the sounds of the drum, the flute, the fiddle and the guitar. There are words without sounds, and pearls without shells. There is lightning without a cloud, and light without the Sun. Brahman, which is shining forth, is putting to shame all luminosity whatsoever. And then, says Kabir, beyond all these, there is an Incomprehensible Infinite : आगे अगम अपारा. "The territory which very few pilgrims have reached—that", he says, "is our habitation. It is only he who is initiated by the Guru, and who is dear to his Guru, can understand the meaning of what I say" : कह कबीर वहँ रहनि हमारी । बूझै गुरमुख प्यारा. On the whole, therefore, we may say that the song we are considering contains the mystical experiences of Kabir about light, form and sound, while his suggestion that words must arise without sounds is an experience which is almost unique.

To give a further touch to the growth of spiritual experience in Kabir, let us add another song from him : चुवत अमीरस भरत ताल जहँ. The final state of his spiritual experience we shall not discuss here. We shall consider it later, when we shall be speaking about his Dohas, and there see how far it tallies with the experiences of the great Saints of the world. Kabir tells us in the present song that when the lake becomes full on account of the oozing of the mellifluous juice, then a sky-reaching sound breaks forth as a submarine volcano in eruption might send its waters into the sky: चुवत अमीरस भरत ताल जहँ सबद उठै असमानी हो. We should note the connection between these two points— the oozing of the mellifluous juice from the cells into the lateral ventricle, and the rise of the sky-reaching sound therefrom. In the next verse, which we shall discuss presently, we shall find that the position is reversed. When such a sky-reaching sound breaks forth, then the lake of the lateral ventricle becomes full with mellifluous juice. At a later stage, we shall discuss what the connection between these two points is. At present, it is enough to say that as every cell begins to discharge 'Amirasa', or mellifluous juice at the time of meditation, the fullness of the lake breaks itself out into the sonorous sound which reaches the sky. A second point which Kabir discusses in this poem is that the river overflows, and engulfs, and even soaks up to ocean: सरिता उमड़ि सिन्धुको सोखै. This is as much as to say that the Self in the aspirant becomes so expansive that it envelopes the Brahman itself. This phenomenon of the river absorbing the ocean cannot be explained, says Kabir, in adequate terms : नहिं कछ जात बखानी हो. Then he says that, in such a state of spiritual experience, there are neither the Sun nor the Moon, nor the stars, neither day nor night. नहिं वहँ रैन विहानी हो. Those who have read the Upanishads can see the parallelism of this to the passage where we are told : न तत्र सूर्यो भाति न चन्द्रतारकं नेमा विद्युतो भान्ति कुतोऽयमग्निः ।।. Then again we are told that, in such a state, various kinds of musical instruments produce each its own harmony : बाजे बजें सितार बांसुरी, and further there is a ररंकार of soft words : ररंकार मृदुबानी हो. What is this ररंकार ? We do not know of any mystical treatise which describes this ररंकार. It may stand either for ॐकार, रमरमकार, or राम राम ध्वनि. So, it is not merely the sounds of musical instruments that break forth, but veritably the words "Rama Rama" with slender tunes at the time of the Samadhic experience of the aspirant. Then, further, we are told by Kabir : दस अवतार एक रत राजें. Now this is open to two interpretations : all the ten Avataras are incessantly and continuously present before him, or otherwise, all the ten Avataras pass before him in a cinematographic show in one night. There are thus outbursts of involuntary praise : अस्तुति सहज से आनी हो. How could one describe the value of that experience ? Words fail to describe it adequately ! It is the experience of eternity being compressed in a single moment, which fills the aspirant with the consciousness of the infinite power of God. These, says Kabir, are serious and secret matters, which rarely any one is able to comprehend : कह कबीर भेद की बातें, बिरला कोइ पहचानी हो ।

After having discussed the rise and growth of spiritual experience in Kabir, though not yet its culmination, we pass on to the psychological and moral effects of spiritual realisation in Kabir, with which the descriptions of Charandas already alluded to bear close resemblance. There is a very fine verse in Kabir : रस गगन गुफा में अजर झरै, which we may now consider. As we said while discussing the former verse, we are told in the present one and possibly more plausibly, that as a consequence of hearing the Anahat sound, the cells of the brain begin to discharge mellifluous juice in the lateral ventricle which becomes like a lake. So, here, we see that the sound becomes the cause of which the mellifluous juice becomes the consequence. How are the two statements in the preceding verse, and in the present one to be reconciled? Those who have read Kant's Critique of Pure Reason know that there is something like Reciprocal Causation: Anahat Shabda having its influence on the oozing of the mellifluous juice, and the oozing of Amirasa having its influence on the rise of the Anahat Shabda—these are the two sides of what Kant would call Reciprocal Causation. We are absolutely at our wit's end in discussing which is the earlier and which is the later. Another way of explaining the two phenomena would be from the point of view of their co-existence, but whether reciprocal causation or co-existence may be true, there must necessarily be between them a unity of apperception – a Homo-Ousion or a Homo-aitia—call it the brain, call it the mind, call it the Self or Spirit if you please, the two phenomena cannot be explained without an ultimate unity.

Kabir proceeds to tell us that such a man in Samadhi enters the tenth cavity : दसवें द्वारे ताली लागी, अलख पुरुष जाको ध्यान धरें. This is a particular mannerism of Kabir in regard to the experience of God in the head. ' Tāli ' might be interpreted either as Samadhi or even as key. In another place, Kabir says खिड़की खुलवावो. The lateral ventricle must be opened before one is able to see God. In a Kanarese verse of the famous saint Vijayadāsa we are told हरि करुण वेंबंथ कीलि कै दोरेयितु : the Grace of God was the key by means of which he could unlock this lateral ventricle.

Whatever their rationale may be, we are placing these experiences of the great saints before our readers. There are two famous lines in the poem of Kabir which I do not know how adequately to evaluate or to praise :—

काल कराल निकट नहिं आवै
काम क्रोध मद लोभ जरै ।

जुगुन जुगुन की तृषा बुझाती
करम भरम अघ व्याधि टरै ॥

These two lines must be carved on his heart by every aspirant. What is the use of our Samadhic experience unless it resolves itself into psychological, moral, metaphysical, and even eschatological consequences ? Terrific death is afraid to come near us when we are thinking about God. Lust, anger, arrogance and avarice must cease. Also, all desires, all actions, all illusions, all sins and all diseases must disappear. When such a state is reached, says Kabir, true immortality is attained : अमर होय, कब हुं न मरै. These are in short the moral and the psychological effects of spiritual realisation.

4. *Flavourism and Beatification : Kabir and Dadu*— We have seen in the preceding paragraphs the manifold experiences of Kabir which are in a line with the experiences of other mystics described in the earlier sections of this chapter. There is, however, one special feature about Kabir's mystical experience, namely, that in addition to the experiences of sound, light and colour, he mentions particularly the experience of flavour. Now this conception of flavour he develops in certain Padas which we shall proceed to discuss in the present group. Along with Kabir, we shall also have to discuss his compeer, Dadu, who also

contributes some new ideas to what we may call 'Flavourism'. The three padas, therefore, to be discussed in the present group are :—

(1) ऐसो है रे हरि रस (Kabir)

(2) हो तो कोई पिये राम रस प्यासा (Kabir)

(3) राम रस मीठारे (Dadu)

These padas on flavourism by Kabir and Dadu, on रामरस or हरिरस as the case may be, would be the connecting link between the padas of Kabir which have gone by in which he has mentioned Amirasa, and the padas of Kabir which are to follow in which he develops his conception of Madirā. Let us, therefore, put the above three padas together and deduce therefrom the doctrine of flavourism which Kabir and Dadu advocate.

There seem to be four chief characteristics which belong to the experience of Divine juice as advocated by Kabir and Dadu. In the first place, we are told by Kabir that the draught of रामरस or हरिरस experienced during the state of Samadhic meditation is a rare and valuable commodity. Kabir even advises every man who feels thirsty to slake his thirst by this Rama Rasa : हो तो कोइ पिये रामरस प्यासा. This expression would mean that if a man felt thirsty, why should he not partake of the divine juice ? It is almost in the manner of Akbar in a reported incident between himself and his minister, Birbal, who had placed before him conditions of famine in the land. Why should not people take to rice and milk, asked Akbar, if there is famine in the land? At least these commodities are available! A similar story is told about the departed Nizam that when his minister told him about the conditions of famine and dearth in his state, he said, why not people partake of 'khichadi' and ghee? These Emperors in a very high position did not understand the conditions in which ordinary humanity has to live. Similarly, Kabir from his lofty spiritual heights could not understand the difficulties of the ordinary seeker. If such a man feels thirsty, says Kabir, why should he not partake of Divine Juice? Then, Kabir goes on to tell us that only a Gurumukh can avail himself of this valuable commodity, while a Manmukh has to go diasppointed. Let us remember in this connection what the Great Nanak said about the Gurumukh and the Manmukh :—

गुरमुखि रंगि चलुलिआ रंगि हरिरंगि राती ।
देंदे थावहु दिता चंगा मनमुखि ऐसा जाणिए ॥

Coming back to Kabir, it may be remembered that the Guru might give only the potentiality of the draught, instead of the draught itself. It depends upon the disciple to utilise the gift according to the best of his powers. Further, both Kabir and Dadu tell us that as a result of this draught of Divine juice, the seeker becomes fearless and immortal : ऐसा अलख अभेव । सो अविनासी प्राण says Dadu; जाके पिये अमर व्है जाई says Kabir.

Secondly, we have to note that this divine juice cannot be obtained, except at the price of desperate devotion to God. A great deal of torture and trouble must be experienced before one gets even a small quantity of this divine juice. Kabir tells us, it is only when we first throw ourselves in a conflagration, that we experience green verdure next : आगे आगे दावा जलै रे, पीछे हरिया होय. This is exactly in the spirit of the Gujarathi poet, Preetam, who tells us : प्रेम पंथ पावकनी ज्वाला, भाली पाछा भागे जोने । मांही पड्या ते महा सुख माणे, देखणारा दाझे जोने, which means that the way of God's love is the way of fire. He who throws himself in to it will be saved, and he who will merely look on and keep aside will be burnt to death. It is the active part in this meditation which will enable us to get out of difficulties and perils. Kabir's account in this connection is in his own usual antithetical manner. He tells us that such a divine juice could be partaken of only by a man who has no head over his shoulders : धड़ पै सीस न होय, calling to our mind a similar utterance of Kabir elsewhere : सीस उतारे भुइ धरै. This would be an illustration of the Vibhavanā Alankara, where the effect is produced without a cause. It is only when we throw down our life that we can rise to the heights of God's experience.

The third characteristic of this thirst for the divine juice is its unquenchability. An attempt to slake the thirst, says Kabir, will lead to further thirst. 'Listen to me, O Saints,' he says, 'your thirst for the Name of God can never be quenched.' This we might regard as an illustration of the विशेषोक्ति Alankara, where the cause is present but the effect is not. So said Tulsidas also. Those who say that they have drunk Rama Charita to satiety have never drunk it at all : राम चरित जे सुनत अघाई । रसविशेष जानत ते नाहीं. This might be taken to be an illustration of the Pratīpa Alankara. In fact, the poetical descriptions of these great Saints seem to be filled with a series of Alankars which enrich the mystical value of their songs.

The last characteristic of the experience of this divine juice is, as Dadu tells us, that he who partakes of the divine juice becomes one with the juice itself : सो रस हि रहा समाय. This is a great idea, and its implications we must examine a little. God is the source of this Rasa; the Rasa is the quality which oozes from Him; and the Saint receives it and enjoys it to his heart's content. The Triputi of God, flavour and saint is exactly on a par with the Vedantic Triputi – ज्ञेय, ज्ञान and ज्ञाता. The implication of Dadu's utterance is that God and devotee would cease to exist, and only the Rasa would remain. This is exactly as the Vedantins would put it. ज्ञाता and ज्ञेय would vanish and ज्ञान alone would remain. These are illustrations of what we may call Triputī Laya in Mysticism and Metaphysics. The same idea has been brought out with great force in that cryptic utterance from the Upanishads, रसो वै सः। The ultimate upshot of flavourism would thus be that flavour alone would remain, neither he who imparts the flavour, nor he who receives it.

On a general consideration of the songs on divine juice by Dadu and Kabir, it may be noted that the following Saints have been mentioned by them as having received the divine juice. Among the ancient saints, Dhruva and Pralhad have been mentioned dy Kabir, and among modern saints Matsyendra, Goraksha and Raidas. Dadu mentions the names of Namadeva, Peepa and Sukadeva as having partaken of the divine juice. Kabir particularly mentions Mirabai as having been never satisfied by the draughts of divine juice, as she continuously repeats the performance, cup after cup. Dadu returns the compliment on Kabir, whom he describes as having been never satisfied by the divine juice and as feeling thirsty even today : पिवत कबीरा ना थक्या, अब हूँ प्रेमपियास. Whatever may be the position in regard to the historic relationship of the names mentioned herein, it is certain that Kabir and Dadu laid great stress on the enjoyment of the draughts of divine juice by the Great Saints.

5. *God intoxication : Kabir*— We have said above that the conception of Rasa leads on to

the conception of "Madira" in Kabir. Madira is veritably the intoxtcating spiritual wine. In the song which we shall now discuss, है कोई सन्त सहज सुख उपजै, Kabir gives us a very sustained account of the production of this intoxicating spiritual liquor. The present Pada may be supposed to be one of the best continued metaphors in Kabir or even in Hindi literature. It may be taken to be a very good illustration of what we may call महारूपक.

The six points in the present song in connection with the production and the enjoyment of this intoxicating spiritual liquor are: (1) the value of the spiritual liquor in satiating and stabilising the mind of the aspirant; (2) the components that go to make up the liquor; (3) the method by means of which the manufacture of the spiritual wine is to commence; (4) the sacrifice that is to be offered for the successful production of the divine liquor—in the present case, the sacrifice of the goat of Eros; (5) the actual oozing out of the divine liquor from the pipe of the Sushumna; aud (6) eulogy of the man who is an expert in the production of this liquor.

In the first place, Kabir throws out a challenge to any so-called Saint to produce this divine liquor. He knows that those who can produce this divine liquor are very few indeed. है कोइ सन्त सहज सुख उपजै is the challenge which he throws out. "Is there any saint", he asks, "who can evoke in us the beatificatory experience called Sahaja ? As a liquor-woman gives us filled cups of liquor, can such a Saint give me even a drop of Rama Rasa ? " " If he can, I shall be prepared ", says Kabir, " to give him the brokerage of my entire life-long penance."

In the second place, Kabir tells us that for the actual production of the spiritual liquor, we have to cut to pieces all our evil passions—काम, क्रोध, लोभ, मोह, मद and मत्सर— and to mix their essence with the Gur of the Guru's word. Psychologically speaking, there is an energy underlying all these emotions. The emotions cannot come into play unless there is a psychic energy to serve as their substratum. When these emotions are cut to pieces, their essence is to be gathered. That essence in psychic energy. This psychic energy is to be mixed with the Gur of the Guru's word. The mixture is to be put into the body-pot, and the pot is to be closed, and no outlet is to be kept for it. This is as much as to say that further stages in the process must be accomplished entirely inside a man's heart. "Mauna" is probably one of its chief characteristics.

The next stage in the production of the divine liquor, says Kabir, is the construction of a fire-place and the igniting of fire. Let all the fourteen worlds now constitute the fire-place, and let the fire of Brahman be lit inside it. Let the closed body-pot be now kept on this fire, so that it will begin to boil to the realisation-point. Without extreme toil and turmoil, no high achievements are possible.

It may be remembered that, in all ceremonial production, it is customary to offer a sacrifice before the process of production is started. In the present case, it is the goat of Eros that must be sacrificed. Madana is proverbially regarded as a goat. The great Ekanath in a famous song has spoken about the exploits of this undaunted goat in subjugating even Shankar and Narada, and its ultimate conquest by Shuka : एडका मदन तो केवळ पंचानन । धडक मारिली शंकरा । केला रावणाचा चुरा । नारदासारिखा ऋषी नाडिला जेणें । शुक देवानें ध्यान धरोनि । एडका आणिला आकळोनि । एकाजनार्दनाचे चरणीं । बांधिला जेणें ॥. Kabir is not satisfied with the mere conquest of this goat ; it must be sacrificed before the fire of Brahman. We are told by Kabir that the way to sacrifice this goat of Eros is to throttle it, and not to kill it, so that it may give out the Anahat Sound before it dies.

Fifthly, says Kabir, when the body-pot has been kept boiling for a long time on the fire of Brahman and a proper sacrifice has been made, then the divine liquor will begin to trickle down from the topmost part of the body by way of the distilling pipe of the Sushumna, which will act as a distributing agent of the nectary wine to the various parts of the body, so as to keep them satiated, powerful, and equanimous. In the case of other liquors, a man feels intoxicated and loses his head and senses. In the case of divine liquor, a man keeps his head cool, and has a complete control of all his sense-organs and mind.

This happened in his own case, says Kabir, when the nectary wine he enjoyed kept him in perfect equanimity and beatification. Such a life, he says, is a very difficult one, and he alone, who has obtained a knowledge of the process from a proper spiritual teacher, can become proficient in it.

Let us now proceed to consider three famous songs from Kabir in which he speaks in detail about the satiety, the freedom, and the equanimity produced in him by the state of divine intoxication. In these songs we can trace somewhat the influence of Sufism on Kabir, as well as an admixture of Urduised and Punjabi words instead of Khadi-Boli or Bhojpuri. In the poem दरस दिवाना बावला, we are told by Kabir that the spiritual aspirant becomes बावला, or mad after the vision of God. Then, we are told, he becomes अलमस्त फकीरा and अस्मतका धीरा. Thus, entirely maddened by the vision of God, such a Saint leads a life of solitary independence. The body clings to him, as described in a famous verse of the Bhagvata as an उत्तरीय to a drunken man.

देहं च नश्वरमवस्थितमुत्थितं वा
सिद्धो न पश्यति यतोऽध्यगमत् स्वरूपम् ।
दैवादपेतमुत दैववशादुपेतम्
वासो यथा परिकृतं मदिरामदान्धः ॥

Those who have read Pali literature know how, in one dialogue of Buddha, we read the description of a खग्गविसाण or a rhinoceros. The name of the सुत्त is खग्गविसाणसुत्त. The Saint of Kabir becomes such a खग्गविसाण or a totally detached person. Kabir tells us further that every breath of the Saint is almost like a cup of wine. This is under Sufistic influence. In every breath that the Saint dedicates to God he is drinking a cup of immortal wine. A Hindu would have said nectar. But we do not mind it, because wine here is nectar. What are the effects of drinking this cup of immortal wine? पियत पियाला प्रेमका, सुधरे सब साथी. The Saint drinks wine while his associates are improved. This is a sort of an असंगति अलंकार. 'Prima facie', these two things are unconnected, and yet one rises from the other. A man has to lead a pure and spiritual life, and this will result in improving the character and ideals of those who come into contact with him. Kabir also tells us that such a Saint moves and nods like an elephant in ruts : आठ पहर झूमत रहे जस मैंगल हाथी. This, of course, is not an ideal to be kept, or attained by every aspirant. Rarely a man like Kabir can hope to reach that stage. Finally, he tells us that when a Saint takes this wine of God-love he becomes free from infatuation and doubt. He reaches a state of perfect equanimity. The pauper and the prince are to him alike : बँधन काट मोह्का बैठा निरसंका। वाके नजर न आवता क्या राजा क्या रंका. The Saint lives in such a perfect state of equanimity. He has a hidden vision. Valuing his own soul, he cares for nobody, and sits in divine contemplation. The Saint in Kabir sitting in posture in divine ecstacy is definitely on a par with the Upanishadic sage who sits singing to himself the "song of universal unity."

In another verse, हमन·हैं इश्क मस्ताना, Kabir describes his love towards God, using the famous word इश्क. The word इश्क carries a double sense. It may mean love to the beloved, as well as love to God. Many so-called mystics have spoken as if they could institute a comparison between sexual love and divine love. The present writer has shown in his work on " A Constructive Survey of Upanishadic Philosophy " how this comparison is totally faulty. Even one of the Upanishads has said : तद्यथा प्रियया स्त्रिया सम्परिष्वक्तो न बाह्यं किंचन वेद नान्तरम्। एवमेवायं पुरुषः प्राज्ञेनात्मना सम्परिष्वक्तो न बाह्यं किंचन वेद नान्तरम्. In spite of the dictum that all Upamas involve a difference or भेद, it is very desirable to remove all appendage of sexual relationship from the conception of divine love. To describe God as the beloved, whether in the masculine or in the feminine sense, is equally wrong. The love of God stands in a category altogether apart from any sexual relationship.

It was with this divine love that Kabir was filled to the brim. As a consequence of his intoxication by God-love, he remained totally independent of the world, and there was no necessity for him to wander like a beggar from door to door. He was absolutely self-poised and self-sufficient. It was, therefore, unnecessary, he says, that anybody should awaken him from his slumber, and impose any होशियारी on him. Now the word होशियारी might have been employed here in either of two senses. Kabir tells us that as he was entirely filled with God-intoxication, it was not 'possible' for anybody to rouse him from that state. Also, as he had attained to unison with God, he knew his duties very well and it was 'unnecessary' for anybody to bring him to the consciousness of his duty. होशियारी in his case thus was neither possible nor necessary. Kabir wondered how the whole world was breaking its head for the sake of fame. To him, the Name of God was all in all, as also the Form of God, which was always present before him, and he was never separated from his Lord even for a single moment.

Three consequences followed from this continuous vision of God. In the first place, there was no necessity for him to have friendship (यारी) with the world. Secondly, it was not necessary for him to entertain any expectations (इन्तजारी) whatsoever. All of his desires were fulfilled, and there was no necessity for him to expect anything from anybody. Thirdly, all his anxiety (बेक़रारी) was at an end, as he knew that God would always protect him, support him, and vindicate him. On the whole, therefore, it may be seen that Kabir's divine love made him rise superior to all ideas of यारी, इन्तजारी and बेक़रारी.

Finally, Kabir says, the reason why he was able to attain to this state was that he had entirely unburdened himself of the load of duality. Duality was a very heavy load indeed. As unity of experience had in Kabir taken the place of duality, he could walk on the slender path of spiritual life with great ease. Had he taken the load of duality on his head, the razor-edge of spiritual experience (क्षुरस्य धारा) might have mortally injured him, and made all spiritual progress impossible.

In another verse, Kabir tells us how such a Saint acquires an absolute equanimity through God-possession. Those who have read Greek Philosophy know that 'Epoche' was regarded as the greatest moral virtue by the Stoics, Epicureans and Sceptics alike. Silence, 'Maunam', speechlessness is 'Epoche'. मन मस्त हुवा तब क्यों बोले, says Kabir. What necessity is there for a man to speak, when he has reached that spiritual stage? It is much better to be silent than to move the lips. Kabir is describing in the above verse the state of 'Epoche' after God-realisation. He gives us four illustrations. In the first place, he says, a man who is in possession of a diamond and has tied it in a knot,— is it necessary for him to open it from time to time, and see whether the diamond is there or not ? The diamond *is* there. Similarly, " the diamond of God is inside me," says Kabir, " I am in sure possession of it. Why should I open it now and again ? " Secondly, Kabir gives us the illustration of a balance with two pans. So long as an aspirant has not attained to God-vision, we may say that in his case one pan is up and the other is down. हलकी थी जब चढी तराजू । पूरी भई तब क्यों तोले. By the attainment of God, however, the upper pan comes to a level with the other, as in the case of Krishna. What now remains to be weighed? पूरी भई तब क्यों तोले. The Saint in all ways thus becomes equal to God.

Then Kabir tells us that such a Saint always lives in a state of God-enjoyment. In Uttar Pradesh, it is customary for women to sell liquor. Who can prevent a liquor-woman from drinking as much liquor as she likes ? Similarly, who can prevent the Saint, who has once attained to the vision of God, from enjoying that vision as long, as much, and as often as he likes ? Kabir also gives a fourth illustration : हंसा पाए मान सरोवर, ताल तलैया क्यों डोलै. A Hansa has reached his final habitat, the Manasa Sarovara. Why should it be necessary for him now to hunt out small ponds and tanks? When we have reached the highest God inside our heart, why should we open out our eyes? — बाहर नैना क्यों खोलै ।

In the end, Kabir tells us that he has found God even behind a sesamum. Another variant of this idea is to be found in a maxim which tells us तिल ओले पहाड़. 'There is a mountain behind a sesamum'. In the same manner, says Kabir, "I have found the great God behind the tiniest thing like a sesamum. Tukaram also has told us that the great God, who fills the universe, makes his home even in a sesamum: तिळा एवढे बांधुनि घर । आंत राहे विश्वंभर. The tiniest particle in the universe and the smallest cranny, according to Carlyle, is filled with the presence of God. The macrocosm is fully present in the microcosm. The microcosm according to Kabir fully reveals the presence and the power of God.

6. *Lifting of the cosmic deceit : Kabir*—After having discussed the Sufistic influence on Kabir, let us now proceed to consider a few Vedantic ideas in him. One such is his description of Maya as a great temptress (ठगनी). In the poem रमैया की दुलहिनि लूटल बजार, he calls Maya the wife of Ramaiyya (रमैया). In another connection we have discussed in Kabir the relationship of Maya and Ishwar in

his doctrine of Niranjana. At present we may say that this great Maya tempts every person in the world. As the Marathi verse says, ठगडी बायको आली रे गडयांनो । भल्याभल्यासि ठकवुनि गेली. She wields her great power in the celestial world, the nether world, and the mortal world, and causes consternation in the minds of everybody. Gods and Sages have suffered alike. Gods like Brahma, Vishnu and Mahesh, and sages like Narada, Shringi and Parashara, have all fallen a prey to this temptress. Narada had to become a Naradi. Shringi had perforce to marry Shanta, the adopted daughter of Dasharath. Parashara had to fall a prey to a fisherman's daughter Matsyagandha, from whom the great Vyasa was born. Saints and Sadhus in spite of their religious austerities have suffered equally from her temptation. Those who impart the Mantra in the ear (कनफूंका), thus falling an easy prey to the temptress, as well as those who have by their presence brought light to Kashi (चिदकाशी), have equally suffered from this temptress. The so-called great Yogeshwaras are no exception : they are also equally tempted by Maya. On being so tempted, they begin to ponder how this should have happened, reflexly combing their beards. The whole world has suffered by the enchantments of this Maya. "Myself alone," says Kabir, "have been fortunate in being saved from her clutches. I caught hold of the rope of

Shabda and by its help have been able to cross the river of existence : सवद डोर गहि उतरे पार.

Then in another verse साधो सहज समाधि भली, we have a further contribution to Vedantic thought by Kabir. Some time back, we discussed the physiological side of Sahaja Samadhi. Here we shall explain the distinction between an absolutistic interpretation of Sahaja Samadhi, and a mystical enjoyment of it. The true Sahaja Samadhi, says Kabir, goes on increasing in intensity in a geometrical ratio. It is the culmination of spiritual wealth. In the poem of Kabir which we are considering, we find two different strata. It is just the difference between an absolutistic philosophy, and an enjoyment of mystical experience. In a fine Sanskrit verse, we have an exact illustration of the absolutistic description of Sahaja Samadhi :

आत्मा त्वं गिरिजा मतिः सहचराः प्राणाः शरीरं गृहम्
पूजा ते विषयोपभोगरचना निद्रा समाधिस्थितिः ।
संचारः पदयोः प्रदक्षिणविधिः स्तोत्राणि सर्वा गिरो
यद्यत्कर्म करोमि तत्तदखिलं शंभो तवाराधनम् ॥

" All that I talk is in prayer to you, O God. Every step I take is a perambulation about you, O God. My enjoyment is your worship, and my sleep is ecstasy." This might be the philosophy of an idler. What are the characteristics of mystical enjoyment ?

आंख न मूदौं कान न रूँधौं, तनिक कष्ट नहि धारौं ।
खुले नयन पहिचानौं हँसि हँसि, सुन्दर रूप निहारौं ॥

Do not shut your eyes, do not close your ears, but see God, recognise Him and laugh. This is just the meaning of the mystical enjoyment in Sahaja Samadhi. Then, Kabir tells us that by the enjoyment of mystical experience, all dirty emotions must come to an end, even on account of the physical influence of Shabda. "If I get up or sit down, my mind is fixed on God". This is the way of life which Kabir calls उन्मनि रहनी, ecstatic life or life in the superconscious state. We have known the distinction between कथनी, करनी, and रहनी. What is the use of mere talking, what is the use of thinking? We must live philosophy. "I sing it in living", says Kabir : कह कबीर यह उन्मनि रहनी, सो परगट करि गाई. In that state which passes beyond happiness and sorrow, we should remain absolutely attuned and merged in God : दुखसुखसे कोइ परे परमपद, तेहि पद रहा समाई ।

7. *Ecstasy and the Sustenance of the world—Maula and Sakha.* We have seen in the preceding poem that Kabir advises us to remain in a state of mergence, whether actually in Samadhi or out of it. There are two very fine poems pertaining to this kind of experience—one from Maula, and the other from Sakha. The poets may not be very much known to fame but the poems are exceedingly fine. The first of them refers to the state of Samadhi itself, and the second to the state

व्युत्थान. Both the poems contain a description of the height to be reached in spiritual experience. But the special features of the two are, that while in the one case, there is an addition of psychological and metaphysical thought, in the other, there is an addition of poetical and social reflection. On the whole, the two poems may be said to give us the experience of the mystics at the height of spiritual realisation,

In the poem जो पीर मेरा बडा औलिया, taken from the posthumous diary of the Saint of Umadi, we shall consider six important points. In the first place, the poet tells us that God gave him an ensign, an emblem, a mark, by means of which his spiritual progress became smooth, and he was ultimately enabled to reach the goal of his spiritual endeavour. The word used in the poem is Nishāṇa which means an emblem, or even a banner in Hindi, and in Marathi a flag or a banner. Tukaram, for example, said : पैल दिसे निशाण विटोबाचे । पांडुरंग भेटे भरंवशानें, that having seen the Nishana of God, he could know that the temple of God was approaching, and that thus he was sure to meet his deity. In the Kannad language, we have a very fine word कुरुहु to signify this idea. There is a maxim in the Kanarese language कुरुहु कंडरे मरळि भवक्के बरलारी, which means that if you may see the ensign once, you will never more return to this earthly existence. The difference between this ensign and the star in

Tennyson's 'Voyage' is that while in Tennyson the star is merely a 'telos' for the sailor, towards which he might constantly direct his ship, in the present case, it becomes a constant guide and companion to carry us to the destination through all the toils and turmoils of life.

The second point of importance in the poem is the very great suggestion which is made therein that the so-called form, light, sound, and colour, which a mystic experiences, are merely the outward correspondences of the qualities of his heart. Whatever we spiritually visualise is ourselves. According to the mystical law, whatever a mystic perceives at any time by any form of sense corresponds exactly to the stage of development of his own spiritual temper and capacity. The Sanskrit expression तत्त्वमसि which, in the case of the present song, is put as तत्तु त्वं असि tells us exactly that what a mystic sees is, really, what he is, and that his spiritual status is to be measured by what he is able to see. This interpretation dawned upon the present writer when he was reflecting on the famous lines of Manikaprabhu तत्त्वमसि महावाक्य केळि हारि होदितु द्वैतद धूळि. This might be elaborated later on in a forthcoming work on Karnatak mysticism. At present, it would be enough to say, that, for all practical purposes, तत्त्वमसि consists merely in the correspondence of the mystical experience with the spiritual quality of the heart.

The author of the poem जो पीर मेरा बडा औलिया seems to be what might be called a colorist, so far as one of his principal experiences is concerned. He talks of four different kinds of colour—the red, the dark, the white, and the blue. It may be remembered by students of Indian Philosophy that these colours correspond exactly to the Raja, Tama and Sattva qualities, and to the state which carries us beyond these three qualities, namely निस्त्रैगुण्य. Also, Indian psychology tells us that these colours correspond respectively to the states of dream, deep sleep, the waking state, and the 4th unnameable state, Turya or the superconscious. Besides the correspondence of the colours with the qualities and the states of consciousness, we must take into account their correspondence with the emotions also. It is a famous doctrine of Theosophy, and perhaps one, in which that system may be said to have made a good contribution to psycho-mystic analysis, that redness would represent rage, darkness would represent vice, whiteness would represent purity, blueness would represent intelligence, yellowness would represent devotion, and greenness, in exact correspondence with the Shakespearean dictum, jealousy. It is very peculiar how nature is filled with all these colours. 'Vibgyor' would be merely a miniature way of accounting for the complexity and extent of the colours. In any case, it is worth while considering to what extent the colours which a mystic sees correspond to his own internal emotions.

A fourth point of importance in the present poem is the way in which the author speaks about his awakening of the Lord in the Unmani state. This kind of conception is familiar to the students of mystical poetry. It is not God who needs awakening, but it is the man who has to awaken himself to God. The Lord is always awake. How would it be possible for a man to awaken Him? Man is to awaken himself to the consciousness and presence of God, and keep himself awake in that state All Prabhatis and Bhupalis would therefore seem to be out of place. As we shall later see when we come to the poems of Raidas, God does not need any lights or sounds ; similarly, he does not need any awakening. A famous saint of the South used to say that by काकड आरती, which is only another name of the Prabhati or Bhupali, we ought to understand that we have to drive away the काक or canker of sleep from our own eyes, and rouse ourselves to the consciousness of God instead of making any attempt to awaken God Himself.

At the end of the poem, we meet with two very significant metaphysical points which are made to correspond, in the present case, with certain mystical experiences. We have already read accounts of the spiritual bath in Charandas and the mellifluous juice in Kabir. (1) As a consequence of the first, we understand from the present poem that the difference between Slave and Master, Self and God, vanishes. The two names become one, and the whirl-gig of existence ceases :

आनन्द नहाया, बन्दा खुदा, दोनो विसर गया ।
वेनाम का नाम होकर, रहटाना राहा ॥

(2) As a consequence of the drinking of the mellifluous juice, the poet takes us a step further and tells us that the mystic in that state is able to reach the *Vāhid*, the One reality, namely God: प्याला लेवे जाने, वाहिद जान पाई ।

Now, in the next Pada, बन्धनोंकी शृंखलाको तोड़कर यह पार आया, which we proceed to discuss, we have a fine description of what we may call the व्युत्थानदशा, or the post-ecstatic state. The seeker, who was hitherto imprisoned in the bonds of existence, has now been set free. He has attained to that particular breath of wakefulness which has put an end to all sleep, sloth and stupor. The poet gives various analogies to describe this condition of the freed soul, and compares him 'seriatim' to a bee, a bird, and a fish. The bee, which was hitherto imprisoned in a lotus, as in a Pandora's box, spreads its wings, hums, and flies away as soon as it is released. The bird, which has been set free, will not now live in a limited cage, but take its flight into the infinite empyrean. The self, which was pent up inside a tenement of bones, will now, like a fish, swim in the sea of joy as soon as it envisages the Form of God. The expression भूमसागर रम रहा है which is used in this connection may be noted. भूमन् is the highest stage of happiness about which the Upanishads speak. We are already familiar with the expression 'tenement of bones' in the famous Vedic passage अस्थन्वन्तं यदनस्था बिभर्ति, or in Tulsidas's phraseology, अस्थिचर्ममय देह मम. So far about the analogies that we meet with in this poem.

Let us now proceed to consider the contribution which the poem makes to the doctrine of Self-realisation. The released person has to thank his very earthly vesture because it paved the way for his spiritual realisation. "The earthly life which was nevertheless the support of spiritual light and form and sound has now fulfilled its raison d'etre." The poet now proceeds to a very fine and acute description of the musical experiences of such a person. "The tune and beat and the pitch of spiritual sound having reached the limitless, a state of creative equanimity has been produced." Here, the conception of the सम or creative equanimity is a remarkable one, and is the Berecynthia of all further mystical experience. Consequently, we are told by the poet that such a mystic automatically begins to sing the song of unison. We are also told that, in a state of self-unison, an indescribable and inexplicable hymn is emerging out of his organ of speech. We can very well realise that this is like that Upanishadic description, एतत्साम गायन्नास्ते हावु हाऽवु हाऽऽवु. As the final act of his spiritual experience, we are told that, in a state of eloquent silence, the priest now worships his own form. Analogies from Patanjali and the Bhagvadgita are not wanting to confirm this experience of the saint :

तदा द्रष्टुःस्वरूपेऽवस्थानम् ।

यत्र चैवात्मनात्मानं पश्यन्नात्मनि तुष्यति ॥

We finally come to the social aspect of mystical experience. The Saint is surrounded not merely by a number of devotees, but also by those who are indifferent to his activities. Our friend, the frog, cannot appreciate the pervading fragrance, even though he is in the midst of a hundred full-blown lotuses. Also, the poem compares the Saint to a celestial tree, which, overladen with ambrosial fruit, is reclining towards the earth, and he who has been blessed to come under its shade is partaking of the juice without ever having gone in search of it. Finally, we are told that the affection of this perfected Saint has descended to the very gravel of the earth, while his luminosity has transcended the limits of the earthly horizon. It may not now look wonderful if the mystic says as the Upanishadic passage has described it :

अहं विश्वं भुवनमभ्यभवाम् । सुवर्ण्ज्योतिः ॥

8. *Post-ecstatic ejaculations : Gulal, Naraharinath and Raidas*— (i) *Gulal*— We have referred towards the end of the above song to the post-ecstatic ejaculations of an Upanishadic seer. We shall now consider a few of such post-ecstatic ejaculations from Hindi saints. Gulal has given us a very fine poem in the Hindola Raga, namely,

तत्त हिंडोलवा सतगुरु नावल.

It is remarkable to see that while the poet is discussing about the Hindola or the cradle, he is also expressing it in the Hindola Raga. It is a very beautiful musico-mystical performance. The Bhojpuri dialect adds even a little more sweetness, simplicity, and directness to the contents of the poem. Gulal calls upon us in the first place to sing the Anubhava Mangal on the pattern of the Janaki Mangal and the Parvati Mangal. Let us sing the auspicious song of self-realisation, he says. He compares the Self to a child in the cradle of Reality, and describes the spiritual Teacher as giving a swing to it. Readers of Kannada mystical literature could easily recall to their minds that famous song of Kudaluresh अळुतिद्या कंदा, one of the most beautiful compositions in Kannada Mystical literature which we may review in course of time. The cradle in which the child is lying, says Gulal, is a very miraculous one, having no poles to support it, nor any ropes to bind it. The bells attached to the cradle are ringing continuously day and night, in order to put the child to spiritual sleep. These might veritably be the harmonious and subtle musical sounds of the Anahat to lull a person to Samadhi. One of the most wonderful things about the cradle is, Gulal tells us further, that while the spiritual teacher is giving it a swing, the cradle leaves the world altogether, flies into the empyrean, and the child in the cradle, namely, the Self, which is the supreme object of love, becomes dissociated and transcendent. These utterances, we may say, are wonderfully full of Upanishadic reminiscences. When Gulal tells us that the Self is the supreme object of love (प्रेमपदारथ) he is recalling to our mind the Upanishadic dictum तदेतत्प्रेयः पुत्रात्प्रेयो वित्तात्प्रेयोऽन्यस्मात्सर्वस्मादन्तरतरं यदयमात्मा, as well as the dictum that the Atman is प्रेष्ठ, the most loveable of all things. But the question arises when the Self is described as the supreme object of love, whether this should be regarded as a fact or as an ideal. In other words, the most important question to settle is whether the Self is an object of love actually, or whether it ought to be the object of supreme love. It would not be an easy matter to regard the Self actually as the supreme object of love, but there is no harm in saying that the Self should be regarded as an ideal to which all must aspire. Then again, when Gulal is speaking of the Self as leaving its connection with the world, and becoming dissociated and transcendent, we are reminded of another Upanishadic passage

अस्मात् शरीरात्समुत्थाय परं ज्योतिरुपसंपद्य
स्वेन रूपेणाभिनिष्पद्यते सोऽयमात्मा ॥

Aristotle was not wrong in describing the highest Reality or God as transcendent. In such a transcendent state, it is no wonder that Gulal might be justified in saying that there is no return for the Self again to the world : अब नहिं अवना जवना हो, recalling to our mind the famous Sūtra of Badarayana अनावृत्तिः शब्दात् अनावृत्तिः शब्दात् ॥

(ii) *Naraharinath*— Another post-ecstatic ejaculation of a somewhat different type – the socio - mystical type – may be found in a fine song of Narharinath, the teacher of Mahipati, whom we have already metioned in the song

क्या वे किसीसे काम, हम तो गुलाम गुरु घरके.

Narharinath describes the Saint, who has reached the highest state of experience, as calling himself merely a bondsman of his spiritual Teacher. The Saint calls himself a beggar who lives merely on alms, and therefore is not in need of help from anybody. He describes himself as a lunatic who lives in the enjoyment of his spiritual intoxication. Finally, he calls himself the king of his mind, in fact, the king of all he surveys.

Narharinath proceeds next to give us some of the mystical utterances of such a Saint. The Saint describes himself as in the enjoyment of the ten different sounds in the Gagana Mandal, the circle of the heavens, in the present case the top of the brain. The Sun and the Moon walk as torch-bearers before him, he says. Kabir has described God walking like a sepoy before him (और वह एक सिपाही). In the same way, Jnaneshwar speaks about God as walking with a torch in his hand in front of himself : दिवटा पुढा पुढा चाले. Thirdly, the Saint describes himself as enjoying the delicious nectar from the अर्धचन्द्र, which we may take as representing the pan of the cranium. The चान्द has already been described above along with the सूरज. So, in the present case, the अर्धचन्द्र, which has got a Yogic and occult connotation, may be taken to imply the pan of the cranium, in which the mellifluous juice is stored, and from which the Saint drinks to his heart's content.

Finally, the mystic describes himself as sitting by the side of a smoking fire (धुनी), and as having gone beyond the 'triplets'. Now the triplets might signify either the qualities, or the states of consciousness. The mystic might have described himself as in the निस्त्रैगुण्य state, having gone beyond the three qualities of सत्व, रजस् and तमस्, or as having come to live in the Turya state, which is beyond the three states of consciousness जाग्रत्, स्वप्न and सुषुप्ति. It would be perfectly psychological to regard this fourth state as the Turya, which passes beyond the three states of consciousness, but further to go on to describe the Unmani state as the fifth is only an unneeded venture in the region of the 'ad infinitum'. Some Vedantins have regarded the Unmani state as a fifth, and if this process were allowed, one does not know where one might stop. It is best, therefore, to suppose the superconscious state as one — call it the Turya or the Unmani or by whatever other name you please. Narharinath describes the Turya as having been inverted into the Unmani, thus suggesting that the Turya and the Unmani are the obverse and the reverse sides of the same state. In any case, it is in that state, call it the Turya or the Unmani, that God is attained : मिल गई जाकर के.

Finally, we have a fine passage in the poem in which the teacher is giving advice to his spiritual disciple. We cannot do better than quote it in the original. "Take care of every moment. Allow not a single eye-lash to beat in vain. Burn your sins. Awaken the Invisible Lord : पलखमें रहना, अलख जगाना, कलख जलाकर के. You have not to live here for ever. Work unceasingly, for you do not know when the tent may fall". It is wonderful to see how the teacher of Mahipati tells him not to sit silent but to work : नाहीं रहना काम करो कुछ, डेरा गिरता है. In modern parlance, we hear of great encouragement being given to secular work. In the poem under consideration, our mind is called back to spiritual work. It would not be incompatible to combine the two. The truest advice would be a combination of secular and spiritual work together. This same idea is expressed by Kabir elsewhere : कर से काम करो, हरि से ध्यान धरो, मकडी के जाल में तंता। चढ़ते उतरते दम की खबर रखो, भूलो नहिं गुणवन्ता ॥. We should not allow even a single breath to pass unutilised. It would not be impossible to fasten your mind on God, while your hand is doing its work.

(iii) *Raidas*— We shall now proceed to two celebrated poems of Raidas in which there are four important points, and which we may discuss together, two physical and two moral. In the first poem, आरती कहाँ लौ जोवै, Raidas is in a way criticising his spiritual brother Kabir. Kabir already talked about Arati. "Where shall I kindle my light, O God," asks Raidas : आरती कहाँ लौ जोवै, "That is filling thy servant with wonder : सेवक दास अचम्भो होवे. Thou art present everywhere, where shall I then plant my lights before Thee ? Secondly, is it not a parody to wave lights before Thee, O Resplendent God, when, through every one of Thy hairs, dazzles the brilliance of a thousand Suns ?

कोटि भानु जाकी सोभा रोमैं ।
कहा आरती अगनी होमैं ॥

Even supposing a Bairagi were to use vessels made of the highest quality of gold and place lights in them, God will not appear to his foolish vision. What is then the use of your golden vessels or brilliant lights ? They will not help you. " In a similar style, the present writer is reminded of an utterance of a great Kannada saint – the saint of Nimbargi – who, when his disciples went to him, and waved lights of camphor in his house, said " What is the use of burning this quantity of camphor ? If God could be attained by burning huge quantities of camphor, people would spend vast sums of money on the purchase of camphor. But God is not to be bought so cheaply. " In a similar manner, waving lights in golden vessels is of no use, says Raidas.

In an analogous vein, an anonymous absolutistic Hindi poet has said in a poem which is very popular in Uttar Pradesh, "It is a great problem to me, O God, how to appease Thee. There is no article which I can use for Thy service. Thou art present, O Lord, in the image, and Thou art present in the flowers. Placing flowers on Thy image is like placing God upon God. If I were to make an invocation to Thee, it would be doing injustice to Thy omni-presence, because Thou art present here as everywhere. If I were to ring a bell in order to wake Thee up, it would be an act of great disrespect, because Thou art always wakeful. If I were to make any offering to Thee, It would be carrying coals to New Castle, because Thou art the master of everything in the world, and thus no offering could be made to Thee. Waving lights before Thee would be entirely ridiculous because any light that we might place before Thee is like darkness before that great luminous Being which Thou art, before whom the Sun, the Moon and the Stars look only like dark bodies." We might see from this poem how its author regards God not merely as omnipresent and as the source of all light, as Raidas did, but also as the source of all sound, fragrance, and energy. The line of argument, however, is only in continuation of what we have seen in Raidas above.

Let us now proceed to two further points in Raidas – those which deal with the moral questions of sin and liberation. In the celebrated poem पावन जस है माधो तेरा, Raidas says, "Our sacred books have rightly bestowed praise on Your Holy Name, O God, as Saviour from our sins. What sins however, can you save me from, if I have no sins to my credit?

जो हम पाप करत नहिं भूधर,
तौ तू कहा नसावै ॥

How can water wash off mud from a man's feet, if they have never been immersed in mud at all?

जब लग अंग पंक नहिं परसै,
तौ जल कहा पखारै ॥

When the mind of a man is in the grip of sensua- ity, then alone can the Name of God save him rom its compelling might

मन मलीन विषयारसलम्पट,
तौ हरिनाम संभारै ॥

You can never take away the spots from an immaculate mind :" जो हम विमल हृदय चित अन्तर, दोष कौन परि हरि हौ. "And lastly", says Raidas, "people are imploring Thee to give them salvation or liberation. I am not going to pray to Thee at all. I am thankful to you, O God, for your kindness, but how can you release a man who is already free : अबन्ध मुक्त का करि हौ. I am perfectly free already; how can you bestow freedom on me ?" Independence will come to those who are dependent, but cannot come to those who are already free. So Raidas does not want to put himself in a prayerful attitude towards God at all.

We can see from these poems to what lofty heights a realiser like Raidas could go. From the lofty pedestal of mystical experience, he would see the omnipresence, and the universal resplendence of God. Also having attained to heights of mystical and moral perfection, he would say to himself that he had lived a sinless and spotless life, and that therefore he was not in need of any liberation. विदेहमुक्ति in short would be of no value to him whatsoever before जीवन्मुक्ति. विदेहमुक्ति would be liberation after death, जीवन्मुक्ति liberation while living and though living.

9. *Apostleship and Prophethood : Kabir*— We shall next proceed to consider the highest

watermark of जीवन्मुक्ति in Kabir, namely his apostleship, or prophethood. In the poem कहूँ रे जो कहिवे की होइ, there are three very important points. In the first place, Kabir asserts that the world is indifferent to the Saints, second, he analyses the causes of this indifference, third, he proclaims his apostleship to the world. Kabir begins by saying cryptically, "I will tell you only if it can be told by word of mouth. I am astonished at people's indifference, in spite of my continued endeavours for their betterment." These remarks of Kabir put us in mind of similar utterances from other great writers. Jesus Christ has told us that the prophet is not honoured in his own time and country. The great Vyāsa said in the Mahabharata ऊर्ध्वबाहुर्विरौम्येष नहि कश्चित् शृणोति माम् : "with my hand uplifted, I am telling the whole world to listen; but nobody is so good as to listen to me." Ramdas has said :

> सांग सांगोनि दमलों । पाठीं जगाच्या लागलों ।
> जन ऐकेनासें झालें ।

"I am tired of teaching the world. People have remained listless and indifferent, in spite of my repeated efforts to better them." Who will not recall Mahatma Gandhi's utterances in this connection towards the end of his career?

Kabir goes on to analyse the causes of this indifference. He finds that people are following each his own whim. They are corrupted by arrogance and avarice. The Bhagvadgita has characterised such men as लोभोपहतचेतस:. They are filled with attachments both personal and impersonal to the very end of their life, and are losing their own selves :

मैं मेरी करि यह तन खोयो, समझत नहीं गँवार ॥

Kabir tells us that many such people become exhausted in the middle of the sea of life, and innumerable others go to the bottom.

Lastly, with great pity for this condition of the world, Kabir unmistakably proclaims his apostleship or prophethood. " God in his graciousness gave me the mandate and the power to save some at least, and thus to bring light into the life of some. If you are not now saved, you have to blame yourself and not me. " The great Tukaram said in a famous Abhanga in the same spirit :

वचनाचा अनुभव हातीं । बोलविती देव मज ॥
परी हें न कळे अभाविकां । जड लोकां जीवांसी ॥
अश्रुत हे प्रासादिक । कृपा भीक स्वामीची ॥
तुका म्हणे वरावरी । जातो तरी सांगत ॥

" It is not I who is speaking to you ", says Tukaram : " It is God who is speaking through me. Those who may not put their faith in me may not regard this as true. I am telling you words which are filled with the Grace of God. " " It fills me with wonder ", says Tukaram, " how in spite of my repeated warnings the world is not listening to me." Kabir's message was not different from that of Tukaram.

We now come to the last Pada in this collection, namely, गुरुने मोहि दीन्हीं अजब जड़ी, wherein Kabir may be said to have summed up his entire spiritual life. "My Guru", says Kabir, "gave me a miraculous herb. It was full of mellifluous juice : अमृत रसन भरी. I deposited it in a mysterious vault inside my heart: कायानगर अजब इक बँगला, ता में गुप्त धरी. Now the value and power of this herb is that all the five Nagas and the twenty-five Naginis die an instantaneous death as soon as they smell it." What are these five Nagas and twenty-five Naginis ? It is interesting to find Kabir talking here so much in terms of Sāmkhya Philosophy. We have a famous passage in Ishwara-Krishna which describes the twenty-five Tattvas :

मूलप्रकृतिरविकृतिः महदाद्याः प्रकृतिविकृतयः सप्त ।
षोडशकस्तु विकारो नप्रकृतिर्नापिविकृतिः पुरुषः ॥

If we just think of the lacuna in this enumeration of Kapila, we shall see that he has not made any mention of five Pranas. The five Karmendriyas are there : the five Mahabhūtas are there : the five Tanmatras are there ; and five other entities are there, but there is no mention of the Pancha Pranas. The five Pranas are Nagas, and the twenty-five Tattvas are Naginis. All these die an instantaneous death when they smell this mystic herb. The power of this herb is thus superior to the five Pranas, and the twenty-five elements. Beyond these five Nagas and twenty-five Naginis, there is also a dark great Cobra which is representative of Death. This Kaliya, who threatened even Krishna, of course does not die by means of this herb. Death cannot ' die ', but he becomes terrified. He is terrified by the vision of the Sadguru : सद्गुरु देख डरी. Thus, said Kabir, he was saved by the power of the Sadguru. Not merely was he himself saved, but he was also able to save those who were his associates : लै परिवार तरी ।

The conception of Parivara-Mukti which Kabir has in mind is different from the conception of Sarva-Mukti which has occupied a prominent place in contemporary Indian thought. We think that the conception of Sarva-Mukti is wrong. It breaks the law of Sufficient Reason. It is too much to believe that when one Saint is born, the whole world is saved. The Parivara-Mukti is understandable, but Sarva-Mukti passes beyond our comprehension. It is all very well for Lord Buddha to say poetically :

कलिकलुषकृतानि यानि लोके,
मयि निपतन्तु विमुच्यतां हि लोकः ॥

In contrast with such a conception of Sarva-Mukti stands the conception of Eka-Mukti which is familiar to students of Vedantic thought. Has not Carlyle told us to look to our own saving, and leave the saving of the world to its Maker ? The conception of Parivara-Mukti of which Kabir is speaking takes a 'via media' between Sarva-Mukti and Eka-Mukti. The Eka-Mukti and the Sarva-Mukti are the thesis and the antithesis, of which Parivara-Mukti is the synthesis. The Sadguru, according to Kabir, is therefore one who liberates not merely himself, but also his associates. His associates in Leibnitziean fashion get the benefit of a spiritual vinculum with him. Do not the iron filings catch up the power of the magnet? Do not the planets derive their illumination from the Central Orb? It is following some such line of argument that Kabir was able to say that on account of the presence and the power of God in him, he was able to save not merely himself, but all those who had been fortunate to come into spiritual communion with him.

PART TWO

Pathway to God in

DOHAS

CHAPTER I

Incentives to Spiritual Life

Introduction

We have seen in the first part of our work how an aspirant rises, step by step, from certain incentives to spiritual life to the culmination of spiritual experience. The five chapters in the first part, namely, on the Padas, we may say, constitute the macrocosm of spiritual experience as found in Hindi literature. The five chapters in the present part on the Dohas constitute the microcosm, with the same head-topics, seriatim, which are to be met with in the first part of the work. In this division between Padas and Dohas, we have followed the time-honoured tradition in Hindi literature, which separates the Shabdas from the Sakhis. Probably, this method is to be commended, because a bigger thing cannot naturally go with a smaller, especially when the bigger thing contains reflective sentiments, and the smaller didactic epigrams. It is for this reason that the present writer has styled the Doha literature in one place as 'Epigrammatic Mysticism'.

The great Saint Tulsidas has made an original use of the Dohas, as containing the 'quintessence' of the narrative in the Ramayana and connecting,

Janus-wise, the Chaupais that precede and the Chaupais that follow, in the progress of the narrative. The word Doha thus signifies, by a sort of a श्लेषालंकार, not merely a metre, but also the 'churned or condensed milk' of the narrative fully expounded in the Chaupais. Elsewhere, as in other Hindi writers of Doha literature, the Dohas become symbols of highly ethical, spiritual, and even worldly-wise 'bon mots'. The present writer does not think that in any other provincial literature of India, there is this peculiar combination of epigram, wit, humour, sarcasm, love, devotion, service and general advice to humanity, which we find in the Dohas. There are only two parallels which we can cite for the Dohas. In Marathi literature we have the Abhangas, and in Kannada we have the Vachanas, which may offer a parallel to the Dohas in Hindi litetature. Just as the Dohas can rise to the highest spiritual experience, so the Abhangas and the Vachanas can also rise to the same level. The Dohas are smaller than the Abhangas, and poetic instead of prose as is the case with the Vachanas. Moreover, every writer of Vachana literature does not write at the highest level. The only author in Kannada literature to compare with the Dohas of Kabir is the epigrammatic Kannada saint 'सर्वज्ञ'. The Abangas are more sentimental as in Tukaram, and more expressive of spiritual experience as in Jnaneshwar; but the entire Abhanga literature of Maharashtra does not rise to the level attained by Tukaram or Jnaneshwar, just as the Dohas of writers in Hindi literature do dot always come up to the level attained by Kabir.

As far as possible, we have selected only such Dohas as would supplement the ideas in the Padas, unless the Dohas are so brilliant that they cannot be omitted. In the present chapter of the Dohas, we are enumerating only two incentives—the incentive of flux or perpetual change, and the incentive of decrepitude and death. The second is to be found in the Padas, but the first is to be found in the Dohas only. To take one more illustration, the Dohas in our second chapter will contain ideas which are only supplementary to those contained in the Padas, for instance, ideas such as those of the combination of material and spiritual welfare, valuation of fine arts, God-love in its individual, social and spiritual aspects, and so on. We are stating these facts only in order to show that our Dohas are not merely replicas of our Pada Literature.

1. *Perpetual flux*—We have said above that the idea of flux in the Dohas constitutes a new incentive to spiritual life. There are three such Dohas which are devoted to the consideration of flux or perpetual change. In the Doha सदा नगारा

कूच का, Rahim is playing upon the word 'कूच', by a sort of a श्लेषालंकार. The army is always on the march, the war-drum being continuously beaten. This is symbolic of change or perpetual flux in the world. A great English poet has said "The moving finger writes, and having writ moves on". Rahim, however, is using the word कूच, by a sort of a श्लेष, for Death also. The God of Death is always moving forward. He is pursuing humanity with his drum being constantly beaten. "Under these circumstances," asks Rahim, "What solace can we have? Taking resort to the maxim that nothing abides in this world, and all things are always changing, our only approach to reality would be a contemplation on the nature of flux or death." We shall illustrate this advice of Rahim by taking a few instances. (1) The advice of Rahim is exactly on the lines of the great Stoic philosophers. The Stoic philosophers, for example, were never afraid of death. On the other hand, they made death the platform of their contemplation of Reality. Philosophy to them, in other words, was merely a contemplation on death. Even Epicurus has said "Death is when we are not, and we are when death is not. Why then be afraid of death?" In fact, death and ourselves never meet at all. (2) The story of Damocles, the jester of Dionysius who was the tyrant of Syracuse, teaches us the same lesson. In spite of regal happiness which the king was enjoying, we are told, a sword was continuously hanging over his head at a banquet, suspended by a single hair, which might mean death at any moment, and end to all regal pomp. (3) The great Satyavrata of mythological fame has been credited with telling us the same story. Contemplation on death led him, we are told, to spiritual realisation. (4) A great Kanarese saint has also said that the cemetery should be a proper place for our meditation, because when we see the bones and ashes of dead men, we are powerfully put in mind of death, and that leads us to a contemplation on God. (5) Finally, we have to note that Kashi, the great centre of spiritual pilgrimage in India, has been described both as a महाश्मशान as well as an आनंदवन. It is a place where God Shankara lived in a cemetery, and where he enjoyed supreme bliss, and became a source of bliss to all those who offered their prayers to him at the great spiritual centre.

Another illustration of the doctrine of flux is to be found in the famous Doha 'पाती झडती देखते'. When the old foliage of a tree is falling down, the new foliage laughs at it. The old foliage retorts, "Be a little patient, Oh foolish fresh foliage. Thou wilt have soon to follow." To the Tree, which seems to be unmoving and unchanging, the falling foliage addresses, "Even thou, Oh tree, will have to follow the same universal law. Thou seemest unchanging and unmoving, but some day the same inexorable necessity will overtake you also. God has ordained that one goes ahead, and another follows." This Doha might be taken as an excellent illustration of the Nigaraṇa Alankara. Just as the Chaddar in Kabir's famous song stands both for itself as well as the human body, similarly, the leaves and the tree stand here both for themselves as well as for members of an Institution and the Institution itself. When the old head of an institution is retiring, the new head may laugh at him. The old head retorts, "Be a little patient, Oh new head, you will have to follow the same law. Remember, even the so-called Institution to which all of us belong will have some day to follow the same inexorable law. Nothing abides in this world. All things change." The greatest apostles of the doctrine of flux are Heracleitus in olden times, and Bergson in modern. "There is a cinematographic change", says Bergson, "in all things. Nothing stands still." Heracleitus tells us, "The Sun that shines to-day will not be the Sun that will shine tomorrow." "You cannot put your foot twice into the same waters," he says, "for when you go to put your foot a second time in the water, the water has already run off." To this the nemesis came from a disciple of Heracleitus himself who said, "You cannot put your foot even once into the water, for in the process of your putting your foot into the water, the water has already run off."

Our third Doha to illustrate the momentariness of all things is somewhat poetic in character: क्षणभंगुर जीवनकी कलिया. We are told in this Doha that just as we are not quite sure whether a bud of this evening will blossom into a flower tomorrow, so also we do not know whether the bud of life will blossom into a veritable living being. This is as much as to say that one cannot be sure whether the fœtus in a mother's womb may be born as a child or come out still dead. All things are transitory. The sleep, which a man is enjoying on a particular night, might also mean Biblical sleep, or death. The poet further goes on to ask whether the cool and fragrant breeze, which is blowing today from the Malaya mountain, the abode of sandal trees, will contitue to blow tomorrow. It may be that the breeze might stop altogether. The poet tells us that the God of Death (Kali-Purusha) has his Empire everywhere. In mythology he appeared before King Parikshit in order to kill the cow of religion, but Parikshit succeeded in limiting his activities to spheres like drinking, gambling, and so on. When that same Kali-Purusha will appear before you, you will have to consider whether your tender body will be able to bear the blow. "Beware, therefore, betimes," says the poet, "begin to think about God even today." The famous Sanskrit verse रात्रिर्गमिष्यति भविष्यति सुप्रभातम् tells us how the bee, pent up inside a lotus flower at night, had to meet its doom along with the lotus plant itself, when the lotus plant was uprooted by an elephant in the early hours of the morning. The poet, therefore, addresses the tongue thus : " Even now, Oh tongue, begin to utter the Name of God, for thou dost not know whether thou wilt be able to move at all at the time of death ".

2. *Decrepitude and death*— After the consideration of perpetual flux as an incentive to spiritual life, we go on to the next incentive, namely, that drawn from considerations of decrepitude and destruction. In the three Dohas that follow, it may be seen that there is an increasing 'Nirveda,' implied in the following excerpts :

(1) पाकि गए कड़ुवाय
(2) कौन खाड़ मे हाड़
(3) जगत पजरता देखि कै कबिरा भया उदास.

This will become apparent as we proceed. The first Doha that we have to consider is कच्चे में नीका लगै. This is a Paheli, a riddle, where certain questions are asked, and their solution sought. The solution, of course, is unexpressed, which adds to the beauty of the Paheli. In the present Doha, the poet asks, " What is that fruit which is liked when it is raw, which tastes extremely delicious when it comes to a half ripe condition, and which becomes bitter when it fully ripens ?" The solution of the riddle, of course, is that the fruit is the human body. When a person is in childhood he is liked by everybody, in youth he becomes the object of ardent love, and in old age he is the target of hatred for everybody. In fact, the process from childhood through youth to old age might be summarised in the three words – 'liked, loved and hated'. This is the first stage of Nirveda.

In the second Doha, which we shall now consider, कहँ जाये, कहँ ऊपने, कहाँ लड़ाए लाड़, five states of existence are enumerated, the last state leading to a further stage of Nirveda. "Have you ever considered, O man," asks the Doha, "how you first came into your mother's womb, and then how you came out of it. (This is indeed the second birth according to the Upanishad–द्वितीयं जन्म). In your third stage, you became an object of endearment for everybody and were consequently fondled. Later, in youth, you reached the zenith of your prosperity and power, and after having done all this, your ultimate fate is to be consigned as a mere mass of bones into a ravine, creek, or river. This should fill you with the consideration as to whether you have given a proper account of your life." Kabir has said elsewhere अपने खातिर महल बनाय। अपहि जाकर जंगल सोया. The practice in Northern India, unlike that in Southern India, is very often to throw the dead body in a ravine, creek. or river. We may compare also the practice among the Zoroastrians of exposing their dead bodies to kites and vultures in the Tower of Silence. Having risen through the height of power and prosperity, says the Doha, your ultimate fate is to descend into a ravine as a mere mass of bones.

What happened in the case of the great Emperors of Dehli? Humayun had to lie in his secluded tomb at Dehli. Akbar was born on the way to Mecca, but was ultimately buried in Secundra. Jahangir ruled at Agra, but his bones were buried at Lahore. Shahajahan, the great Moghul Emperor, in his last days, had to be interned, and buried by the side of his beloved Mumtaj. Aurangzeb, in his power, vanity, and glory, having ruled the major part of India from Delhi to the Deccan, had to die at Ahmednagar, and his bones had to be removed and buried at Aurangabad. Such is the fate reserved even for great Emperors. This is Nirveda at the second stage.

"If, on the other hand, you have been born a Hindu," says Kabir, "Your body will be cremated, your bones will burn like wood, and your hair will glow like burning grass." Kabir had said elsewhere also हाड़ जलै जैसी लकडीकी मोली, । बाल जलै जैसी घासकी पोली. Kabir saw the whole world afire, and was filled with consternation and concern as to how to escape both burial and cremation, and reach a permanent state of existence, which would be beyond the pale of both. This is Nirveda at its peak.

If we may be permitted to make a classification of philosophers who have sought the spiritual life, we may say that there have been three kinds of such philosophers, the sad philosopher, the weeping philosopher, and the shouting philosopher. From the Doha we have discussed above, it may be seen that Kabir belonged to the first category. He is filled to the brim with sadness when he sees the whole world on fire : जगत पजरता देखिके कबिरा भया उदास. Tukaram and Ramdas may be described as the weeping and the shouting philosophers respectively. There is a story connected with these two great Saints of Maharashtra, which might be briefly mentioned here. It has been reported that Tukaram and Ramdas met only once during their life-time, and that too, on the opposite banks of Bhima at Pandharpur. As Ramdas, with his band of disciples, was coming from the other side of the river, Tukaram went with his disciples from the side of Pandharapur to receive him. Tukaram began to weep, and Ramdas began to shout. Not knowing the reasons for these strange acts of their spiritual teachers, their disciples asked them what prompted them to act so strangely. Tukaram said he was telling the world with tears in his eyes that they should leave away their futile mundane pursuits and follow God, and nobody listened to him. Ramdas said that he was shouting to the world that the course they were following was a vain one, and yet nobody listened to him also. " Of what value would be your tears ? " asked Ramdas to Tukaram when they met. " My very shouts and howls are drowned in the hue and cry, which people raise in their bustle of life. " We have spoken about Kabir as being a sad philosopher, Tukaram a weeping philosopher, and Ramdas a shouting philosopher, aud yet none of these characteristics would ultimately belong to these great Saints. Behind the semblances with which thcy approached humanity for its spiritual upliftment, there was the attitude of a potent Beatificism which was the very core of their being.

CHAPTER II

The Necessity of Moral Preparation

After the discussion of the incentives to spiritual life drawn from the Dohas, namely, those of flux, decrepitude and death, we now proceed to discuss the help which the Dohas give for the formulation of the moral life. What moral preparation are we asked to make in order to fit ourselves for the spiritual life?—that is the question. Analysing the present chapter we may see that we shall have to discuss the following points seriatim : (1) Material and spiritual welfare ; (2) Original temperament and formation of character ; (3) Fine arts, their moral and immoral aspects; (4) Charity and work ; (5) Love of God as the supreme virtue in its individual, social and spiritual aspects; and (6) Self-annihilation as the only road to God.

1. *Spiritual welfare and material welfare*—Let us proceed to the first question, namely, the relation between material and spiritual welfare in the Dohas. It seems as if in the Doha literature we are told that we can follow only one path—either the material path or the spiritual path, either the path of pleasure or the path of virtue. We are told in the Doha चींटी चावल ले चली that an ant was once carrying a grain of rice in her mouth. On

the way, she encountered a grain of pulse. Now evidently, as she was already carrying a grain of rice in her mouth, she could not accommodate the grain of pulse also in her mouth, even though she wanted to do so.

The ant was in the veritable position of Buridan's ass. This ass was once feeling both hungry and thirsty at the same time, and happened to be placed between a stack of hay on the one hand and a pool of water on the other. Now, as it could not choose between the two, nor could make any reconciliation between the two, it had to die of hunger and thirst in the midst of plenty.

Kabir tells us, as the conclusion of the story, that we cannot get material and spiritual welfare together. We have to take only one of them, and cannot have both. In its wider application, we are to understand from the Doha that it would not be possible for us to reconcile the irreconcilables; for example, it would not be possible for us to combine the historical and the philosophical methods, nor the analytical and the synthetical, nor even the descriptive and the interpretative.

So far, however, as Ethics is concerned, this conflict between material and spiritual welfare is known as the conflict between hedonism and asceticism. The conflict between the Epicureans and the Stoics in ancient times, and Bentham and

Kant in modern, is too well known to need detailed description. It is enough to say that a number of eminent moral philosophers have accepted the doctrine of Eudaemonism as the reconciliation of asceticism and hedonism. This is also the doctrine which याज्ञवल्क्य propounded in the बृहदारण्यक Upanishad. Janaka called a number of philosophers for intellectual contest at his court, and the prize for the winner was a thousand cows with golden coins attached to their horns, as well as victory in the contest. When याज्ञवल्क्य entered the court of King Janaka, Janaka asked him whether he had come there for winning the cows and the coins on the one hand, or winning the victory on the other. The answer which याज्ञवल्क्य gave was very characteristic. " I have come for both, O king, " he said, उभयमेव सम्राट्, " for cows and the coins, as well as for intellectual victory." This attitude is the attitude of Eudaemonism. We need not deny material welfare even if we pursue spiritual welfare, and a true moral philosopher would be he who would reconcile them in a proper perspective.

2. *The place of Company in Spiritual Life* — The next point for our discussion in this Chapter is the question of the relation of temperament to character, and of actions to consequences. We shall be considering three Dohas under this head :

(1) कदली सीप भुजंग मुख ।

(2) जो रहीम उत्तम प्रकृति ।
and (3) कबिरा तेरी झोंपड़ी ।.

There is an antinomy between the first Doha on the one hand and the next two Dohas on the other, inasmuch as the first Doha tells us that company does affect temperament, while the next two Dohas tell us that company cannot have such an effect on a morally formed character. In the Doha कदली सीप भुजंगमुख, we are told that the same drop of water can become either a pearl, red colour, or poison, according as it comes to be lodged in a shell, or in a flower of the Kadali tree, or in the mouth of a serpent. It may be noted that the three colours belonging to these objects—the pearl being white, the Kadali flower being red, and the poison in a serpent's mouth being dark—are symbolic of the three qualities Sattva, Rajas and Tamas, so that the import of the Doha is that an original constitution is capable of being affected by company and become either of the Sattva, Rajas or Tamas type. We have a famous verse in Sanskrit similar in idea to the Doha we are discussing :

संतप्तायसि संस्थितस्य पयसो नामापि न ज्ञायते ।
मुक्ताकारतया तदेव नलिनीपत्रस्थितं राजते ॥
स्वात्यां सागरशुक्तिमध्यपतितं तन्मौक्तिकं जायते ।
प्रायेणाधममध्यमोत्तमगुणः संसर्गतो जायते ॥

According to this verse, a drop of water which falls on red hot iron vanishes, that which falls on the leaf of a lotus gets the semblance of a pearl, while that which comes to be lodged in a shell becomes a real pearl. The three qualities that the poet wants to speak of are theअधम, मध्यम, उत्तम Gunas, which respectively belong to the three states of the drop of water. On the whole, therefore, it may be seen that according to this Doha and according to the Verse, company does have an effect upon temperament.

On the other hand, we are told in the two Dohas – one by Rahim and the other by Kabir – that company can have no effect upon a morally acquired character. The question is whether our natural constitution can be affected by bad company. Rahim goes to the length of saying that even bad company cannot affect our original constitution : का करि सकत कुसंग. This is questionable because we do find that people born with a good temperament do become subject to the evil effects of bad company. Rahim's illustration is that the inside of a sandle tree cannot be affected by the poisonous fangs of an encircling serpent. The analogy may be good, but not true.

Kabir tells us, in the same style, that he cannot be affected by the company of butchers, even though his hut might be situated near a locality where butchers live : 'गलकट्टन के पास.' To be in bad company, says Kabir, does not mean to be an accomplice. A Karnatak Saint, who used to get his clothes washed by a leper, was asked whether the company of the leper would not affect him physically, and replied exactly as Kabir does : जो करता सो पावता : he who does receives. Kabir is a firm believer in the law of action and consequence, even like the author of the धम्मपद, who says "ततोनं दुःखमन्वेति चक्कमिव वहतो पदम्". Good consequences would follow good conduct and evil consequences evil conduct, exactly as the wheels of a cart would follow the heels of the bullocks. It is very peculiar to note that the Doha of Kabir, which contains the word गलकट्टन, came to hand exactly on the day on which the massacre of Calcutta began, namely, the 17th August 1946, as if to show the similarity of pronunciation between गलकट्टन and Calcutta. Apart from this, however, the two Dohas we are considering involve an antinomy to the first, as they tell us that bad company can have no effect upon a morally formed character, though an original temperament is susceptible of being influenced by it. Also we learn from the Doha of Kabir that the law of actions and consequences is paramount, and one who does good actions is sure to be rewarded some day — if not in this life, at least in a future existence, as Kant would say.

3. *Fine arts and Mysticism* — Let us now proceed to consider the place of fine arts in Mysti-

cism. We are discussing here only two Dohas, one concerned with the dancing art, and the other with the musical art. In the Doha मृदंग कहै धिक् है धिक् है, we have the description of an exhibition of dancing art by a courtezan. We are told that the मृदंग is giving out interjectory sounds of धिक् धिक्. This means that the मृदंग is saying "Fie upon all those who are spectators of this dance." We have a similar expression in a Sanskrit verse, which tells us "धिक् तान् धिक् तान् धिगेतान् कथयति नितरां कीर्तनस्थो मृदंगः." The onomatopœic sound धिक् is here made to import deep censure. Then the jingling bells on the ankles of the courtezan are giving out interrogatory sounds किनको किनको. Then lastly, the विश्वयोषिता or the courtezan, lifting up her hand, says in answer to the query of the किंकिणी, "Fie upon everyone of those who are assembled to see me dance. (इनको इनको)". The author of the Doha seems to have conceived the dancing art as nothing but an object of censure.

In the Doha that follows, गाया है बूझा नहीं, we are told that a musician, who does not understand the end of his own art, has not bade good bye to infatuation, just as a piece of iron, which has not reached the touch-stone, remains only a piece of iron. This means that the end of all music must be regarded as something more than mere pleasure of the hearer or the singer. According to the author of the Doha, all music should be a glorification of God. One who does not look at music from this point of view, does not understand the real nature of music. Music without Mysticism would be a dangerous thing. Surdas and Tulsidas escaped the danger. They were Musicians as well as Saints.

In the above two Dohas, we have a criticism of dancing and music as generally tending to increased erotic tendencies. This is not wrong criticism, but there is another aspect also from which the fine arts must be looked at. The erotic element must be necessarily condemned, but if the fine arts are used in the service of God, there could be no better means to help devotion. Take, for example, Music. A musician, who sings very devotional songs, will help the God-devotion of the hearers as much as their own actual meditation would. A dancer, who can exhibit devotional attitudes, will be a great asset to the devotional life. It is not merely dancing and music with which we are concerned. When we are speaking about fine arts, we must remember that poetry, painting, sculpture and architecture are equally liable to the same kind of censure and to the same kind of praise. All these fine arts have both moral as well as immoral aspects. The immoral tendencies are to be checked, and the moral tendencies are to be developed. We must compliment the Indian Radio Department for having recently taken the lead in abolishing the lascivious aspect from Indian Music. As with morality, so with mysticism. As to whether the moral and the spiritual aspects are stressed in the practice of fine arts depends entirely upon the attitudes with which they are practised and received. It is not necessary that the aim of the fine arts should be the service of Eros. A study of the rhetorical science would convince us that the fine arts can be placed in the service of the development of the Rasas and the Bhāvas. Heroism, affection, God-devotion, humour, pathos, terror, wonder, and tranquility could all be exhibited in the fine arts. The highest end of all art should be, as Bacon has put it, "the glory of God and the the relief of man's estate."

(iv) *Charity*—Let us now take the question of virtues, and of these we shall consider only two from the Dohas, namely, Charity and God-love. In the Doha ऋतु वसन्त याचक भयो charity is illustrated in the act of giving their foliage by the trees, when Vasant comes and asks for them, and in return the Vasant endows them with new foliage. There seems, however, generosity on the part of the trees in handing over the foliage, and a sense of barter on the part of Vasant. The Doha refers to the natural phenomenon of trees parting with their old leaves when spring sets in, and immediately afterwards, the spring endows them with new foliage. What will not God do, if we offer all our wealth to Him ? A famous Doha tells us that it will go on increasing in a geometrical ratio day by day :

" राम नामके कारन, सब धन डाला खोय ।
मूरख जाने गिर गया, दिन दिन दूना होय ॥.

Another aspect of the act of charity is illustrated in the Doha सहज मिलै सो दूध सम, in which we are told, that what we obtain easily, automatically, unconsciously, and without asking for, may be compared to milk. What we obtain by begging and spreading out our hand may be likened to water, and what we obtain by means of a tug-of-war process with our donor, may veritably be compared to blood. This Doha implies that we may not refuse what comes to us automatically, but if we engage ourselves in a tug-of-war in getting our desired object, it will be merely a bloody act.

A third aspect of the act of charity is illustrated in the Doha तुलसी कर पर कर करै, in which Tulsidas tells us that we should always hold our hand aloft in the position of giving, and never down in the position of receiving. It is better to die, says Tulsidas, than to spread out one's hand for the sake of begging. This idea in the Doha is illustrated by a very interesting story from the life of a great Karanatak saint. The saint of Umadi was once performing a Community Bhajana, along with a number of disciples, among whom was the

Swami of Kannur, a Jangam by caste, whose profession was to beg. While the Bhajana was going on, the Saint of Umadi went to the Swami, and held both of his hands aloft in the air. Surprised at this act, the Swami asked why it was that his Spiritual Teacher had held his hands over his head. The Saint replied that even though the Swami's profession was to beg, he must always hold his hand above, and never down. He had held his hands aloft in the air in order to communicate to him symbolically this piece of advice. It so happened later, that, when the Saint of Umadi had been to Kannur, the Swami told him that he had left off his profession of begging; the Saint then went to his farm, and showed him a place where he should dig a well, initiating the act of digging by a trumpet. Even though the locality was generally without water, the well that was sunk there gave immense water, which has been an ornament to the village, giving land-products on a huge scale. This has entirely dispensed with the act of begging by the Swami, and he is himself in the position now of giving, instead of receiving. His farm has been to him a veritable mine of fortune.

5. *Devotion to God in its individual, social, and spiritual aspects*—After charity we shall pass on to the virtue of God-love, which we shall notice

in its individual, social, and universal aspects. The Doha अस्थिचर्ममय देह मम, which is put into the mouth of Tulsidas's wife, can be translated in a Wolseyan manner as follows: "Had you but loved God with the same intensity with which you are loving my skin and bones, God would not have handed you over to the dangers of life." If you just substitute the word यह for मम in the Doha, it becomes a universal proposition and is applicable to all. Instead of Tulsidas, it would then apply to the whole of humanity. Actually, it was a remonstration of Tulsidas's wife to her husband for his ill-timed and unwanted overtures. It is very peculiar to note that this remonstration became the chief incentive for spiritual life for Tulsidas. We have seen cases where remonstrations of father, mother, brother, and relatives have proved incentives for higher purpose to young men, but in this case the remonstration of a wife became the chief incentive to Tulsidas's spiritual life, and from that time onwards he regarded her as his धर्म की माता. We have an elaboration of the above Doha in the following famous song भज मन तुलसी राम कहो रे, in which occur the following noteworthy lines:

> "जितना हेत कियो तुम हमसे, उतना हरिसे हेत करो रे ।
> चल जात्यो वैकुण्ठधाम को, जँह ठाकुर दरवार लगो रे" ।
> "तुम तो हो मेरी धर्म की माता, हमको ज्ञान दिया रे ।
> जात अहीं प्रभु भजन करन कूँ, अव तिरिया तेरी सेज न चढो रे" ॥

The remonstration and the reply may be regarded

as very classical pieces of spiritual literature.

Let us now pass on to the social aspect of God-love. Tulsidas advises us in the famous Doha तुलसी यह जग आय कै, "having come into this world, we should run to meet and embrace every human being. For, we do not know in what form Narayana may appear." It is interesting to remember that Tulsidas here uses the word Narayana, and not Rama. Of course, there was no distinction to him between Narayana and Rama as forms of God. The use of the word Narayana, however, here may be noted. Tulsidas advises us to believe that the whole world is filled with God, and that all beings are His manifestations. Actually, however, when God appeared to him twice in a personal form in his life, he could not recognise Him on both the occasions. - Of course, there was no lack of love or respect in him for the forms in which God appeared to him, but the fact remains that he did not recognise these forms as God Himself. Once upon a time, Hanuman appeared to him in the form of an old man, attending his sermon at the Sankata-mochan temple at Benares, but Tulsidas could not recognise him and be aware of the fact that the old man he had met might be God Himself in the form of Hanuman. On another occasion, (as we shall see in Chapter III of our Dohas) when at the Chitrakoot fair, Shri Ramchandra was engaged in giving the 'tilak' in the presence of Tulsidas, Tulsidas could not recognise him as God Himself. It is of course one thing intellectually to regard all human beings as divine manifestations, and quite another actually to recognise God when he presents Himself in body-form. There might be a higher manifestation still, namely, that of a supersensuous character. This would be superier to a personal manifestation, and when once we have attained to that, we can see the truth of Tulsidas's remark that all human beings are the embodiments of God Himself.

God–love in its spiritual aspect could not be expressed more brilliantly than by Tulsidas in his famous Doha घर राखे घर जात है. Tulsidas advises us to leave the house, and leave the forest, and live in the City of God. There is a व्यंजना here in the contrast between गृह and पुर, which suggests that, if we leave the house, we shall get the City of God in its stead. Such a 'civitatis dei', says Tulsidas, you have to build for yourself, and for the devotees of God. Of course, you will have to leave your connection with the house, and connection with the forest in which naked Fakirs might stay. The entire expanse between the house and the forest will have to be occupied by your divine city (राम-प्रेम-पुर). You have to build and thatch the city of God-devotion, give shade and protection to all those who may come to stay in it, and live in it yourself along with your brother devotees. It is, as the present writer has called it elsewhere, a "theopolis" where God is the supreme ruler, and all humanity, bound together by the spiritual tie, become equal and aspiring denizens, whose only vocation is to fill the world with the praise and glory of God.

6. *Suffering, as the ladder to God*—Let us now proceed to our final section of the Dohas in this chapter. Let us first consider the two Dohas कबिरा खड़ा बजार में and साधु कहावन कठिन है, and then proceed to the Doha by Mansur चढ़ा मन्सूर सूली पर, at the conclusion of the chapter. All these relate to self-annihilation in one form or another, and we are told that, unless we annihilate ourselves completely, we have no hope of reaching God. Kabir tells us that he takes his stand in the market-place and proclaims his message to the world. Now there have been three great philosophers of the market-place—Socrates, Chokhamela and Kabir. It seems that it is important to go in the market-place, because then you can communicate your message directly to the masses. Socrates used to visit the Agora, and discourse on all philosophical, practical, national, social, and ethical topics. Chokha-mela gave his life in the market-place at Mangalvedha. Kabir, on one occasion, took his stand in the market-place with a firebrand in his hand and said, "He alone need follow me who will set fire to his

house, property, and possessions." Elsewhere, we are familiar with the assertion of Kabir, which has been repeated by him so many times in his writing, सीस उतारै भुइ धरै. Unless you cut off your head, and place it on the altar of God for the cause you have in view, you cannot hope to accomplish it. It is not enough to lose your property and possessions, you must be prepared to lose your very life also, says Kabir.

In a similar spirit, we are told, in the Doha साधु कहावन कठिन है that to be called a 'Sadhu' is not a simple matter. You must be able to ascend the date-palm of existence. Now the date-palm is very well known in Arabia as a tree which reaches to the centre of the sky. He alone, who can ascend to the top of the date-palm, can partake of the nectary juice of its palms. If he fails in reaching the top, he will shatter himself to pieces. In a similar style has Warwick told us, in a Shakespearean drama,

> " Those that stand high have many blasts
> to shake them, And, if they fall, they shatter themselves to pieces."

Both these Dohas tell us that preparedness for self-annihilation is a necessary condition of spiritual success.

William I did not hesitate to burn his boats, when he landed in England to conquer it. The Hero of Sinhagada, Suryaji Malusare, cut off the ropes and ladders from the slopes of Sinhagad in order to give battle to the enemy at the top of the mountain. His soldiers at first hesitated and wanted to get down, but when all the ropes and ladders had been cut down, they had no alternative except to fight the enemy to the last which they did with great success. In that way was Sinhagad conquered. Unfortunately, Tanaji the brother of Suryaji, had fallen in the conflict. "गड आला पण सिंह गेला" is a well-known maxim in Maratha history, which tells us that Tanaji was lost, but the fort was conquered. In the early years of the present century, the Japanese were able to conquer Port Arthur from the Russians, only by ordering the soldiers in the front rank to throw themselves on the spikes and spears in the moat, making a way for soldiers in the rear to tread upon their living dead bodies, which made possible the triumphant entry of the Japanese into Port Arthur. The famous Montgomery had to play a similar trick. He reversed the Italo-German method of sending the guns and cannon first, and then make the soldiers follow them. Montgomery first made the soldiers to go ahead and sacrifice themselves, to a man, on the Italo-German mines, and then opened the guns and cannon to achieve success in one of the most remarkable battles of contemporary history — the battle of Almein. Finally, the Anglo-American armies could not rout the Germans in the last battle of the War on the Continent, until armies and guns had come to their help from the other side of the Channel, but this could not be accomplished until a flotilla and an army in the English Channel had been sacrificed to entice the enemy away by putting them on a false scent. Thus was the remarkable victory of Eisenhower and Montgomery made possible on the Continent, the last greatest victory which put an end to the great Global War. History thus amply proves that self-annihilation is the only road to victory.

This did really happen in the case of Mansur, the absolutistic mystic philosopher of Islam, who had in the opinion of his opponents the audacity to proclaim that he was none but Reality, that he was God, अनलहक. The question arises whether the the reader of the present work would prefer to be a Mansur, or an Alamgir. Would he rather try to conquer his mind, or conquer the universe ? The second is impossible. The first may be possible under proper direction, and with continuous effort. Hence 'Mansur' would be a far more elevated title than 'Alamgir'. As it happened, Mansur went to the stake on account of his absolutistic assertion. When he was going to the stake, he called upon the 'soi-disant' lovers of God to follow him if they chose. But none followed him. This showed that Mansur was the King of the martyrs, and others merely idle spectators..The sharp-pointed pillar upon which he ascended to death, he proclaimed, was merely the staircase to the terrace of Reality, or God. Readers of Indian Rhetoric will not fail to understand here the presence of an अपन्हुति अलंकार, which hides the 'staircase to God' in the 'stake of death'. Mansur did really believe that by ascending the staircase of the stake, he would reach the topmost part of existence. It is customary to believe that mystics and god occupy such topmost plateaus, and carry on from these high altitudes their own contemplative and governmental work. Himalayan heights has become a phrase of everyday parlance in contemporary Indian affairs. The Upanishadic philosopher said that Reality was like ths topmost terrace of existence, कीर्तिः पृष्ठं गिरेरिव, himself being its mover and enveloping it with light as of the Sun. We are also familiar with the conception of Zeus in Greek mythology, where on the unreachable heights of Olympus, he reigned as the supreme ruler of the Gods, assigning to the subordinate deities the Government of different parts of the Universe. Aristotle has also told us that his God took His throne in an entirely transcendent sphere, beyond the pale of all existence, looking at the past, present, and future as an eternal Now. Mansur's ambition was evidently to reach such unimaginable heights.

CHAPTER III

The Relation of God to Saints

In our last Chapter we have tried to ascertain what the path to sainthood is. In the present chapter, after first discussing the rarity of the phenomenon of sainthood, we shall proceed to some points in the doctrine of God according to the Dohas, particularly the doctrines of the Immanent and the Transcendent, the अंतर्यामी and the बहिर्यामी, the latter being a very notable contribution of Tulsidas to the Philosophy of Religion. After having discussed these conceptions, we shall next proceed to the ten ascending stages of Tulsidas's Philosophy of Devotion. The topic will be dealt with specially at this place because no general survey has hitherto been taken by us of the contribution which Tulsidas has made to the Philosophy of Bhakti. We shall next proceed to discuss the relationship that exists between Saints and God, both practical and philosophical. Under the first head, we shall consider the question of (i) the proximity to God, which means protection, and (ii) of personal autonomy under the suzerainty of Divine power. We shall next proceed to consider (iii) to what heights, according to Tulsidas, a Saint can reach starting from a life of abject poverty, as well as (iv) the service which God renders to such a Saint as in the case of Tulsidas in North India, and Ekanath in the South. The last two other points to be considered in this connection would be (v) the fore-fulfilment of a devotee's desires by God, and (vi) the ideal of eudaemonistic attainment by the Saint of combined material and spiritual welfare. Under the second head, we shall proceed to the concluding Dohas of this Chapter, wherein we will be told about the philosophical relationship that subsists between a Saint and God. Here three stages will be indicated, first the Saint's indentity with the साकार form of God, second, the Saint as reflecting the निराकार, and third the eschatological mergence of spirit with spirit to which the Saint ultimately attains.

1. *Sainthood, a rare phenomenon* — We shall begin with the rarity of the phenomenon af Sainthood. We have been told in the Bhagvadgita that one out of a million ever reaches God. Many seek, but few are chosen. In a similar spirit, we are told in the present Doha by Kabir, संत संत सब एक है, that in a field covered by opium poppies, rarely one yields red capsules. Others yield only white ones. In the assemblage of Saints rarely one is characterised by ardent and burning love of God. Others remain only white and unaffected. Now redness and whiteness are respectively marks

of ardent love, and an unimpressionable indifference. Elsewhere, whiteness and redness are compared to सत्त्वगुण and रजोगुण, for example, as in the Bhagvadgita, or in Samkhya Philosophy, the dark being reserved for the तमोगुण. In the present case, however, Kabir reverses the conception, and tells us that redness is the mark of ardent and passionate love for God, while whiteness a mark of an unimpressionable *tabula rasa*. Even redness has been credited with three kinds of emotions in the history of psychology. Redness in the Bhagvadgita means activity; in the language of contemporary Communism it signifies violence; and in the language of Kabir, as we have pointed out, it means a burning love for God, or the highest devotion. Kabir in a famous passage talks of the redness of God as well as his red love of God :—

लाली मेरे लाल की जित देखौ तित लाल ।
लाली देखन मैं गई मैं भी हो गई लाल ॥

If you ask Kabir of what this redness is the outcome, he would have no hesitation in saying that it is the outcome of God's Grace – कोई कुदरती लाल है. In fact, कुदरत might be taken to mean one of the three things—nature, fate or the will of God. All these things have been mixed up promiscuously by Greek philosophers. Occasionally, one has been stressed, occasionally another, and occasionally a third. In the present context, we have no alternative except to suppose that it may be the outcome of the Grace which God sends on His devotee.

In another Doha, सिहों के लेंहड़े नहीं, Kabir gives certain illustrations to support this rarity of the phenomenon of Sainthood. A real saint is a rare being. You can find him only on occasions. How many saints have been produced in the world since the beginning of time ? Lions, says Kabir, do not move in flocks, there are no processions of swans, and rubies are not collected in bales. Even so there are no caravans of saints. Kabir has described elsewhere in the manner of the खग्गविसाण-सुत्त that a saint is like a rhinoceros who delights in living alone to himself. In another Doha of Kabir,

सब बन तो चंदन नहीं शूरों का दल नाहिं ।
सब समुद्र मोती नहीं यों साधू जगमाहिं ॥,

we are told that the forest does not abound in sandal trees. There are not many generals in the army. The sea is not replete with pearls. This has also been said in a famous Sanskrit verse :

शैले शैले न माणिक्यं मौक्तिकं न गजे गजे ।
साधवो नहि सर्वत्र चन्दनं न वने वने ॥,

which speaks in the same manner of rubies, pearls and sandal trees. By a comparative consideration of these three passages, we may find that almost the same illustrations have been employed by them, and the rarity of the phenomenon of sainthood stressed. A Saint when born shines in his own native lustre even like a superb form of spiritual experience to which nothing else can be compared, and which stands supreme above all other forms.

2. *The immano-transcendence of God* — We next proceed to consider the immanence and transcendence of God as taught in the Dohas. Tulsidas gives us two very fine Dohas, both on the subject of Immanence and Transcendence. In the Doha तुलसी मूरति रामकी घट घट रही समाय, we are told how the form of God remains latent and immanent in all human beings, as well as in all things of the world. The analogy that he cites for this immanence is the way in which red colour lies latent and hidden in the myrtle-leaves. Now, this colour cannot be brought out unless the leaves are pounded in a mortar, or with a stone. The implication is that the form of God will not appear to our vision, unless we pass through difficulties and perils. Perils or difficulties are the source of wisdom and realisation. In a very similar Doha we are told by Kabir :

रँग लाती है हीना पत्थर पै घिस जाने के बाद
अक्ल आती है वशर को ठोकरें खाने के बाद ।,

that wisdom (अक्ल) will not dawn upon a man, unless he has passed through perils. We are also told in the Mahabharata how, when Kunti was asked by Krishna what she wanted, Kunti said " adversities " :

विपदः सन्तु नः शश्वत् यासु संस्मर्यते हरिः ।

That was the boon she asked from Krishna. It is only when we pass through adversities that we are reminded of the presence of God, and then we know how we can surrender ourselves to him. The above Doha has spoken of red colour being immanent in the myrtle-leaves. Another Doha from Kabir, कस्तूरी कुण्डल बसै मृग ढूण्ढै वन माहिं, tells us how musk lies hidden in the navel of a deer, and yet the deer roams in a forest from place to place in order to find it. Probably, it is the scent of the musk inside that makes the deer run about to find it in the outside world. Immanence may thus serve as an incentive to transcendence. On the other hand, transcendence itself may serve as an incentive to immanence. In the Doha हरिको ढूंढन में चला जा पहुंचा हरिद्वार। हरि मिले ना, पग थके हरि थे मेरे द्वार॥, we are told how, not knowing the presence of God inside, the whole of mankind wanders about to find Him in the outside world, and when their patience has been tried in finding God in the outside world, they return to themselves to find God at their very door, in fact, inside their own mind. In this case, transcendence serves as an incentive to immanence. Finally, in the Doha under consideration तुलसी मूरति रामकी, Tulsidas uses a very important word समाय. The form of God lies pervading both the internal and the external worlds. We might note the use of this important word in the perorative hymn of the ऋग्वेद which tells us समानीव आकूतिः समाना हृदयानि वः।

समानमस्तु वो मनो यथा वः सुसहासति ॥. Let your hearts, wills, and minds be all pervaded by the presense of God. This is the supreme boon that the author of the ऋग्वेद asks at the end of his great work.

In his famous Savaiyya अन्तर्जामिहु ते बड़ बाहरजामि है राम, Tulsidas introduces a new category in the philosophy of religion, namely, that of the बहिर्यामी. This is a word which, so far as the present writer is aware, occurs nowhere in any earlier literature, even Sanskrit literature. Tulsidas contrasts the word बहिर्यामी with the word अन्तर्यामी. The word अन्तर्यामी is known to every student of Indian philosophy. It first occurs in the बृहदारण्यक Upanishad when याज्ञवल्क्य is expounding his doctrine of the अन्तर्यामिन् in the famous passage :

यः पृथिव्यां तिष्ठन्, पृथिव्या अन्तरो, यं पृथिवी न वेद, यस्य पृथिवी शरीरं, यः पृथिवीमन्तरो यमयत्येष त आत्माऽन्तर्याम्यमृतः। अप्सु, अग्नौ, अन्तरिक्षे, वायौ, दिवि, आदित्ये, चन्द्रतारके, तमसि, तेजसि, प्राणे, मनसि। एष त आत्माऽन्तर्याम्यमृतोऽतोऽन्यदार्त्तम्।

This doctrine of अन्तर्यामिन् was later made the foundation-stone of his philosophy by Ramanuja. Tulsidas adopts the category of अन्तर्यामी, and introduces a new one, बहिर्यामी. The transcendent God, according to Tulsidas, is, in the present Savaiyya, declared by Tulsidas to be higher than the immanent God. His justification for the introduction of this category is that when Prahlad was asked by his father as to where his boasted God was, Prahlad replied 'everywhere'. God, however, Tulsidas tells us, did not reveal himself from the heart of Prahlad but from a pillar of stone, thus proving the supremacy of the बहिर्यामी to the अन्तर्यामी. Tulsidas was not probably aware of the defects of the बहिर्यामी doctrine, namely, that he was playing into the hands of the deists and the pantheists. There has been a great deal of discussion in the contemporary philosophy of religion about the immanence and the transcendence of God, and a reconciliation is offered by the theists in the conception of God's immano-transcendence. Spinoza regarded God as identical and co-existent with the world. Aristotle made God live in a transcendent sphere. Modern Theists make God simultaneously immanent and transcendent. Of course, Tulsidas does not mean that God was only बहिर्यामी. He only wanted to stress the outward presence of God. So the conception of बहिर्यामी, instead of being taken as antithetical to the अन्तर्यामी, must be taken as complementary to it. The famous Jain sage Pujyapada of the fifth century gives us in his Samadhi Shataka a fine reconciliation of अन्तर्यामी and बहिर्यामी. He tells us that the conceptions of the अन्तरात्मा and the बहिरात्मा could very well be synthesised in the conception of the परमात्मा. Of course, this conception of the परमात्मा does not fit in with the Jainistic doctrine proper; but it may very well go in with the philosophy of Tulsidas who could then reconcile the conceptions of the अन्तरात्मन्

and the बहिरात्मन् in the doctrine of the परमात्मन्.

3. *The Ascending stages of Tulsidas's philosophy of devotion*—We have hitherto considered the doctrines of Immanence and Transcendence in Tulsidas. We shall now proceed to a somewhat detailed treatment of the different stages in the development of Tulsidas's philosophy of Devotion. This has been suggested by the consideration of the Doha that follows, अगुनहिं सगुनहिं नहिं कछु भेदा, in which Tulsidas arrives at the non-difference, or even the identity, between Sugana and Nirguna. People read Tulsidas for his poetical, literary, and even religious significance, but they do not judge his philosophy as a whole, nor do they see how the different parts of Tulsidas's philosophy could be fitted into each other. We have not hitherto taken any general survey of this problem. We have discussed only a few aspects of the same at various places in this work. Before we proceed to a somewhat fuller consideration, we shall begin with an outline of the different ascending stages of Tulsidas's Philosophy of Devotion, following it up with an authentication from original Sources. Tulsidas, as would befit a true devotee, begins by saying that the Saguna form of God must be regarded as superior to Nirguna. From this point of view, Bhakti, which is the very essence of Saguna worship, has no concern with Maya, which infects and

even infests the Nirguna philosophy. Tulsidas however is compelled, as we shall see, by his own grammatical device to recognise that there might ultimately be an alliance between Jnāna and Bhakti, leading to an identity. Following this, the next point in Tulsidas's programme would be to recognise the non-difference between Saguna and Nirguna, which is tantamount to an identity. We thus see how Tulsidas began by saying that the Saguna was the fundamental category, and he now reaches the stage when there can be no distinction between Saguna and Nirguna. Not content with this, Tulsidas soon goes on to regard that the Nirguna might be the source from which the Saguna might spring, as occasion and necessity require. So far then about the relationship between Saguna and Nirguna. The next stage in the developmental programme would be the reconciliation of Nama and Rupa both with Saguna and Nirguna, as well as 'inter se'. Tulsidas here again begins by telling us how Nama is the schematiser between Saguna and Nirguna, and ends by saying Nama is superior to both. When we next come to the relation between Nama and Rupa, Tulsidas begins by asserting the parity between Nama and Rupa, and ends almost unconsciously, and by force of logic, by asserting the superiority of Nama. This veritably constitutes Tulsidas's Philosophy of Devotion, of which the Name of God is the pinnacle, its very alpha and omega. After these points have been considered, we shall delve into a small comparative consideration of the relationship of Tulsidas and Kabir on this head, so far as the meditational process by means of the Name is concerned, as well as the ideal to which it points, namely, the realization of the लक्ष्य or the अलक्ष्य as the case may be.

Let us now try to amplify a little the points we have raised in the preceding paragraph, as well as authenticate them by drawing on the original Sources. Nothing we can say here would be of much value, unless we have actual quotations from Tulsidas to support our statements. (1) In the first place, Tulsidas tells us that the Saguna is a higher conception than the Nirguna for the principal reason that while the Nirguna is pervaded by illusion or Maya, the Saguna is pervaded by devotion or Bhakti. If Bhakti is a chaste woman, Maya is only a Nartaki :

(a) निर्गुण रूप सुलभ अति । सगुन न जानहिं कोइ

(b) पुनि रघुवीरहिं भगति पियारी, माया खलु नर्त्तकी विचारी.

(2) This point could be made clear if we just go into the relation of Maya with Jnana on the one hand, and Bhakti on the other. Jnana, says Tulsidas, is a masculine conception, and therefore it can very well make an alliance, if not a dalliance, with Maya. On the other hand, Bhakti which is of the feminine gender, can have no such love towards Maya which is also feminine :

(a) ज्ञान विराग जोग विज्ञाना। । ए सब पुरुष सुनहु हरिजाना

(b) मोह न नारि नारिके रूपा ।.

So far so good, but this quaint grammatical conceit or gender-trick which Tulsidas introduces was likely to act as a boomerang, and make him grant that Jnana might make an alliance with Bhakti, so much so that Jnana and Bhakti might ultimately be regarded as identical : भगतिहिं ज्ञानहिं नहिं कछु भेदा । उभय हरहिं भवसम्भव खेदा ।

(3) This teaching, however, has a bearing upon the doctrine of Nirguna and Saguna, whose central conceptions they respectively are. Hence Tulsidas is obliged to postulate an identity between the Nirguna and the Saguna themselves. Not only because they are ब्रह्मन् in their own nature, but also because they are aspects of the same underlying substance, the Saguna and Nirguna might well be regarded as identical :

(a) अगुन सगुन दुइ ब्रह्म सरूपा । अकथ अगाध अनादि अनूपा

(b) सगुनहिं अगुनहिं नहिं कछु भेदा ।
जलु हिम उपल बिलग नहिं जैसे ।।

Tulsidas gives us an illustration. He tells us that जलु हिम उपल might appear to differ from one another, and yet considered from the point of view of their substance or under-lying unity, they might be taken to be identical. Now this expression जलु हिम उपल may cause some difficulty of interpretation. जलु हिम उपल might be taken to mean (i) water and hail (हिम उपल) or (ii) water, frost (हिम), and hail, or if one may have in mind to designate the three kinds of existences, solid, liquid and gaseous, जलु हिम उपल might be taken to mean water, snow, and cloud (उपल), understanding the word उपल, in the Niruktian sense. In any case, all these may be regarded as the multiform products of the same underlying substance. Even so, with the Saguna and the Nirguna.

(4) Tulsidas is not satisfied simply with postulating an identity between the Nirguna and the Saguna, but goes on to the length of saying that Nirguna might be even regarded as the cause of Saguna. Was not the Nirakara Niranjan God, he says, obliged to take on the form of a Bhūpa, and is not the Nirguna reality obliged to shape itself in Saguna forms in order to satisfy the spiritual aspirations of men?

(a) निर्मल निराकार निर्मोहा, नित्य निरञ्जन सुखसंदोहा
राम धरेउ तनु भूप।

(b) अगुन अरूप अलख अज जोई। भगतप्रेमवस सगुन सो होई।

(5) Let us now proceed to consider what relation the Name bears to the Saguna and the Nirguna. One fundamental proposition which Tulsidas puts forth is that the Name may be regarded as a schematizer between the Saguna and the Nirguna. It may be called उभयप्रबोधक, सुसाखी, and दुभाखी. It is an illuminator, a witness, and an interpreter of the one to the other: अगुन सगुन बिच

नाम सुसाखी । उभयप्रबोधक चतुर दुभाखी ।

(6) Further, as the Name sits in a judicial tribunal over Saguna and Nirguna, it exercises an authority over them and brings them under its control :

मोरे मत बड़ नाम दुहूं ते । किय जेहि युग निज बस निज बूते ।

As a judge is higher than the disputants, as imagination in Kant is higher than perception and understanding between which it intervenes, and if we may be allowed to cite an illustration from Contemporary Indian politics, as Mountbatten might be regarded as superior to the parties he reconciles, similarly, the Name might be regarded as superior to both Nirguna and Saguna whom it brings under its power. This function of schematism, which has been attributed to the Name by Tulsidas, has been attributed by a Kannada saint to the Rupa; for example, Shesha which, according to Kanakdasa, intervenes between Shiva and Vishnu and schematizes them both. This point has been made clear by the present writer in a lecture on Karnatak Mysticism delivered at the Karnatak University, Dharwar. This, however, is not our present concern. We are concerned here with showing how the Name intervenes between Saguna and Nirguna, and is superior to both. Very many people may admit that the Name might be regarded as superior to Nirguna, but Tulsidas has no difficuly in positing that it is superior even to

Saguna itself, a point at which, says Tulsidas, he has arrived after mature consideration :

निर्गुन तें एहि भाँति वड़, नाम प्रभाव अपार
कहेउँ नाम वड़ राम तें, निज विचार अनुसार.

(7) Further, we come to the relationship of Nama and Rupa. In the first place, we have to remember that Tulsidas regards Nama and Rupa as the two attributes of God, a point which we have already discussed in a previous Chapter of this work. There is a sort of a parallelism between the conceptions of Nama and Rupa, and if, perchance the question be asked which of them is superior, Tulsidas tells us that the philosopher knows the answer in his heart and sits 'mum'.

नाम रूप दुइ ईस उपाधी..........
को वड़ छोट कहत अपराधू । सुनि गुनभेद समुझिहहिं साधू ।

(8) Soon, however, the inner meaning of Tulsidas becomes apparent, and he is compelled to say that the Name may be regarded as superior to Rupa, for the reason that the Rupa is dependent upon the Name, the Name being its cause. Further, Tulsidas tells us that God comes with greater force and love to the heart of a devotee who meditates merely on the Name of God without caring for the Form, a superb illustration of what may be called Nishkam Bhakti :

(a) देखिए रूप नाम अधीना । रूप ज्ञान नहिं नाम विहीना ।।
(b) सुमिरिय नाम रूप विन देखे । आवत हृदय सनेह विसेखे ।।

(9) By considering the progress of the argu-

ment hitherto, we might come to the conclusion that the Name of God might be regarded as the pinnacle of Tulsidas's Philosophy of Devotion. If we may compare this with a similar conception in Kabir, we may point out that to both of them, the Name of God is the most fundamental category, though they differ from each other in the way they make use of it. Both of them insist on the Name of God as the fundamental vehicle of meditation. But they differ from each other when Tulsidas insists on a रसनाजप being the chief way of meditation, while Kabir insists upon a श्वासजप :

(a) काहे न रसना रामहिं गावहिं, says Tulsidas.

(b) विन ही मुखके जप करो नहिं जीभ डुलावो, says Kabir.

We may say, on the whole, that there are four such kinds of Japas : रसनाजप, ओष्ठजप, श्वासजप, and मानसजप ; the first belongs to Tulsidas, the second to Manu who characterises it is उपांशुजप, the third to Kabir, and the fourth, मानसजप, might be regarded as underlying all these, so far as the fructification of the process of meditation, namely, the realisation of God, is concerned.

(10) Tulsidas was so much enamoured by the importance which he attached to the Name of Rama that he had no difficuly in making a tirade against all those who followed the path of अलख, calling their minds back to the conception of Rama-Nama as the only way of salvation : तुलसी अलखें क्या

लखै । राम नाम जपु नीच. On the other hand, Kabir veritably says that the अलख may be regarded as the highest goal of experience, and that it may be possible for man to supersensuously visualise it :

अलख पुरुष निर्वाण है, वा को लखै न कोय
वा को तो वाही लखै, जो उस घरका होय.

It is in this way that we might have a comparative understanding of the ascending stages of Tulsidas's Philosophy of Devotion, particularly so far as the relationship between such fundamental conceptions as Saguna, Nirguna, Nama, Rupa and Dhyana, are concerned.

4. *The office of God for the Saints*—We have referred in the initial paragraph of this Chapter to to the twofold relationship that exists between God and Saints, both practical and philosophical. Under the practical relationship we shall discuss six points, and under the philosophical relationship three points, as aforementioned. Coming to the first, we shall first discuss two Dohas of Kabir, then two Dohas of Tulsidas, and then two Dohas again,—one from Kabir and the other in the Surdasian style. In the first Doha under this head, चलती चक्की देख के, we are told that Kabir began to weep when he saw the two pans of a grind-stone reducing all grains of corn to powder. Kamal, who was present, rejoined that his father need not weep because those grains of corn which lay near-

est the central peg remained unpounded. Now, this is an allegory which is full of high moral and spiritual significance. From the point of view of Rhetoric, we might say that in the two Dohas under consideration there is a great Nigaraṇa Alamkara, in which the two grind-stones stand not merely for themselves but also for heaven and earth, the grains of corn for human beings, and the central iron peg for God, who might well be called the Centre of the Universe, or in Archimedean terminology, the spiritual "fulcrum" of the world, proximity to which means protection as a reward for devotion.

The Doha चक्की चक्की सब कहै is sometimes attributed to Ramanand; but in our opinion, it would be better to attribute it to Kamal, in view of the humility of utterance चक्की चक्की सब कहै, कीला कहै न कोय. It would befit a good boy like Kamal to speak these words in a spirit of humility, but further, it would not be desirable to accuse Kabir of not having believed in such a central peg. It would be an act of malignment to suppose that Kabir did not believe in this great centre of the universe which moves all creation, – the great centrifugal and centripetal Reality which sends out and draws in all the existences in the world according to its laws. Kabir thanked himself that he believed in such a protecting centre of the universe. Among numerous other Dohas attributed to Kabir is the following which shows his attitude to Reality :

एक न भूला दोइ न भूला, भूला सब संसार ।
एक न भूला दास कबीरा, जाके राम अधार ॥.

Many stories are told about the relationship of Kabir and Kamal. A particular line of Kabir, बूडा वंश कबीरका उपजा पूत कमाल, has however caused some difficulty of interpretation. It is said that Kamal was a bad boy, and on account of his having led a vicious life, Kabir is supposed to have said that his whole lineage had gone to ruin. On the other hand, it is also possible to construe the line exactly in an opposite manner. When Kabir was convinced that Kamal was sure to be liberated on account of his spiritual life, it is no wonder that he should have exclaimed that there was a termination to his physical lineage, the whole lineage having been saved by his only remaining representative.

On the Maharashtra side, particularly, there is a well known story about Kabir and Kamal, which, so far as the present writer is aware, does not find a place in the tradition of Northern India. In that story, Kamal is made to shine even more than Kabir. While Kabir was going on a road and Kamal was following him at a distance, Kabir saw a piece of gold on his way, and for fear lest Kamal when he saw it might be tempted to pick it up, Kabir stopped a while, covered it with dust, and then pursued his course. Kamal, who was looking forward, stopped at the place where his father had stopped, and called to his father and asked him what he had done. Kabir returned and told him that he wanted to save Kamal from appropriating the piece of gold which lay there. "Do you think that is a piece of gold" asked Kamal, "To me it appears nothing more than a slab of yellow stone." This is just in the spirit of the great Vyāsa and Shuka in the Bhagavata, a story about whom tells us, in a similar manner, how, when Shuka was going ahead, naked, the ladies in the lake, who were bathing without clothes, took their bath in that condition without minding the presence or peregrination of Shuka. When Vyasa, who was fully dressed, followed behind Shuka and came near the lake, the ladies hastily covered their bodies with their Sarees. Vyasa was astonished that this was not done by the ladies when the naked Shuka was going ahead. The Apsaras as replied that in his eyes there was a distinction between man and woman, masculine and feminine – तवास्ति स्त्रीपुंभिदा – while Shuka was incapable of such a distinction. The following verse in this connection is worthy of attention and may be carved by every aspirant on his heart:

दृष्ट्वाऽनुयान्तमृषिमात्मजमप्यनग्नं
देव्यो ह्रिया परिदधुर्न सुतस्य चित्रम् ।
तद्वीक्ष्य पृच्छति मुनौ जगदुस्तवास्ति
स्त्रीपुंभिदा न तु सुतस्य विविक्तदृष्टेः ॥

Another Doha of Kabir, कबीर कूता रामका, tells us about the limits of human freedom. Kabir describes himself, like Nanak at a latter date, as the dog of God. These two words dog and God remind us, on account of their proximity, of a very famous utterance from Spinoza which students of philosophy might remember. Kabir says that he is dear to his Master like the pearl, like the spiritual pearl, मुतिया मेरा नाउँ, that his neck is tied by the cord of God's Name, and that he goes wherever his Master pulls him. This suggests to us, that, according to Kabir, all the actions of man may be determined by the power of God. On the other hand, readers of James's "Will to Believe" will remember that in his essay on the 'Dilemma of Determinism', he has used a similar example to illustrate the doctrine of indeterminism. A falcon, to whose leg a tether has been tied, could fly anywhere within the orbit described by its tether, and not outside. This, says James, betokens ethically the limits of human freedom, or in the language of political science, a restricted autonomy under the aegis of a suzerain power. The word which Kabir uses is जेवडी and not शृंखला, which should indicate the flexibility of a cotton cord, and not the inflexibility and regidity of an iron chain. While, therefore, the Doha may have been intended by Kabir to designate the determinism of all actions by the Divine Power, James's illustration, that it might also involve indeterminism and a limited freedom is also worthy of consideration.

In this connection, the present writer is reminded of a very famous Abhanga in Marathi literature अनंत जुगाचा देव्हारा....पहा तुकें भुंकविलें. Tukaram considers himself to be the dog of God, and tells us that his function is fivefold so far as the spiritual sphere is concerned. The jingling bells round his neck constitute the Anāhata sound; like a faithful dog, he shows the path to the spiritual pilgrims; he becomes possessed by the spiritual 'guist', and becomes subject to the epilepsy of God-devotion; and in that condition he almost onomato–pœically barks out the name of his spiritual teacher गुरं, गुरं.

After considering the above two Dohas from Kabir, let us now pass on to two other Dohas from Tulsidas, concerning the service which God renders to the Saints: (1) घर घर मांगे टूक (2) चित्रकूटके घाटपर. "At that time Tulsi used to beg, now Emperors fall at his feet. At that time, Tulsi was without Rama, now Rama has become his helper and guide". In this way does Tulsidas tell us how the attainment of the Grace of God has made all the difference. It is questionable to whom the authorship of the Doha घर घर मांगे टूक belongs. 'ते तुलसी तव राम विनु, ते अब राम सहाय' indicates a respectful plural, which shows that the Doha might have been composed by some worshipful admirer or devotee of Tulsidas. For the substance of the present Doha, we might compare the autobiographical सवैया from Tulsidas's कवितावली which tells us how Tulsidas in his childhood used to beg from door to door, sorrowfully craving and weeping, and when he was fortunate to get even four grains of gram, he felt so glad as if he had attained the four goals of human life, namely, धर्म, अर्थ, काम and मोक्ष :

बारे ते ललात बिललात द्वार द्वार दीन ।
जानत हो चारि फल, चारहि चनक को ॥.

We might here compare exactly the naked Fakir as Mahatma Gandhi was during his life-time, and his magnificient Samadhi on the Rajghat at New Delhi, on which wreaths are placed by Consuls and Ambassadors, Presidents and Plenipotentiaries.

The other Doha of Tulsidas चित्रकूट के घाटपर tells us in an admirable manner how God serves the Saints. On the Ghat of the पयस्विनी river at the foot of the Chitrakut hill, Saints were taking their bath with a view to ascend to the top of the hill after their holy ablutions. It is customary in Northern India to have a tilak (तिलक) put on the forehead after the bath. The occasion of the Doha raises the question as to by whom and to whom this holy sandal mark was applied. Three explanations may be offered in regard to the holy mark of Chandana to which a reference has been made in the Doha. In the first place, Tulsidas might have been rubbing sandalwood, and God Rama like a faithful servant rendering him service in putting the holy mark on the foreheads of the saints who had taken their bath. This was exactly in the spirit of Shrikhandyā in Ekanath's house, who was supposed to be an incarnation of God, and who was doing similar service in rubbing the sandalwood himself and bringing pitchers of water to the house of Ekanath : स्वकरे चंदन घासी, गंगेचे पाणि कावडी भरितो. A second explanation may be that God in order to test whether Tulsidas knew Him or not came to him and put the holy sandal mark on His own forehead, and then went back, being glad that Tulsidas could not recognise Him. A third alternative may be that Rama might have put the holy mark on the forehead of Tulsidas himself, who on account of the brilliant 'Chhabi' of Shri Rama remained unconsciously glaring without knowing that it was Rama himself who was putting the mark on his forehead. A similar practice is also followed in South India at Pandharpur, where the Bukka, instead of the Sandal mark, is put on the chief Kirtānkara by those who attend the Kirtana. ब्राह्मणो मम दैवतं, says the proverb. Rama himself put this mark on the forehead of Tulsidas regarding him as his Deity. These are the three possible explanations, that could be offered in regard to the Doha.

We should not try to attach too much mystical value to these interpretations. Many stories have been told concerning Tulsidas in regard to his great desire for the vision of Rama. The story of the ghost (प्रेत) who showed Hanuman to Tulsidas, Hanuman's assuming the body of an old man while Tulsidas was performing Kirtana at the Sankata Mochan temple at Benares, the efforts of Hanuman to bring to the notice of Tulsidas the figure of Shri Rama either in the shape of a warrior with a bow and arrows, or in the shape of a charming boy who came to Tulsidas and asked him for a little quantity of sandal paste to be put on his forehead, बाबा हमे चंदन दो, all these are stories interesting from a narrative point of view, but not of much importance from the mystical standpoint. The psychological element in the third interpretation certainly deserves our consideration. A physical manifestation of God, however, would be too much to believe in, philosophically or scientifically. On the other hand, a mystical vision of God is not impossible, but that experience might be couched in a different manner.

Two other Dohas — one from Kabir and the other in Surdasian style - are also available, wherein we are supplied with some valuable observations in regard to the questions of fore-fulfilment of desires, and of a eudaemonistic combination of material and spiritual welfare. In the first of these Dohas, पीछे माँगे चाकरी, which we find in the Gujerathi collection of Kabir's Dohas, we are told that God is not like other masters. His reward precedes service, as in the case of other masters it follows. This indicates the forefulfilment of the desires of the saint by God. Before any desire arises in the mind of the saint, it is already fulfilled by God. This question of the forefulfilment of desires is an ethical counterpart of the doctrine of foreknowledge in the epistemological sphere. James tells us in his "Will to Believe" how God is the great expert, who can anticipate any moves of a novice in a game of chess, and thereby manipulates his moves in such a manner that ultimate victory is gained for Himself. On the other hand, in the case of fore-fulfilment, the events are so manipulated by God that the desires are fulfilled before they arise in a man's mind and victory is gained for the Saint.

Similarly, it is the function of God eudaemonistically to combine the material and the spiritual welfare for his devotee. We are told in a Doha written in the Surdasian manner how the cowherdesses of Gokul went to Mathura not merely for the sake of the sale of their milk-products, but also and particularly for the vision of Krishna – गोरस बेचत हरि मिले, एक पंथ दो काज. Similarly, many seekers want to have not simply either material welfare or spiritual welfare singly, but their combination. Greatness in the world may not be incompatible with greatness in the spiritual life.

Even a Vice-Chanceller's chair may not be incompatible with the vision of a spiritual Form. It was not impossible for King Janaka to have his mind fully engrossed in the spiritual life, while he was at the same time ruling the entire world. When याज्ञवल्क्य came to the Court of King Janaka, Janaka asked him whether he had gone there for victory in argument, or for winning the cows and coins, which was the prize set for the victory. उभयमेव सम्राट् was the characteristic reply which याज्ञवल्क्य gave to King Janaka. King Janaka had not any cause for dissatisfaction with such a reply. No better reply than that of याज्ञवल्क्य could have been given to King Janaka who was himself an embodiment of the highest eudaemonistic combination of material and spiritual greatness.

5. *The Saint as personal and God as impersonal Reality* — We now come to the question of the philosophical relationship that exists between the Saints and God. Under this head we shall discuss three Dohas

(i) जो चाहे आकार तू
(ii) निराकार की आरसी
(iii) भजन भरोसे राम के

and shall see towards the end how they rise one at the top of the other. In the Doha जो चाहे आकार तू, we are told by Kabir, that if we are unable to see the form of God in this world, the bodily form of the Sadhu would be an excellent substitute for it. In fact, to Kabir the Sadhu would be a fully representative personal and physical replica of the Godhead. On the other hand, says Kabir, if we are anxious to see the Nirākāra, we have to take recourse to the Nijarupa. By distinguishing between the two, namely, Sākāra and Nijarupa, Kabir tells us that we should give प्रेम to the one, and प्रीति to the other, personal love and impersonal devotion respectively. We have also parallels for both of these conceptions elsewhere. Kabir has already said जाके दरसन साहब दरसै : to see the Saint is fully equivalent to seeing God; while Patanjali tells us in his aphorism तदा द्रष्टुः स्वरूपेऽवस्थानम् that the ultimate aim of the seeker is to abide in his own Form, the स्वरूप or निजरूप. The question might arise here as to whether the निजरूप could be described as निराकार at all, as Kabir does. The triad is of course, form, formless, and transcending form. Saguna corresponds to the first, Nirguna to the second, and गुणातीत to the third which transcends both form and formlessness. According to Patanjali and others, the निजरूप might be characterised as गुणातीत instead of निर्गुण.

The elevation of the Saint to the pedestal of the God-head had been anticipated by Jain philosophy, when it denied God and raised the तीर्थङ्कर himself to the status of the God-head. The nemesis of the denial of God in Jainism was in effect the apotheosis of its founder. As Hopkins has put it, the Jain philosophy dethroned God, and made the तीर्थङ्कर reign in His place. Jain philosophy is what might be called an atheistic, spiritualistic pluralism, and in such a scheme there is no place for God at all. On the other hand, in a famous verse from the Kannada poet सर्वज्ञ, we are told that the formless not being satisfied with living in an isolated condition, came and took on the form of a Saint to confer the highest spiritual boons on humanity :

परमना रूपदलि नेरवीयलरियदे
नरनागि बंदु वरवीव गुरुविगे
सरि यारु काणे सर्वज्ञ

In सर्वज्ञ, as in Kabir, deity is recognised, but it is made to assume the form of a Saint, and the highest aspiration for Sainthood is declared to be assimilation with the deity.

The Doha that next follows – निराकार की आरसी– goes a step ahead of the Doha we have discussed above. In the former Doha, the Sadhu was regarded as a physical embodiment of God. In the present Doha, we are told that the Sadhu is like a mirror, in which one can see the Nirākāra reflected. This Doha introduces the conception of mirroring or reflection. We shall consider fully the implications of this conception when we come to a Doha in the Fifth Chapter – हृदया भीतर आरसी. In the meanwhile, we shall be concerned with the reflection of the Nirākāra as we find it in the Sadhu himself. Jnaneshwar goes even a step ahead of Kabir and tells us in his famous चांगदेवपासष्टी that God and Saint serve as mirrors to one another and forget their difference in seeing each other's reflection.

ज्ञानदेव चक्रपाणी ऐसे । दोन्ही डोळस आरसे ।
परस्पर पाहतां कैसे । मुकले भेदा ॥.

In this state it becomes impossible to describe which is the बिंब and which is the प्रतिबिंब, which the original and which the reflection. Two mirrors placed in front of each other, as physical science would tell us, reflect each other 'ad infinitum'; even so, the Saint and God reflect each other infinitely. Thus, the ultimate difference between the two vanishes, and a state of absolute unison is created.

We now come to the final Doha of this Chapter, the Doha of Kabir, भजन भरोसे रामके. The question arises whether the authorship of this Doha could be attributed to Kabir. It describes the state of union of Kabir with God after his death, and therefore might well have been composed by some disciple of Kabir, unless we suppose that it might have been composed by Kabir himself in full anticipation of the state in which he might exist after death. In the first case, it might be taken to be a tribute paid by some worthy devotee to the memory of his Master, and in the second it might be taken as a fully anticipatory Doha. It is very significant to see how Kabir and Tulsidas agree with each other in regarding भरोस as the highest virtue of which man is capable :

भजन भरोसे राम के, says Kabir

एक भरोसो एक बल, says Tulsidas.

Unless we place our fullest reliance upon God, it will not be possible for us to reach the state to which we aspire.

The passing away of Kabir at Maghar near Gorakhpur, and the Doha which is composed in that behalf, have been matters of classical significance. It was traditionally supposed that one who died at Maghar was born as an ass in his next birth. " By all means, then " said Kabir, " Let me die at Maghar, for I know that I have no future birth for me, far less that of an ass ". A man who leads a sinful life, says Kabir, even if he dies at Benares, cannot be saved. On the other hand, a virtuous man, though he died at Maghar, might escape the clutches of death :

हिरदै कठोर मऱ्या बनारसी, नरक न वंच्या जाइ, ।

हरिको दास मरै जो मगहर, सेन्या सकल तिराय ॥

The tomb and the Samadhi of Kabir which exist at Maghar will stand as an eternal monument of the unity of spiritual realisation to be attained in Hinduism or Islam, and for that matter in any other form of religion. The present writer is tempted to believe that the place should be called अघहर instead of मघहर. It is a place where our sins will be washed away, and which will, therefore, enable us to advance on the path of spiritual realisation.

In the Doha we are considering, we are told how Kabir is lying like a 'child' on the lap of the Immutable : अविनाशी के गोद मे खेलत दास कबीर. The Bible tells us that unless we become as little children, we cannot enter into the kingdom of God. The present writer pointed out for the first time in his essay on Herakleitos how this Biblical conception was borrowed from an aphorism of Herakleitos who lived about four hundred years before Christ, and who tells us "paidos hē basilēiē", the kingdom belongs to the child. Kabir was in perfect accord with these dicta of Herakleitos and Christ, and realised in his person what they so passionately taught. A simple, unquestioning, and implicit faith in our Maker is the only guarantee of an unimpeded and progressive realisation of the Godhead.

If we just look at the three Dohas that have preceded, we shall see that the first Doha जो चाहै आकार तू represents the thesis, of which निराकार के आरसी is the antithesis, while भजन भरोसे राम के constitutes a synthesis of the two. The true solution of the antinomy of the Saint's body being either the Sākāra form of God or as hiding the Nirākāra is the conception of an eschatological unison between the Saint and God. We need neither say that the Saint is a physical metamorphosis of God, nor need we say that he fully mirrors the Absolute.

On the other hand, it would be perfectly legitimate for us to suppose that when the Saint has passed away, his spirit merges with Absolute spirit. This would be a perfectly scientific conception, which would displace the poetic conceptions of the two preceding Dohas. There might be limitations of body and mind so long as the Saint subsists upon earth, and hence we can never fully identify the Saint with God. On the other hand, when the Saint has left off his body, there is nothing to prevent his spirit from merging into the highest Spirit. From that point of view, in spite of much Vedantic speculation on the subject, विदेहमुक्ति might be regarded as even a higher conception than जीवन्मुक्ति.

CHAPTER IV

The Beginnings of the Pilgrimage

We are going to discuss in this chapter the beginnings of the spiritual pilgrimage as found in the Dohas of the great Hindi saints. We shall begin by discussing the nature and function of the spiritual teacher in the scheme of spiritual realisation. Next, we shall proceed to discuss two important topics :

(1) first, the method by means of which the spiritual teacher instructs us to begin and perfect our endeavour for God-realisation. This, of course, is meditation by the Name, which he communicates to us from a high spiritual altitude, from which it must descend and be conduited in the minds of his disciples.

(2) second, the power that lies in this Name and the function it performs in the spiritual development of the disciple.

Afterwards, we shall proceed to discuss four important requisites for the perfection of this methodology : what physical, mental, moral and mystical requirements are necessary for this perfection ? Finally, that inner spring of devotion, that longing for self-realisation, that passionate attachment to the spiritual life without which we can never rise to the sublime heights of realisation, will be discussed briefly from these Dohas in Hindi spiritual literature.

1. *The nature and function of a Guru* — Let us begin by considering the nature and function of the Spiritual Teacher as found in the Dohas. Here, we shall first discuss the analogies which are to be found in Doha literature for the function which the Spiritual Teacher performs.

There are three excellent analogies to illustrate this function, first, the analogy of the swan; second, the analogy of the Sikligar; and third, the analogy of the potter.

After discussing these analogies, we shall proceed to consider the difference between the Guru of the 'Peras' and the Guru of the 'Apeiron.' Finally, we shall consider the supremacy of the Spiritual Teacher even to God Himself.

From the Doha, क्षीररूप सत नाम है, it may be imagined that it is Kabir who is comparing the Spiritual Teacher to a swan. The expression सतनाम is to be found in Kabirite and allied theology, and stands for the ultimately real Name, and even for the ultimate Reality itself.

In another passage of Kabir, we know how he tells us :

सत नाम का भरभर प्याला आपु पिये मोहि प्यावै ।.

Hence, in Śankarite terminology, we might regard

the सतनाम in its aspect of ultimate Reality as equivalent to परमार्थ itself, with which Kabir is contrasting व्यवहार in the Doha.

The Guru separates Vyavahara from Paramartha, matter from spirit, just as the swan separates water from milk. This is the principal function which a spiritual teacher performs. Not every bird is capable of performing this miraculous function. In the same manner, not every so-called Guru can separate matter from spirit for the upliftment of his disciple.

The second analogy which is to be found in the Dohas for the spiritual teacher is that of a सिकलीगर. Now this word 'sikligara' seems to have had an Arabic origin, and it is interesting to see that the same word in a slightly modified form (सिक्कलगार) is to be found in Kanarese.

The function of a 'sikligara' is to sharpen instruments of iron or steel; so does the Guru sharpen the mental instrument of his disciple. The second function which a 'sikligara' performs is that he takes away all rust from the iron instruments; similarly, the spiritual teacher takes away all the dirt and rust of passions and desires from the mind of his disciple.

We are told by Kabir that a 'sikligara' does this within the span of a single moment, छन में डाले धोय. Even so, the spiritual teacher has been credited with the power of taking away all the hindrances in the spiritual path of the disciple so as to confer on him immortality and liberation in a single moment.

There are, of course, two views on this head. In the first place, the disciple has, by a process of self-purification, to continue his effort to perfect himself on the path of realisation. On the other hand, we are told that in a single moment the disciple can reach the goal of his endeavour by the Grace of his Guru. जेच्चि क्षणीं अनुग्रह केला । तेंचि क्षणीं मोक्ष झाला । बंधन कांहीं आत्मयाला । बोलोचि नये ॥ says Ramdas.

Kabir seems to be of the same opinion. The very moment that the disciple comes under the grace of his Spiritual Teacher, he finds the door of liberation open to him. What these doctrines imply we may not discuss at this place, the full meaning and implication of these being reserved for a later occasion.

The third analogy for the spiritual teacher is that of a potter, or a कुम्भकार. A spiritual teacher performs for his disciple the same functions which a potter performs for his pot. In the first place, he takes away all the depressions and protuberances of his jar, and rounds off all its angularities. In the second place, he enlarges the potential vacuum of the pot, and gives it the shape and size he wills.

In a similar manner, a spiritual teacher takes away all the defects and deficiencies of his disciple's mind, enlarges his receptivity, and makes of him a worthy disciple capable of performing the functions he wills.

Then, again, a kumbhakār gives continuous strokes to the pot from the outside, but gives it a constant and unfailing support from within. Similarly, in the midst of the calamities and misfortunes which might fall to the lot of his disciple, the spiritual teacher gives him internal and continuous support, and enables him to face boldly his trials and tribulations. Every misfortune, every calamity, has now a silver lining for him. The Sun of his Guru's grace shines through the edge of his misfortunes, though these for a while might darken the luminosity of his spiritual life.

This analogy of the pot and the potter, the giving of continuous strokes from the outside and support from the inside, the taking away of all angularities, and the giving of any shape and size that the potter might will, was a very peculiar phenomenon to such a highly-placed and well-informed Bishop like Westcott, who had never seen this phenomenon, and who, after studying this Doha, asked his Hindi Pandit if he would take him to a place where the potter was performing this miracle, and it is very interesting to note that the photograph of the potter and the pot on which the potter was giving his strokes is to be found in the famous book of Bishop Westcott on 'Kabir and Kabir Pantha'.

After considering these analogies, we go on to discuss how the real Teacher is a teacher of the Limitless, the Apeiron, and other teachers are teachers of the limited, or the Peras. The expressions which Kabir often uses in this connection are the हद and बेहद, the Peras and the Apeiron of Pythagoras.

We shall see later at the end of this work how Kabir tells us

हद हद पर सबही गया, बेहद गया न कोय ।
बेहद के मैदान में रमै कबीरा सोय ॥.

At this place it is necessary only to bring out the distinction between the Guru of the Limited and the Guru of the Unlimited, the साधारण गुरु and the असाधारण गुरु.

The Guru of the ordinary कनफूंका type is the Guru of the limited; his sole function is to breathe into the ears of his disciple his so-called Mantra. The function of the real spiritual teacher is not the breathing of this Mantra into the ears of his disciple, but the showing of the form of God to his vision. What is the use of imparting a Mantra to a disciple, if it does not result in the vision of the God-head ?

The real Guru is he, therefore, at whose instance his disciples have walked on the path of God, taking note of the landmarks and the signboards on the way until they have reached their ठकाना ठोर, their final destination from which there is no return. Veritably, this ठिकाना ठोर is the Hindi way of putting what Bādarayana has called अनावृत्ति at the end of his Sutras.

We finally come to the discussion of the primal supremacy of the Spiritual Teacher in the Doha गुरु गोविंद दोऊ खड़े. We do not know whether the Hindi world knows the story connected with this Doha; but the Saint of Umadi used to expound it in the following manner. Kabir had once a simultaneous vision of God, and his Guru. A question might not be irrelevantly asked here as to whether it is mystically possible to have a simultaneous dual vision of this kind, or whether the two presentations might not coalesce into one. But this question apart, supposing that God and Guru made a simultaneous appearance before Kabir, Kabir was placed in a dilemma as to whom he should owe his primary allegiance.

It is said Kabir chose his spiritual teacher because it was on account of him that he was able to realise God at all. God was not satisfied with this decision of Kabir and so He made an appeal to the teacher of Kabir, viz. Ramanand.

The qnestion was whether God was to be regarded as superior to the spiritual teacher or not. Ramanand like Kabir himself voted in favour of his spiritual teacher, and so God was left supportless. God then went from teacher to teacher until ultimately he was absolutely ruled out of the spiritual court.

In a similar style, the saint of Nimbargi has been credited in a peom एनु माडिदी केळेन देवा with having drawn God to the bar of his Spiritual Teacher, and the judgment was of course that God had to fall prostrate at the feet of the Spiritual Teacher in order to exonerate Himself from His sins of commission and omission.

This is, of course, a spiritual story clothed in a poetico-legal imagery. As regards the question of the 'regresses' of spiritual teachers 'ad infinitum', it is possible to resolve it only on the lines of Spinoza who had postulated an original hammer in order that all the later hammers might be produced. No hammer can be produced without a hammer, this without a second, and so on ad infinitum. In this way an original hammer, a 'causa sui', or 'substance' might be postulated before other hammers are produced. We have talked elsewhere about the God-Guru complex, and instead of a simultaneous vision of two, let us be satisfied only with one entity, call it God or Guru. It was from this point of view probably, that the great Patanjali has identified God and Guru by calling God the Parama Guru in his Sutra परमगुरुर्हि देवानाम्.

2. *Meditation by means of the Name* — We now proceed to our second group of Dohas—those concerned with the process of meditation by the

Name. We are told by Kabir that it is only by the word imparted by the Guru, that we are able to dispel our spiritual and mental darkness :

विना सवद गुरुदेवके कवहूं तिमिर न जाय.

तिमिर also signifies cataract, and for the matter of that, the cataract of ignorance.

This innate cataract of ignorance cannot be removed by any other means except by the Name imparted by the Guru. This assertion finds justification in a famous stanza from Sanskrit spiritual literature which tells us :

अज्ञानतिमिरान्धस्य ज्ञानाञ्जनशलाकया।
चक्षुरुन्मीलितं येन तस्मै श्रीगुरवे नमः ॥

One important point, however, which Kabir stresses is that this Name, Word, Sound, or Shabda is capable of dispelling this physical and metaphysical darkness.

We might note the property contained in the Shabda or the Sound which has the power of producing illumination or Light. More than any other writer in Hindi spiritual literature, Kabir stresses the Sound aspect or the Shabda aspect of the Name. Tulsidas and others stress the devotional aspect. Kabir being interested in the Science of spiritual life could very well credit the Word with the production of illumination. This might veritably be called a Sphotism in the terminology of of the great अलङ्कारिक s and वैयाकरण s.

Nominalism which is used by the Schoolmen

even though it signifies a stress on the Name would be a word entirely out of place in this context, because that word is used by the Schoolmen in contrast to Realism, or Subjectivism. Sphotism would be a good word; but one might say Sonnanism would be even better to signify the idea conveyed by Kabir in his philosophy of the Spiritual Sound. As Christianity stresses the Logos aspect of the word, Kabir stresses the Sound or Anahata aspect, and credits it with the power of dispelling our intellectual darkness. It may even, in modern scientific terminology, be called 'Luminous Sound'.

Let us now harp back to the teaching of Tulsidas about the Name of God. Tulsidas waxes eloquent over the superiority of the Name to both Saguna and Nirguna. Saguna and Nirguna, he says, are no doubt both अकथ, अगाध, अनादि and अनूप. They are unfathomable, and ineffable.

Granting such high predicates to Saguna and Nirguna, Tulsidas feels no difficulty in exalting the Name above both Saguna and Nirguna. The Name of God is superior to God with form, as well as to God without form.

It might easily be granted that Tulsidas might recognise that the name of God is superior to the formless God; but he excels himself in saying that the Name of God is superior even to God with Form. He tells us that this superiority of the Name to the personality of God is established by the 'Setubandha'. Rama felt a little self-conscious that his Name was able to make stones float on the surface of the sea. But when he personally went and placed these stones on the water, they went to the bottom of the sea.

Tulsidas is in the habit of occasionally giving expression to his own personal opinions. This is not a bad practice, because very often, from the philosophical point of view, the mention of any personal opinions such as मोरे मत, निज विचार अनुसार are really very welcome expressions. We are really thankful to the great Tulsidas for having been courageous in explaining his own personal opinions in this manner.

The one thing which Tulsidas abhors is the designation of God as अलक्ष्य. In the Doha हम लखि लखहि हमार, it may be supposed that Tulsidas is preaching a tirade against Kabirism, Gorakshism, and allied theology.

Have done with your अलक्ष्य, says Tulsidas. Meditate on the Name of God, O Fool : राम नाम जपु नीच.

The word अलख which is used by the बैरागी s and गोसावी s might well be taken from the Arabic words अल्हक़, the Truth, Reality, or God; but it may as well be taken from the word अलक्ष्य. अलक्ष्य लक्षुनि पाहे निजवस्तु is a famous verse in Marathi literature. As to whether it is possible for us to meditate on 'alakshya' is a different matter.

Tulsidas's tirade against the doctrine of 'alakshya' is couched in the following philosophical arguments. God can never be 'alakshya' is the conclusion at which Tulsidas arrives.

How does he argue ? (1) In the first place, he says, we might begin by saying that we see our own selves ; then, we proceed to see the world which is the object of our experience (हमार); and then we see God or the subject-object relation which is intermediate (बीच), and, therefore, the connecting link between the self and the world. This might well be regarded as a philosophy of Introspectionism. (2) Secondly, after having seen the objective world (लखिहि हमार – gerundial construction), we come back to see God, as between the internal world and the external world. This might be called the philosophy of Introvertism in its literal sense.

Those who have studied the philosophy of Descartes will be amazed to see the relation of these arguments to his philosophy. Descartes proceeds by denying the objective world by denying God; but the one thing he cannot deny is the self; so he makes the self the starting-point of his philosophy. Afterwards, he proves that there must be a God, who is the maker of the self, or who is more perfect than the self, or whose existence is involved in the idea of the self, and when once God is proved, Descartes finds no difficulty in saying that the world which is the handiwork of God must also be regarded as real.

In the two alternatives to this Cartesianism which Tulsidas proposes, namely Introspectionism and Introvertism, the existence of God as a Personal Being (लक्ष्य) must be regarded as fundamentally certain. Any philosophy which regards God as अलक्ष्य is to Tulsidas mere 'abracadabra', and therefore he proceeds to tell us it will be the better part of valour to meditate on God by means of His Name.

However, the Name, which Tulsidas regards as the 'par excellence' approach to the Godhead is the Name of Rama. 'There might be a thousand other names of God; I am not concerned with them', says Tulsidas. 'My allegiance is given to the Name of Rama as the supreme God-head. For, does not the word राम contain the two letters र and म, and do not र and म come at the top of all alphabets whatsoever, for example, अर्क and अंक. In the case of both, the रकार and the मकार come at the top, and as the name of Rama is constituted out of these two letters, that Name stands supreme above all other names of God'.

र and म also constitute the pre-eminent insignia of royalty. The रकार is the royal umbrella, and the मकार is the crest-jewel of the crown. If, therefore, the word Rama is constituted out of these supreme royal insignia, why should we not suppose that

God Rama is superior to all other gods ?

It is interesting to note that this very clever way of putting the matter which Tulsidas employs for providing the supremacy of Rama is valid only for the Devanagari script, and not for the Dravidian script. For example, in Kanarese, both the रकार and the मकार are collinear with the alphabets—sometimes preceding, sometimes following. In the case of अंक, the मकार precedes, and in the case of अर्क, the रकार follows. Hence unless we are prepared to deny to the Dravidians the privilege of regarding Rama as the supreme God-head, we have to find the derivation of the word राम elsewhere : अन्तः रमयति इति रामः, he who lives inside the heart, and who lives inside the world, moving them and filling them with beatific joy.

In any case, Tulsidas's derivation, though imaginative, might be taken to be a contribution to Niruktism. More often than not, Yaska was successful in tracing words to their proper origins. But he has also given imaginative derivations as in the case of ऋषि and हंस :

यद्ब्रह्मा तानषीनभ्यानर्षत् तदृषीणामृषित्वम् ।
भवेद्वर्णागमाद् हंसः सिंहो वर्णविपर्ययात् ।

On the other hand, might we not regard ऋषि as one who is able to see God, and हंस as the symbol of the identity between the self and the Absolute ?

We have seen how the Name is the ladder

by means of which we might reach God. 'What kind of Name would be effective' is the next question. Does every Name that comes to the lips of the seeker enable him to have the vision of God? One wonders how the various schemes of सहस्रनाम might have enabled the mere verbal pronouncers to have the vision of the God-head.

In this matter, the teachings of Kabir and other Saints who had reached the heights of God-realisation cannot but be regarded with respect. Metaphors have been drawn from agriculture, epistemology, and science to bring out the distinction between two different kinds of names. We have heard the expressions, सबीज and निर्बीज, Name with a seed, and Name without a seed – a name viable and a name non-viable.

From the epistemological point of view, we might have names which come laden with meaning, and others which are not so laden—significant names and non-significant names. From the point of view of science, a name might have the highest potentiality of spiritual energy, and another which has no such potentiality. The first kind of name would be the real atom-bomb of spiritual experience. The great Maharashtra saint Tukaram said everybody calls upon the the name of Rama, but nobody knows who the आत्माराम is :

राम राम अवघेचि ह्मणती । कोणी न जाणती आत्माराम ।

राम हा कालचा सुत दशरथाचा । अनन्त युगाचा आत्माराम ।

रामासी हा राम जरी ठावे असता । तरि कां शरण जाता वसिष्ठासी ।।
तुका ह्मणे राम तुझा तुजपाशीं । विचारोनि घेसी गुरुमुखें ।।

'God Rama, as you know,' says Tukaram, 'was son of Dasharatha; आत्माराम has lived from times immemorial. If 'this' Rama, the son of Dasharatha, had known 'that' Rama, why would he have gone in submission to his spiritual teacher?' It is only the Name, which an aspirant might receive from his spiritual teacher who has reached the heights of spiritual realisation, that can be of any avail in this matter. The real Name is the name which fructifies. It is entirely 'sui generis', unique and in a different category altogether, says Kabir : वह नाम कुछ और.

3. *The function and power of the Name*—We now proceed to our next group of Dohas which discuss the function and the power of the Name. Tulsidas tells us that the Name of God is like a lamp placed on the threshold of the tongue, so that it might illumine both the inside and the outside of man. The tongue, he says, is the देहली. If you place the lamp on the देहली, it will spread light both internally and externally.

This advice is of a piece with the teachings of so many other Saints of India who have insisted that the name be uttered by the tongue — the वैखरी. The real insistence should be on the utterance by breath — whether by परा, पश्यन्ती, or मध्यमा.

It is not simply a mechanical uttering of the name of God that will lead one to illumination. There must be a भाव accompanying the utterance of the name. So, insistence may be laid on the quality of the heart rather than on utterance by tongue.

Elsewhere Tulsidas talks of Bhakti as a Mani and Jnana as a Dīpa. The functions of the Bhakti-Mani and the Jnana-Dīpa consist respectively in warding off and destroying the insects of life, such as sins, diseases and desires. A radical distinction is here made by Tulsidas between Bhakti and Jnana, undetstanding by Jnana philosophical knowledge, or intellectual conviction. Jnana is more than mere knowledge or conviction. It means, or it ought to mean, spiritual illumination. When the Bhagavadgita speaks of ज्ञानदीपेन भास्वता, it speaks of this lamp of illumination, and as this illumination can proceed only from the quality of heart, there is no essential contradiction between Bhakti and Jnana.

In another Doha, Tulsidas speaks about the Name as a कल्पतरु, a wish-fulfilling tree. How many have seen this Kalpataru? This Saint of Nimbargi has composed a very fine poem in Kanarese in which he speaks of कल्लु कल्पवृक्ष काणण्णा, and describes the functions of this Kalpataru. According to Tulsidas, this Kalpataru is the shelter for spiritual felicity in this Kali age. Contemplation on it turns a sinner into a saint, 'Bhang' into 'Tulsi' : जो सुमिरत भयो भाँग ते, तुलसी तुलसीदास.

Another happy reading would be भागते or भागसे, which might imply that it was by great fortune that Tulsi became Tulsidas. It is evident, therefore, that the aspirant must try to realise this 'Kalpataru', seeing that it is the only supreme shelter for spiritual felicity.

Kabir's insistence on the power of the Name is not less strong than that of Tulsidas, though his conception of Rama might differ somewhat from that of Tulsidas. Even though Kabir brings Yogic and occult terminology to illustrate his meaning, his insistence on the power of the Name is supreme.

The name of Rama, he says, is superior to the अनुभव of शून्य, to जप by अजपा, and even to the experience of Anāhata sound. These may have an end, he says, but Kabir has not; because he is unceasingly uttering the name of God.

What Kabir means by Shunya is a little difficult to understand. It is probably not the Shunya of the Madhyamikas. The Kabirites gave the Shunya a technical sense, understanding by it probably the vacuum of the mind, instead of the negation of reality. What Kabir means by ajapa japa is counting the names of God without a tactual or a labial modus operandi. It is counting beads without beads, it is counting beads with breaths.

Also, we need not here enter into a detailed

distinction between Anāhata and Shabda. According to Kabir we may suppose that one of the highest categories of spiritual experience, namely, the Anāhata does not come up to the power of the Name. The uttering of the Name of God has become almost a reflex action with him, says Kabir: राम नाम रट लाय.

A great Kanarese saint called Shishunaladhīsha has also spoken about an aspirant's calling on the name of God almost as reflexly as the barking of a dog:

वसुधेयोळगे शिशुनाळधीशन हेसरु बोगळि ऐदक्षर नुडियलु ॥

Tukaram has evidently called himself the dog of God:

गुरु गुरु करी वेडे चारे । पहा तुके भुंकविलें ।.

The expression which Shishunaladhīsha uses is बोगळि, barking, not पोगळि, praising. This evidently implies as reflex an action as that contemplated by Kabir.

4. *The physical requisites of Meditation*—We next come to the four groups of Dohas, in which we have a discussion successively of the physical, mental, moral, and mystical requisites for perfection in the meditational process.

In the first place, an aspirant must recognise the extreme value of the present moment. What you intend to do tomorrow do to-day, says the Doha: काल करो सो आज कर; and what you want to do today, do just now. You must not lose a single moment of your life in the pursuit of vanities. Death is ever ready to pounce upon you, and he does not care whether you have fiinished your work or not. This Doha is an excellent replica of the famous verse in the Mahabharata which says :

श्वः कार्यमद्य कुर्वीत पूर्वाह्णे चापराह्णिकम् ।
न हि प्रतीक्षते मृत्युः कृतमस्य न वा कृतम् ॥

In the next place, an aspirant must be careful not to lose a single breath, for he does not know whether the next breath will come. Ramdas has warned us not to lose time even for the purposes of sneezing, yawning, coughing, or belching. The time required for the meeting of the eye-lashes, he says, is time lost in vain :

शिंक जांभई खोकला । तितुका वेळ व्यर्थ गेला
पात्या पातें न लगत । तितुकें वय व्यर्थ जात
लागे अवचित उचकी । तितुके वय काळ लेखी.

Jagannathadas, the great philosophic and devotional poet of the Karnatak, has said the only way to escape the clutches of death is to meditate on the name of देवक्किनय – while you are yawning or belching or playing with children मक्कळाडिसुवाग.. ..विक्कुवागाऽऽकळिसुतलि देवक्किनय स्मरिसुतिह नर, सिक्कनेमदूतरिगे आवावल्लि नोडिदरू. Kabir tells us that we must weave a rosary (सुमिरनी) of breaths, instead of beads. Whether the beads be made of wood or coral, they have to be secured together by intermediate knots, and there is also a head-bead. The rosary of breaths steers clear of the impediments both of the knots and the head-bead. These give incessant interruption in the process of meditation; while, in addition, the head-bead puts us in mind of the number. God is numberless, and the number of times we have uttered the Name of God has nothing to do with his realisation. What is wanted is only the quality and intensity of the heart.

'Proceed with the rosary of breaths, not with the rosary of beads; count beads which are no beads' says Kabir; 'Meditate intently on the Parama Tattva, the Highest Reality, and you will soon see that you are that Reality itself."

The last requisite from the physical point of view is to meditate in silence. There is no use in calling upon the name of God aloud. अजान and बांग, the Dohas say, have no value before God. He who hears the sound of an ant's feet, will He not know the quality of your heart?

The Mulla vainly fancies that God is deaf, unmindful of the fact that he is making himself deaf by shutting his ears with his fingers. The poet, Akbar Allahabadi, made fun of such a Mulla. Vainly does the Mulla imagine that loudly calling upon God is indispensable for rousing people from their dogmatic slumber. Does not the steam-engine, he asks, whistle regularly and at the appointed hour, so that people who want to get up for meditation might do so by hearing the whistle? The Sheikh, says the poet, beats his breast because his vocation was now gone. The whistle of the steam-engine is regular, fearless, and powerful, and that should be enough to rouse people from their slumbers to their spiritual duty. There may be other ways of rousing a man from his slumbers. In that way, a braying ass would be better than a Brahman, a barking dog better than an image of God, and a crowing cock better than a Mulla.

5. *The Mental requisites* — Let us now proceed to see what the mental requisites for a successful spiritual meditation are. Kabir tells us humorously that when an aspirant is sitting up for meditation, his tongue is moving in his mouth, his hand is moving on the rosary, and his mind is moving in all the ten directions. This is only pseudo-meditation, says Kabir.

The Bhagavadgita has told :

कर्मेन्द्रियाणि संयम्य य आस्ते मनसा स्मरन् ।
इन्द्रियार्थान् विमूढात्मा मिथ्याचारः स उच्यते ॥

One might control one's motor organs, says the Bhagavadgita, and yet think of objects of desire; such a person is a man of false character. To think of a bad thing mentally is itself bad, according to the Bhagvadgita, even though the motor organs may not move to achieve their object. Elsewhere, Kabir has excused the motions of the mind, but has principally focussed his attention on the motor organs :

मन गया तो जाने दो, मत जाने दो शरीर.

These must not be allowed to go astray as the cattle do. A bad idea occurring to the mind does not necessarily make a man a bad character, says Kabir; but an evil action certainly does.

We are next told that a Sadhak must have his mind fully concentrated upon the Object of his meditation. Rahim advises the aspirant always to look at God intently, as a Chakor looks at the moon.

It may be noted that Rahim is speaking here about Krishna-chandra. He also speaks of the Chakor looking at the moon both by night and by day. It may be possible for the Chakor to look at the moon by night if the moon is shining; but its looking at the moon by day must be a case of mere mental imagery.

Basaveshvar, the founder-saint of Lingayatism, has given expression to the same idea in a very famous verse :

चकोरंगे चन्द्रमन बेळगिन चिंते
अंबुजके भानुविन उदयद चिंते ।
भ्रमरंगे परिमळद वंडुंव चिंते
एनगे नम्म कूडलसंगम देवर नेनेव चिंते ॥

"Just as the one object of the anxiety of the Chakor is the light of the moon; just as the one object of the anxiety of the lotus is the rise of the Sun; just as the one object of the anxiety of the bee is the juice in a fragrant flower; similarly my one object of anxiety', says Basaveshvar, 'is the remembrance of my God, the कूडलसंगमदेव ".

A third mental requirement for successful meditation is the occupation of the mind by only one idea and no other. When the eye is full of the vision of the only one object of our love, says Rahim, no other vision is possible. When the mind is filled with one idea, no other idea dare enter. This is the chief aim an aspirant must always keep in view. Analogies for this description are to be found in a caravansarai which is full of pilgrims not allowing any other pilgrims to enter, a railway carriage full of passengers not allowing any new passenger to get in, and a cinema-house which is full of spectators refusing to admit any further spectator. The seeker, likewise, must therefore refuse to admit within his mind any idea except that of God. It is only when such a thing takes place, that spiritual concentration becomes fruitful. A psychological help that may be offered in this connection is to draw the mind continually from the periphery towards the centre, until it becomes firmly established in the focus of consciousness.

6. *The moral requisites* — As mental concentration is the 'sine quâ non' of a successful meditation, moral qualities are equally, if not more, necessary. In the first place, the aspirant must

make an active search for the Object of his realisation : no inaction would do, no indifference, no mental complacency to allow things to come their own way, and in their own time.

The Doha जिन खोजा तिन पाइयाँ tells us that it is only those who seek, to them comes the reward of their effort. The door shall not open unless you knock it. नायमात्मा बलहीनेन लभ्यः, says the Upanishad. Those who want to take out pearls from the bottom of the sea must make a desperate dive down the waters of the sea.

In a similar style, we learn from the Gujarathi poet, Pritam (or Priyatam) हरि नो मारग छे शूरानो नहि कायरनु काम जोने, that the way of God is the way of the brave; cowards have no place in it. Those, who can afford to dive deep into the bosom of the sea, can alone come out with hands full of pearls; those who stand on the shore will be rewarded only by receiving the shells. Unless, therefore, we make an active effort for the realisation of our ideal, it will continually fly from us like an ignis-fatuus.

Another virtue which a seeker must possess is that he must not care for the derision of the world. In the Doha रकीबोने लिखाई हैं रपटें, we have a sarcasm on the practice of the world to pooh-pooh religion, and religious meditation.

The poet, Akbar Allahabadi, tells us how in his days the C. I. D. reporters used to frequent the 'thana' and report the names of God-meditators. In this age of civilization and culture, what place is there, he asks ironically, for those who meditate on God? This is indeed, he says, atheistic government, with a vengeance. Did not Cromwell in his days decry George Fox, the founder of the Society of Quakers, for having seen Inner light?

The next virtue which the seeker must possess is meditation on God in all mental conditions whatsoever. Tulsidas tells us that we should utter the name of God under all circumstances. The seed takes root whether it faces upwards or downwards. We must not mind whether we utter the name of God with pleasure or displeasure, रीझ भजो या खीज, in happiness or in grief.

Further, we learn from Tulsidas in a very famous passage भाव कुभाव अनख आलसहुं, that belief, unbelief, sloth and even malignity do not matter. Shankar uttered the name of God with full faith; Valmiki, when he began his spiritual career, uttered the name with irradiated faith. The utterance of the name of God was to him a sort of an un-understanding reflex action, tantamount to disbelief. We may compare the line आ मरा ई मरा in a famous song by Purandardas. Kumbhakarna uttered the name of God in sloth, and Ravana with malignity, and yet in all these cases, says Tulsidas, there was an upshot of auspiciousness. Good actions are recorded in the brain, if not in a heavenly register, and in due time they get the full value for their desert. Students of Indian Rhetoric will see in this Doha an excellent illustration of the combination of यथासङ्ख्य and अर्थान्तरन्यास.

The last moral virtue which we gather from the Dohas as essential to spiritual life is from the poet, Rahim, who tells us that the way of egoism is not the way of God. To imitate Prof. James' manner of expression, we might say, Egoism or God, choose! It would be easier for a camel to enter the hole of a needle than for the tall-talker to enter the kindgom of God.

Love and sense of honour, says another Doha, do not go together. The same scabbard cannot hold two scimitars. Unless, therefore, we bid goodbye to all sense of egoism, we cannot prosper in the spiritual life.

To summarise our discussion of the moral virtues essential for spiritual realisation, we might say that the spiritual seeker must have the following virtues. He must make an active effort for the achievement of his ideal; he must not care for the derision of the world; he should utter the name of God with pleasure or displeasure, faith or misfaith, sloth or even malignity. Finally, he must bid good-bye to all sense of self-importance which is often too subtle even for those who are given to heart-searching.

7. *The mystical requisites* — Let us now see what may be regarded as the mystical requisites for the process of full self-realisation. Kabir tells us in a famous Doha that his process of contemplation was concerned not so much with Bhakti or Jnana, but with Dhyana. Bhakti may enable one to attain to the सगुण, and ज्ञान to the निर्गुण, but it is ध्यान alone, says Kabir, which may enable one to attain to the Reality, which is beyond both Saguna and Nirguna. It may be noticed that Kabir has no difficulty in using the word 'Sarguna' to contrast it with Nirguna, as Jnaneshwar has none is using the words सन्मुख and विन्मुख.

Continuing the same idea, Kabir tells us in another Doha, which later became the foundation of the Radhaswami-Mata that the धारा is to be inverted, and then the process of contemplation effected.

The Doha कबिरा धारा अगम की has brought forth a number of interpretations and suggestions. To begin with the Radhaswami-Mata, they tell us that Kabir prophetically announced the coming of the first teacher, Radhaswami, in this important Doha. Put this Dhārā in a reverse order, append to it the word Soami which is a colloquial form of the word Swami, and the whole Mantra Radhaswami is ready, which is the foundation of their spiritual meditation.

It is contended that this Radhaswami-Mata

has got nothing to do with Krishna and Radha as we understand them traditionally. This seems to be a subterfuge by means of which the connection of the Mata with Radha and Krishna is intended to be avoided, but the fundamental fact remains that the founder and his wife were worshipped as Krishna and Radha.

Three other interpretations may be offered instead of this. अगम, the Incomprehensible Reality, sends down a stream; turn it upside down and meditate in the presence of the Lord, स्वामी को साथी बनाकर. Now what is this stream? One explanation is that it may be regarded as equivalent to breath. Turn the breath upside down – उलटाकर – and meditate on God with its help.

A second interpretation is that Dhārā might be taken as the stream of light which the teacher shows to his disciple. Turn your mind away from sense, and meditate by means of that stream of illumination, by taking help of the presence of the Lord. A modern spiritual poet of Marathi has said: विषयापासुनि वळता वृत्ती । सहजचि येइल आत्म्यावरती । जैसा निश्चल दीप निवांती । समाधी पावे ॥

A third interpretation might also be offered. Dhārā might be regarded as a stream of spiritual energy which has emanated from the God-head; turn the current back to its source, and meditate in the presence of the Lord. In any case, the fundamental thing to be noted is the "Swami."

Breathe your Mantra in and out in the presence of the Lord.

Bahiro has told us elsewhere that the process of contemplation would not be finalised until it is done in the presence of the Lord : सन्मुख साँवरा खड़ा हो.

Meditation on God in his presence and meditation on God without his presence may well be related to each other in Spinozistic terminology as God and Dog,– the same alphabets no doubt; but what a difference !

Another way of comtemplation on Ultimate Reality is supplied by the presence of the Anāhata sound instead of the form of God. Your spiritual teacher might be staying millions of miles away, says Kabir, and yet you can send your Self as a messenger on the तुरङ्गम of Shabda, or on Shabda as experienced in the तुरीय state; and as the speed of the Anāhata Shabda or spirit would far exceed that of any entity known to science such as light or electricity, contact would be established between yourself and the Guru, and for the matter of that, between yourself and God, within the twinkling of an eye-lash. In any case, the presence of the Anāhata sound here is just as helpful as the presence of the form of God in the preceding Doha.

This process of carrying on our spiritual contemplation in the presence of the Anāhata sound may be contrasted with that carried on by mere breath. While the latter is pre-realisational, the former is post-realisational. The great Shankaracharya gave them their proper place in the scheme of realisation when he said:

नादानुसन्धान ! नमोऽस्तु तुभ्यं
त्वां साधनं तत्त्वपदस्य जाने।
भवत्प्रसादात् पवनेन साकं
विलीयते विष्णुपदे मनो मे ॥

8. *A devotee's passionate longing for God* — We have discussed hitherto all the main stages of the spiritual pilgrimage – initiation by the Guru, meditation by means of the Name, and the physical, mental, moral and mystical requirements for a life of complete realisation. The crowning piece of the performance, however, is the passionate longing of the aspirant for the realisation of God. It is this inner urge, this one-pointed and passionate search, this life of consecration to the ideal, which crowns the efforts of man for the attainment of God.

Rahim tells us that the devotee must pant for God like a fish out of waters. 'When thou art dried up, Oh Lake!' says the fish, 'the birds and swans can take resort elsewhere; but pinionless as I am, where shall I, whose life is entwined with yours, go to seek resort? In the very process of my search would lie the termination of my endeavour. If that contingency happens, my only fate will be to be dried up along with thee, Oh my habitat!'

In another Doha, we have the heartfelt prayer of a sinking pilgrim in a boat to the all-powerful God: 'My boat is fiilled to the brim by flood-water. In addition, a fierce gale is blowing past. Cast thy gracious glance on me, O Raghuvir, and take me to the other shore of existence.' It is only in such a helpless state of existence that the passionate appeal of the devotee is likely to be heard by God.

We have discussed above two analogies, one of the pinionless fish and the other of the sinking pilgrim, for the prayerful attitude towards God. We shall proceed now to the final analogy on this head, namely, that of a Chātaka. The thirty-four verses which have been written by Tulsidas, entitled the चातकचौंतीसा, are exceedingly symbolical, allegorical, and pathetic. Tulsidas regards himself as a Chātaka par excellence. To him, the Chātaka is a typical embodiment of अनन्यभक्ति, the one-pointed devotion of the aspirant for the attainment of God.

Tulsidas probably regarded this spring of devotion as innate in the devotee. Tukaram regards it, in Alexandrian terminology, as emergent. If a man does not possess it by birth, he may come to acquire it by a life of prolonged moral travail, and then he may be able to realise God: होईल सद्‌भक्ति येणें पंथे । सद्‌भक्ति झालिया सहज साक्षात्कार.

We are not concerned here with the philosophical aspect of the innate or the emergent character of Bhakti. We only want to discuss the type of अनन्यभक्ति of which Tulsidas is speaking. He sets the scene of his appeal, we may say, almost on the meteorological level. The Chataka's one aim is to turn its eyes longingly towards the cloud; but the cloud may easily be accompanied by such destructive phenomena, as lightning, thunder, hailstorm and even a thunder-bolt.

Tulsidas takes advantage of such a meteorological scene to describe the extraordinary devotion of the Chataka for the cloud. The घनश्याम to the Chataka is the 'one belief, one power, one hope':

एक भरोसो एक बल एक आस विश्वास.

"Even if the wings of the Chātaka", says Tulsidas, "be reduced to bits by the falling hail, it will continue to look longingly at the cloud of mercy. Even if the cloud (the उपल of निरक्त) may rumble fiercely, and send down a merciless thunderbolt, will the Chātaka have any other object for its adoration than the cloud itself? Even if the Chātaka were to fall into the holy waters of the Ganges, being shot by the arrow of a huntsman, it will not allow its beak to be contaminated by the holy waters, but will turn it upward to the Cloud of Mercy and give up the ghost. It will never allow its garment of devotion to be even slightly scratched." It would be impossible to add a hue to the rainbow!*

*This Chapter appeared in the two issues of the Leader dated 14th and 21st October 1951.

CHAPTER V

The Highest Ascent

In our last chapter, we have seen the beginnings of the meditational process, which must be crowned by the perfection of mystical experience. This constitutes the highest ascent of man towards the life Divine. We shall begin the chapter by pointing out the chief psychological characteristics of mystical experience, and then go on to the different varieties of supersensuous experience of which the Dohas speak. Of course, these kinds of supersensuous experience are stressed, wherever and in whatever form of literature an attempt is made to climb the ascent. In the Dohas we find in an inexplicable and cryptic form, and at the same time very accurately, all the stages or rungs of the spiritual ladder, which have been spoken of in other Provincial Literatures of India, and which might, therefore, be regarded as the distinct contribution of the Dohas to the psychology of mystical experience. The first thing stressed in the Dohas is the Anāhata sound, the consequent music, and the necessity of coming into contact with the Musician who produces the music. Then, we shall go on to a short philosophical consideration of the nature of Anāhata Shabda, and see how this is accomplished in a supersensuous fashion. Next, we shall proceed to visual experience both morphic and photic, which characterises the rising saint, and then to other supersensuous experiences, such as the spiritual bath, and the spiritual juice and fragrance, about which the Dohas speak. After this, comes the problem of self-realisation. Of course, it cannot be maintained that the Dohas do full justice to such an important subject, but there are definite illustrations in the description of the Dohas, which point to analogies in more developed literatures in connection with the subject of Self-realisation. Then, there are Dohas which contain the description of motor and tactual experiences, which form an important development of one chief form of self-realisation. In order to attain such spiritual heights, however, a great travail has to be experienced. This we might call the travail of unison. The dangers we have to meet, the temptations we have to face, the calamities we have to suffer, all these constitute the travail, through which we must pass before we attain to the crown of spiritual experience. When such a state has been reached, then there are certain marks, especially the moral marks, of God-realisation, by which we may discriminate the highly developed Saint from others. Finally, we shall go on to the doctrines of liberation, beatification, and infinitude which we meet with in the Dohas.

1. *The Psychology of Spiritual Experience* — Let us begin by considering the psychological characteristics of mystical experience. In the first place, we have to remember that this mystical experience is a matter of intuition. It is neither instinct, nor mere perception, nor intelligence, nor understanding. Of course, we cannot enter here into the relation of intuition to other psychological processes, but may point out that intuition possesses the directness of perception, while intelligence warps and distorts, and, in the language of the Dohas, produces an opacity in spiritual vision. After considering the relation of intuition and intellect, therefore, we shall pass on to the supersensuous character of the spiritual experience. Next, we shall proceed to the unity of spiritual experience, which binds and brings together all those who possess a common mystical experience, and makes them recognise each other. Finally, we shall consider the somewhat difficult problem of the inter-incommunicativeness of the sense organs from the point of view of ordinary psychology, and their inter-communicativeness in mystical experience through the unity of apperception.

In the Doha, लिखापढी की बात नहि, we are pointed to a distinction between understanding and intuition, and have been told that it is only the intuition, which, in Bergsonian fashion, leads us directly to real experience. By a sort of Nigarana

Alankara, the Doha tells us that all ceremonial functions come to an end when the bride and the bridegroom have met, which implies that all our formalistic religion would cease, as soon as there comes about the unison between Self and God. The bride and the bridegroom signify not merely themselves, but, on the mystical level, the Jivatman and the Parmatman. All the travail that has been undertaken for their meeting has accomplished its 'raison d'etre' and, therefore, comes to an end. In the same way, Tulsidas tells us that intellect produces an opacity in human beings, तुलसी या संसार को भयो मोतियाबिन्द. Things which are near cannot be seen by a man having a cataract. Similarly, from the intuitional point of view things are so clear, that, by arguing from the point of view of intellect, we can never understand their real nature. The same idea is expressed very finely by Ramdas :

देव जवळीं अंतरीं । भेटी नाहीं जन्मवरी
मूर्ति त्रैलोकीं संचली । दृष्टि विश्वाची चुकली

which tells us that the form of God is near us and inside us, and yet we are unable to see God in our entire life. His form lies pervading the entire universe, but the vision of the seer is warped, and he is not able to see it. In a celebrated Doha, again, we are told by Surdas about his own physical and mystical condition. Blind Surdas was being led by God in the form of a young boy by the hand. When Surdas had gone to the middle of his way, the boy left off the hand of Surdas, and blind Surdas was compelled to manage as best he could. Surdas addresses God by saying that he could very well leave his hand, but not his heart. This means that the supersensuous presence of God is superior to his sensous manifestation. The opening stanza of the Sursagar tells us that the blind man may come to possess the power to see all things by the grace of God : अन्धे कू सवकछु दरसाई : which implies that the heart may, by the grace of God, be the seat of all supersensuous experiences, and that, therefore, God may be found more in the heart, than in the outside world. The fourth mystical characteristic is the unity, which lies behind similar experiences of mystics. It has been said that an aspirant who is able to hear the Anahat Sound is able also to detect the signs of it in another. The Anahat sound must express itself in physiological terms, and this characteristic enables the man, who hears the Anahat sound, to detect its audition in another mystical seeker. From this point of view, we may be enabled also to interpret the unity of God from the one finger which Ramkrishna Paramahansa pointed towards the heavens, implying that the One only exists, namely God. This unity of spiritual experience cannot be accounted for, except by supposing that the same 'homo-ousion', the same spiritual entity, underlies the experience of all similar aspirants.

The last point in the psychology of mystical experience we want to discuss is the inter-communicativeness of sense functions through the unity of apperception. From the point of view of ordinary psychology, each sense is opaque to the other, each is unique, independent, 'sui generis', and non-communicative with other senses. This position is reversed, as we shall see, in the case of super-sensuous experience, where an inter-communication can take place between different sense functions through the unity of apperception. We have illustrations of this in such expressions as नयन को लगी प्यास and बानी फूटी बास, which occur in the Dohas. The Doha from Kabir, जो देखे सो कहै नहिं, expresses, only in terms of ordinary psychology, the non-communicativeness of senses with each other. How shall we, then, explain the inter-communicativeness of sense functions in super-sensuous experience ?

The present writer was conversant, for a number of years, with a story, which used to be narrated by the saint of Nimbargi about Kabir, the origin of which in the Dohas he was not able to trace till 1946. All of a sudden, when he was hearing a Doha from Kabir, जो देखे सो कहै नहिं, while he was proceeding in a motor car, a new light dawned upon him, and he saw in the Doha the foundation of the story he had heard. Kabir, so the story ran, was once a witness in a murder case, where he had seen the husband committing the murder of his unchaste wife. The husband pleaded to Kabir that as he was not entirely unjustified in his act, he may be pleased to help him in the matter. How was Kabir going to do that without telling an untruth ? Kabir was called in the witness box to give evidence in regard to his having seen the murder. Kabir thought that the murderer might be saved, in view of the unchastity of his wife, without his telling an untruth. As soon as Kabir was brought into the court and made to stand before the judge, Kabir turned his face away from the judge, and began to see in the direction in which God was appearing to him. Then the judge said " Why is he looking in that direction? Turn his face towards me." Accordingly, Kabir's face was turned towards the judge. Then the judge asked him the questions whether he had seen the murder, or had heard any authentic report about it. Kabir then uttered the following Doha :

जो देखे सो कहै नहि, कहै सो देखे नाहि ।
सुनै सो समझावै नहीं, रसना दृगश्रुतिकाहि ॥

" He who sees is not able to speak, he who speaks is not able to see; he who hears is not able to make others understand. Vision, audition, and speech are all independent in their own spheres." Kabir pulled out his tongue, and asked " is this able to see ? " Kabir forcibly expanded his eyes by his fingers, and asked "are these able to speak?" He pulled his ears, and asked "will these make you understand?" Hearing this very strange answer from Kabir, the judge remarked that a mad man had been brought to give evidence before him, and thus he dismissed the case, as Kabir was the only witness.

From the point of view of ordinary psychology, it would be a truism to say that he who is able to see is unable to speak, he who is able to say is unable to see. Each organ is independent in its sphere. Each is unique, and each is opaque to the other. From the point of view of supersensuous experience, however, all these functions are related to the unity of apperception. It is not the eye that sees, says an Upanishad, but the self; it is not the ear that hears, but the self. There is an inter-communicativeness in supersensuous functions, which is denied in the sensuous sphere. This exchange takes place on account of the unity of apperception, which lies at the back of all supersensuous functions, or, if we prefer to use a physiological expression, the 'apperception-masse', which may be regarded as responsible for vicarious functions in the supersensuous sphere. It was for this reason that we said above how the eyes of Kabir felt thirsty, and how his speech emitted fragrance. The saint of Umadi used to say that we should hear such news as would give us a sense of fragrance : सुगंध वार्ता कानीं पडो. Purandardas, a great Kannada saint, has also given us a classical Vachana, in which he speaks of the inter-change of physiological functions through the unity of apperception :

कण्णि केळुवलि किवियलि काम्बुव
नासिकदि कांवुव केळुव....लोक-विलक्षण
अप्राकृत-विग्रह्....पुरंदर विठल.

"My great God is absolutely लोक-विलक्षण and अप्राकृत-विग्रह" says Purandardas. "His body is not like the body of mortals, and all his functions are un-human. He hears by the eyes, and sees by the nose, and by the nose he is able both to see and hear. Divine ways are so much unlike human ways." We thus see how the unity of apperception might be responsible for vicarious supersensuous functions in mystical experience.

2. *The music and the Musician* — Let us now begin with the stress, which is laid in the Doha literature, on the significance of sound or Anahat, as a vehicle for God-realisation. The Dohas, which we shall consider, are :

(1) गुण इन्द्री सहजै गए
(2) हाड़ सूखि पिंजर भए,
(3) सब बाजे हिरदे बजैं.

There has been some discussion as to the difference between Anahat and Shabda, and it is supposed that Shabda is a higher entity than

Anahat. The parallel of Brahman and Ishwar may be quoted in this connection. Just, however, as there might ultimately be no distinction between Ishwar and Brahman, similarly also there might be no ultimate distinction between Anahat and Shabda. Kabir, particularly, is very fond of laying stress upon the Anahat Shabda, not merely as being the vehicle for God-realisation, but as being a substitute for Divinity itself. By collecting together all the different passages in the Dohas in regard to Anahat sound, we might come to four important conclusions. In the first place, we are told that the Anahat is resounding like a fundamental note from every pore of the body : रोम रोम सुर उटत है. The bones of the human body constitute the wooden frame of the Tanpura, and the nerves its wires or strings, and from this body, the Anahat shabda sounds forth like a fundamental note. In the second place, all the various musical instruments such as the drum, the guitar, and the flute are also heard in the process of meditation : सब बाजे....प्रेम पखावज तार says Kabir; विनि करताल पखावज वाजै, अणहृद कि झणकार रे says Mirabai. A Kannada poet has also said : घंटा किंकिणि नादं सिहं शङ्खं नादं, भेर्यादिक महानादं अनुभव मन लुब्धम्. By considering these passages, we can see that the various musical instruments which an aspirant hears heighten his devotion. Mirabai, especially, as we have already seen, stresses that she was able to hear all the 36 Ragas without the fundamental note : बिनि सुर राग छतीसूं गावै. In the third place, as a higher stage in this process of hearing the Anahat sound, the Name of God becomes audible to the aspirant. घटमे नाम प्रगट भया says one Doha, and बाजत नाम तिहार says another. Fourthly, not being satisfied with hearing merely the Name of God, a Doha tells us that the aspirant might be able to perceive the Musician behind the music. Where is now the necessity for going from temple to temple, asks the poet : मन्दिर ढूंढत को फिरै, मिल्यो बजावनहार ? We have been familiar with two other similar experiences which emerge from every pore of the aspirant's body. Mirabai tells us that through every pore gush forth varied colours : रोम रोम रंग सार रे. Through every pore of the aspirant's body shines forth a brilliant lamp says Kabir and the great and kind Lord manifests himself therein : रोम रोम दीपक भया, प्रगटे दीन दयाल. We thus see that the culmination of such processes as hearing the Anahat sound or seeing a brilliant light consists in experiencing the great God whose auricular and ocular manifestations they are.

3. *Shabda as 'Substance'* — It is in the same spirit that we are told by Kabir in the Doha अलख पुरुष निर्वाण है वाको लखै न कोय, that it is only when one's affection is centered on Shabda (सबद सनेही), that one is enabled to visualise the अलक्ष पुरुष. Kabir tells us that we cannot visualise this अलक्ष पुरुष unless

two conditions are fulfilled, जो उस घर का होय and तखत तरे का होय. This is as much as to say, that it is only when we are bound, on the one hand, with the Master of the house with ties as those of association, affection, and watchfulness and, on the other, with the ties of humility, secrecy and promptitude that we are able to see this अलख पुरुष. The expression तखत तरे का is a very significant one. It implies, in the first place, that the disciple must sit at the foot of his Master's couch, showing his deep obedience and watchfulness to the Master. In the same spirit, we are told by Bacon that Judges must be lions, but lions under the Throne. Also, if we understand the whole surface of the earth as the foot-stool of God, then the saint must sit beneath it in order to assimilate himself to his Master. In fact, a justification for an underground chamber as a place for meditation on God might come out of such an interpretation. The present writer must confess his gratitude to this Doha which came to him very significantly. On a पुण्यतिथि day of his Master, he was fortunate to have a dream-vision in which his Master was sitting alone to himself in an underground chamber, below the surface of the earth, with his entire mind and affection centered on Shabda (सबद सनेही), and his watchman, Pundappa, attending at the door. The present writer could not understand the significance of this vision until a couple of hours later, when two unknown persons from the Allahabad Cantonment came to him with the Doha :

घर का भया तो क्या भया, तखत तरे का होय ।
तखत तरे का सूरमा, सबद सनेही सोय ।'.

After carrying on a discussion about the meaning of the Doha with these gentlemen, the present writer was convinced that it was the literary and poetic form of the dream vision he had seen, thus giving strength as a third link in the chain of कीर्तन, गान and ध्यान processes, which are involved in enabling one to assimilate oneself to the Godhead. The upshot of the entire story is that unless our affection is centered on God, unless we carry on an intimate meditation by कीर्तन, गायन and ध्यान, we may not be able to rise to the full heights of spiritual experience.

We shall now go on to the final assessment of Shabda in philosophical terms which Kabir offers. In the two Dohas (1) सबद सबद का अन्तरा, and (2) मकडी चढ़ती तारसे, we are given the full philosophical function of Shabda. In the first place, we are told the Shabda is self-immanent सबद सबदका अन्तरा. In fact, it occupies the same position in Kabirite theology which Substance occupies in Spinoza's. The Shabda might veritably be compared to the substance of Spinoza, which 'is' in itself and can be 'conceived' by itself. In the same way, we are told by Kabir, that Shabda is the Lord of Shabda, a Being that draws all its power and strength from itself—सबद सबद का पीर, or सबद सबद का सीर. Thirdly, Shabda is the criterion of itself, or clue to itself. There is no outside criterion by which Shabda can be found—सबद सबद का खोजना. Finally, it is 'causa sui', it is its own cause, both material and instrumental. Like a Makaḍi, which sends forth its thread and absorbs it over again, Shabda sends out the universe and finally absorbs it inside itself. There is no maker of Shabda. It is a self-made and self-producing entity. A hammer, says Spinoza, can be produced only by a hammer. So Shabda can be produced only by itself. It is self-creating and self-absorbing : यथोर्णनाभिः सृजते गृह्णते च says the Upanishad. Shabda, like God, might thus be compared in an Arachnomorphic fashion with a great Spider, self-creating and self-absorbing. Then, finally, the only difference between the spider and the saint which we may conceive of is that while the spider ascends as well as descends by its thread, the saint can only go on continually ascending : सन्त चढ़त है शब्दसे, चढ़त चढ़त चढ़ जाय.

4. *Visual experience, Morphic and Photic*—We next proceed to visual experiences, both morphic and photic, enjoyed by the mystics. These may appear in the shape of some Form, which presents itself to the supersensuous vision of the seeker, or else, in the form of Light which dazzles the eye and the imagination. In the Doha हरि

दरिया सूभर भरा, we are told, by a sort of Mālā Rūpaka, that God is like a great sea, in which the saint is like a shell, and his spiritual experience is like a pearl. Now, this expression 'pearl' has been introduced in the Doha, not merely for the sake of analogy, but to designate a veritable spiritual form, which is experienced probably during the early stages of a man's spiritual career. Kabir has said elsewhere :

नजर न आवै आतम ज्योती । झिलमिल झिलमिल निशिदिन चमकै जैसा निर्मल मोती । तेल न बाती वुझ नहीं जाती । नहि जागत नहि सोती ॥

This experience of a pearl has been stressed by many Maharashtra and Kannada saints : कापसाचे गोळे फिरती पोकळीं । मोतीयाची जाळी विखुरतीं, says a Maharashtra saint. मुत्तु वंदिदे कोळ्ळीरण्णा । अदके एज्जिलल्लेनिल्ल बेलेयागदण्णा says a Kannada saint; purchase this spiritual pearl; no hole has been pierced in it, and yet it remains priceless; it is impossible to make out its value. The brilliance of this pearl may not be valued at the moment, nor the person who experiences the pearl be rated high, but the pearl and the pearl-experiencer have got a value elsewhere : चढै देसावर दीप. Just as a Prophet may not be honoured in his own time and country, so this pearl experiencer whose importance may not be understood at the moment, may be regarded as of high significance at other times and in other places.

We next pass on to two other Dohas :

(1) बूंद समानी बूंद में,

(2) सुन्न मण्डल में घर किया.

In regard to the first, it must be said at once that this Doha was not composed by Kabir, but has been founded upon one of his Dohas. The original Doha of Kabir runs as follows:

बूँद समाना समुद मे जाने सब कोइ ।
समुद समाना बूँद मे, जाने बिरला कोई ॥

Of course, there is some चमत्कृति in this Doha, implying the presence of the sea inside a drop. On the other hand, in the form in which the Doha stands before us, there would be a greater चमत्कृति, because in that case the बूंद coalesces with Shabda. Let us not be too harsh to the prayer of a seeker who demanded three things at once, meditation on God's name, vision of his form, and the experience of the Anahat sound (झिंगुर). Now, a question arises as to whether all these things are possible at once. Possibly, the limits of the psychological process of attention might forbid the simultaneity of these experiences. A question might arise as to how many things we can attend to at the same time. Probably, the answer would be that we can attend to only one thing at a time. On the other hand, there is nothing to prevent other things from coming within its orbit, and be members of the marginal consciousness. Seekers, however, always demand a simultaneous enjoyment of all forms of experience. In the Doha सुन्न मण्डल में घर किया, this promise seems to have been realised. It speaks of an enjoyment simultaneously of the experiences as indicated in the expressions :

बाजे शब्द रसाल, रोम रोम दीपक भया, प्रगटे दीन दयाल.

Of course, this is a consummation most devoutly to be wished. St. Paul was a fortunate man when, during the state of his conversion, a great column of light appeared to his vision on the way to Damascus, and words issued from that column, reprimanding Paul, and bringing him to a sense of responsibility : " Saul ! Saul ! Why persecutest thou me ? "

5. *Other supersensuous experiences*— After the morphic and photic experiences enjoyed by the mystics, let us pass on to other supersensuous experiences which fall to the share of the seeker : experiences such as those of the spiritual bath, juice, or fragrance. There are three Dohas relating to these three different experiences :

(1) गगन गरजि बरसे अमी,
(2) धरनी पलक परै नहिं
(3) पिञ्जर प्रेम प्रकासिया.

In the first Doha गगन गरजि बरसे अमी, we are told by Kabir how he experienced the phenomena of a spiritual thunder, a cloud, and the glitter of a lightning, how ambrosial rain began to fall, and how Kabir experienced a spiritual bath under that shower. These statements only imply, how, under the great power of the experiences of thunder and lightning, the whole body of the aspirant becomes metamorphosed, and lustre begins to shine on the surface of his body. This idea of Kabir is also expressed very finely by Dharamdas. We take the liberty of quoting these lines, because they serve as a full commentary on the statements of Kabir :

झरि लागै महलिया गगन घहराय
खन गरजै खन बिजली चमकै
लहर उठै सोभा बरनि न जाय
सुन्न महलमें अमृत बरसै
प्रेम आनंद व्है साधु नहाय.

These experiences, respectively of Kabir and Dharamdas, are supported by the great Maharashtra saint Jnaneshwar who tells us that this spiritual bath might appear either in the form of drops of perspiration through the pores of the body, or through the tears of joy which an aspirant might shed during the state of the experience which he is fortunate to enjoy. Jnaneshwar says,

शिवतला चन्द्रकरीं ! सोमकांत द्राव धरी
तैसिया स्वेदकणिका शरीरीं । दाटलिया.

Drops of perspiration emerge out of the pores of the aspirant's body, as the moon-stone might give out drops of water under the infiuence of the Moon. Also the saint is described by Jnaneshwar as shedding tears of joy with his eyes half shut : अर्धोन्मीलित डोळे । वर्षताति आनंदजळें.

As regards the experience of the spiritual juice, we have had very fine striking illustrations of that experience already in the two great songs of Kabir : (1) चुवत अमीरस, भरत ताल जहँ, (2) रस गगनगुफा में अजर झरै. These are microscopically related by Dharanidas in his fine Doha, धरनी पलक परै नहीं. Now this Doha could be interpreted in two ways. Dharani might be taken either as the name of the author of the Doha, or it may be taken to mean the earth. In either case, the total meaning of the Doha remains the same. The poet tells us that he is unable to close his eyes on account of their full occupation with the form of God, or otherwise the vision of the eyes does not fall upon the earth in view of its occupation with the form of God. "I have been continually drinking the ambrosial juice", says the poet, "and still my thirst remains unsatisfied". This also reminds us of another poem of Kabir in which he says : और पियन की आसा. As regards the experience of the spiritual fragrance, we are told in the Doha पिञ्जर प्रेम प्रकासिया, that when the body was filled with God-love, there was a great luminosity inside. The self enjoyed beatific sleep. The words that issued from the mouth were tinged with an aroma of fragrance : सुख करि सूती महल में, बानी फूटी बास. This Doha refers to the experience of the Samadhic state enjoyed by the Jivatman, where it is supposed to sleep in a chamber of glittering light, and to enjoy all forms of supersensuous experience. The श्वेताश्वतरोपनिषत् tells us that fragrance is one of the earliest stages of spiritual realisation :

गन्धः शुभो मूत्रपुरीषमल्पं योगप्रवृत्तिं प्रथमां वदन्ति.

The sweet spiritual fragrance that might emerge from the body of an aspirant is one of the earliest signs by which his spiritual progress might also be judged.

6. *Realisation of Self* — The question of self-realisation is tackled in the three Dohas :

(1) सुन्न सहज मन सुमिरते,
(2) हृदया भीतर आरसी,
(3) लागी लागी सब कहें,

from which we may understand how the Doha conception of self-realisation is almost a replica of the Upanishadic conception. In the first Doha, we are told that when the mind becomes devoid of all ideas, we begin to think about God and meditate on his Name. While meditating, a flame appears before us in which a person is seen to whom the Doha asks us to make an oblation of our mind and body. This person is also described in the Doha as the supportless support of all (निरालम्ब जो होत). This vision of the flame, and the perception of God inside, is most classically expounded in that passage of the Upanishad where we are told अस्माच्छरीरात् समुत्थाय परं ज्योतिरुपसम्पद्य स्वेन रूपेणाभिनिष्पद्यते सोऽयमात्मा. This same idea of the vision of the Self in the light, which one sees in such a process of meditation, is expounded in the Doha which follows, namely, हृदया भीतर आरसी, and which may be regarded as a very fundamental Doha which explains the nature of Self-realisation. "Inside our heart there is a mirror, but we are unable to see our face in it. It is only when our sense of duality comes to an end, that we are able to see our face inside the mirror." This is exactly what the Bhagavadgita means in its description of Self-realisation, यत्र चैवात्मनाऽऽत्मानं पश्यन्नात्मनि तुष्यति, and also what Patanjali means by the classical Sutra, तदा द्रष्टुः स्वरूपेऽवस्थानम्. This process of mirroring (आरसी) or transparency (आरपार) is expressed fundamentally in certain classical passages, which it will not be out of place to quote here, in order to throw some light on this conception. In the first place, we are already conversant with the idea in Kabir which tells us that the Nirākāra is reflected in the Sadhu : निराकार की आरसी. The Sadhu serves as a mirror in which one can see the reflection of the Nirākāra or the formless God. Secondly, we have a famous passage in Jnaneshwar which tells us : ज्ञानदेव चक्रपाणी ऐसे। दोनी डोळस आरिसे। परस्परें पाहतां कैसे। मुकले भेदा, from which we gather that Saint and God serve as mirrors to each other, who reflect each other ad infinitum, and when they see each other, each of them sees his reflection in the other, and so the difference between thetwo vanish es. In the third place, and this is the most important of all, the Saint sees himself as reflected in the mirror of his own heart, which is the purport of the Doha we are considering : हृदया भीतर आरसी, मुख तो देखे नाहिं. In an exactly similar manner Jnaneshwar has told us :

नुसधें मुख जैसें, देखिजतसें दर्पणमिसें ।
वायाचि देखणें ऐसें, गमों लागें ॥.

There is no value in seeing our reflection in an ordinary mirror, says Jnaneshwar; on the other hand, when we are able to see the reflection of ourselves in the mirror of our own heart, we can be said to have approximated to the Godhead.

Another Doha, expressed almost in terms of Sāmkhya philosophy, and bearing on the doctrine of Self-realisation is the important Doha, पिया को हेरन में गई. In this Doha the authoress tells us that she went out to discover the Lord, but while she was doing this, she was herself discovered. She did not recognise her Lord, and her Lord entered into her, and became immanent in her. Now, the first line of this Doha tells us, almost in terms of Sāmkhya Philosophy, how प्रकृति would dance before her Lord, and wield power so long as she is not seen. But as soon as she is seen, she retires from the stage, and disappears. The word हेराय, which the Doha uses in this connection, contains a very wonderful combination of two senses : she was seen, and she was lost. This is exactly what happens to the प्रकृति

in Sāmkhya Philosophy. The प्रकृति ceases to exist as soon as she is discovered. Archimedes was filled with joy when he had discovered the law of specific gravity while taking his bath, and went out naked in the streets, saying "Eureka, Eureka: I have discovered, I have discovered", but people told him that instead of his discovering any law, they had discovered him. The same thing happens to the प्रकृति also. She goes out to discover her Lord, but, when she is discovered, she is lost. The second line of the above Doha is couched in Vedantic terms. When प्रकृति went about to see her Lord, the Lord himself entered the प्रकृति, and became fully immanent in her. In any case, the Doha is a good accompaniment, from the point of view of the relationship between प्रकृति and पुरुष, to the doctrine of Self-realisation, and being couched whether in Sāmkhya or Vedantic terms, points to the pervasiveness of the Lord everywhere, including the seeker who seeks.

7. *Motor and Tactual experience* — After discussing the doctrine of Self-realisation, let us now proceed to the motor and tactual experiences of the mystics about which the Dohas speak. The Doha मनुवा मेरो मरि गयो, tells us how, when Kabir's mind had almost ceased to exist, and his body had become weak and emaciated, God followed Kabir as Kabir was walking alone. God called out

'Kabir, Kabir', but Kabir would not listen, and moved on. Now, this is a kind of reference about which a good deal of information is to be found in Maharashtra and Kannada saints, as well as in the Upanishads. Kabir saw God following him. In the same manner, we are told by Tukaram that God was running after him while he was walking along : धावत चालती मागें मागें. As against this, we understand from Jnaneshwar that God went ahead of him, like a torch-bearer, with a torch in his hand : तया तत्त्वज्ञान चोखटा, दिवि पोतासाची सुभटा । मग मीचि होऊन दिवटा, पुढा पुढा चाले. Also, we understand from Jnaneshwar that when God showed his cosmic vision to Arjuna, Arjuna could see God both behind and before him : पाठीं तिये साद्यन्तें, न्याहाळीं श्रीमूर्तितें । आणि पुढती ह्मणे नमस्ते । नमस्ते प्रभो ॥ Then again, we understand from Tukaram that he saw God whirling round him in a circle : तुका ह्मणे वेगळा नव्हे । हरि हा भोवे भोंवताला. References in the Upanishads are not wanting to prove other motor relationships of God to Saints : आसीनो दूरं व्रजति शयानो याति सर्वतः, sitting he moves far off, sleeping he moves in all directions. Finally, Tukaram's famous Abhanga निजल्यानें गातां उभा नारायण in this connection, is paralleled by two Vachanas from the Kannada saints, Purandardas and Jagannathdas, मलगि पाडिदरे कुळितु केळुव, and मलगि परमादरदि पाडलु कुळितु केळुव, कुळितु पाडलु निलुव, all of which point to the motor relationship of God to Saints.

After the motor experiences we come to the

tactual experiences of saints and God. Great mystics have spoken about three such relationships, दर्शन, स्पर्शन and संभाषण, the present one being the second in the list, namely, स्पर्शन. We are told by Kabir that he was fortunate to have only a fragment of God's experience, कबिरा देखा एक अंग, and yet the importance of it was so great that his words failed him for adequate description. I touched the great God, who was full of lustre, and he became immanent in my eyes. Now, this Doha gives us the tactual experience of Kabir about God, but we must remember, at the same time, that according to Kabir it is only a fragment of divine experience. Newton, after spending his entire life in discovering the law of gravitation, said ultimately that he had found only a few pebbles on the shore of time; even so Kabir speaks of his having been fortunate to get only a fragment of divine experience. We must, however, remember that Kabir touched God, which is not a fragment. God remained pervading his vision, which is not a fraction. The fragment and the fraction are merely expressions of Kabir's great humility.

We have got another Doha which tells us more definitely about the tactual experience of Saints about God. In the Doha सुरत उड़ानी गगन को, the author tells us that his mind flew to the topmost part of his body, namely, the lateral ventricle in the brain, and there he came into contact with the feet of the Lord. This kind of experience is paralleled by what we have already spoken about Kabir having a similar spiritual experience, namely when he speaks of दसवें द्वारे ताली लागी, अलख पुरुष जाको ध्यान धरै. The same kind of experience has been expressed by the Kannada poet, Vijayadāsa, in his famous poem अंतरंगद कदवु तेरेयितिदु. There is, however, another interpretation of the Doha which is possible. The Saint having taken recourse to the feet of the Lord upon the ground, went up and saw His face aloft with joy, to which there was no parallel. This experience is supported by the utterance of Tukaram in his famous verse जोडोनियां कर, मुख पहा सादर । पायावरी शिर, ठेवोनियां. With his hands folded and with his body bent upon the feet of the Lord, he looked up and saw the face of God with joy and reverence. In any case, what we are concerned with in the present Doha is the tactual experience of the saint about God. The saint is not satisfied with having merely a vision of God. The Darshana is not enough, he must have स्पर्शन and संभाषण if possible,—things which seem almost to be beyond the limits of attainable experience.

8. *The travail of Unison* — The travail of experience in preparing for the vision of God is nowhere better expressed than in the Doha of Mansur, बड़ा लुत्फ़ है यार इश्कमें, when he tells us that while

experiencing excruciating pain on the stake to which he was fastened, he was also fortunate to have a vision of God. In fact, excruciating pain, in his case, seemed to be the price that he had to pay for that vision. We understand from his poem that his Teacher taught him to say हुकुम है शाह कलंदर का, अनलहक़ तू कहाता जा. Now, orthodox Islam, which maintains an unbridgeable distinction between self and God, cannot tolerate this expression of the unity between the two. It was for this reason that the Muslims wanted to put Mansur to the agony of death. While he was at the stake, he had the vision of God in the midst of his agony. After death his bones began to resound with the words अनलहक़, अनलहक़. Ghalib, the great Urdu poet, has said in his commenting remarks, that Mansur should not have delivered himself over to such a belief in the identity of Self and God. Ghalib calls अनलहक़ a phrase of arrogance. Mansur may have reached a state of unity, said Ghalib, but he should not have expressed that unity by word of mouth. Mansur, in short, left off his humility. Identity, said Ghalib, should be a matter of experience, and not of expression. We can recall to mind what Tulsidas said about the question of the supremacy between Nama and Rupa. A philosopher knows in his heart which of them is superior, but if he is asked the question about superiority, he sits 'mum'. Even so, said Ghalib, Mansur should have desisted from proclaiming his identity with God. Hence Sufism, which posited this identity, was not regarded as an organic part of Islam, but only as a tangential doctrine, and hence the Sufis had to suffer at the hands of orthodox Muslims. Mansur's death at the stake recalls to our mind how, under similar circumstances, Socrates met his death by drinking the cup of Hemlock, Christ ascended the Cross, Cranmer was burnt at the stake, and Guru Arjuna was boiled in a cauldron – a fate which reminds us of the most ferocious atrocities that were committed by the Nazis on their war-prisoners. In any case, the fate of all these religious martyrs tells us that the path to God is not an easy one, and that the highest tortures have to be experienced before we attain to the Godhead.

9. *The moral marks of the God-realiser*—When we have attained to God through suffering and through the various stages of mystical experience, there are certain marks by which a God-realiser may be recognised. It is not merely by his own mystical achievement that a man may be useful to society, but by his consequent moral characteristics. In fact, he may have attained to the Godhead, but, for all practical purposes the world knows him by his moral marks. What are the chief marks by which such a God-realiser may be known? By putting together all the different

concepts from the Dohas, we may arrive at the following five-fold scheme of moral characteristics, which single out the God-realiser from others :

(1) Epoche,
(2) Humility,
(3) Equanimity,
(4) Self-surrender, and
(5) Altruism.

Let us consider these characteristics in order.

(1) As regards the first virtue, namely, epoche, we have two very good Dohas :

(1) रहिमन बात अगम्य की,

and

(2) कबिरा जब हम गावते,

which tell us how the greatest virtue of a mystic is silence. Rahim tells us in the spirit of Augustine's 'Ignorando cognosci, Cognoscendo ignorari,' that those who know do not speak, and those who speak do not know. Mahatma Gandhi once said, after his return from South Africa in 1914, that he was advised by his teacher, the Hon'ble Mr. G. K. Gokhale, to keep his eyes and ears open, and shut his lips. The केनोपनिषद् tells us likewise : अविज्ञातं विजानताम् । विज्ञातमविजानताम् ; those who say they know do not know; those who say they do not know may alone be credited with knowledge. The great sage, Nārada, has also told us in his Bhakti-Sutra स्तब्धो भवति, मत्तो भवति, आत्मारामो भवति, that the perfected Saint remains silent and merged in God;

he remains absolutely mute and dumb, enjoying all the while the vision and the presence of God. In the second Doha of Kabir, we are told that when Kabir sings, God is not; and God is, when Kabir sings not. This may be true so far as a man's heart may be centered on the art of singing as a suitable approach to God, but when his singing comes reflexly and automatically, as a result of his great concentration and feeling of devotion, that criterion may not hold. In that case, we may say that the pitch and power of the singing may be even regarded as an index to his own concentration and realisation.

(2) The second characteristic of a God-realiser is his great humility : बडे बड़ाई ना करें. Those who are great never talk in big terms. When does a diamond say that its price is a 1000 pounds ? Unconscious virtue has been regarded by Carlyle as the highest characteristic of his hero. The present writer has also said in his Essay on "Meditations on a Fire-fly" that the fire-fly is entirely unconscious of its light which is behind it, and which it sheds for the sake of others, and not for itself. It is this great humility and unconsciousness of one's own powers, that constitute another mark of God-realisation. Closely connected with this conception of the unconsciousness of a diamond, is another mark of it which Kabir enjoins on the God-realiser: हीरा तहाँ न खोलिये ; mystical experience is not to be

narrated to everybody. We should not open out our diamond before a vegetable-seller. Prudence thus becomes the chief mark for those who have walked on the path of God. We are told in the Doha :

रतन भरी कोठरी बार बार मत खोल ।
जब मिलेगा जौहरी तभी चढेगा मोल ।।

A room may be full of diamonds, but the owner must not open it from time to time. It is only when a great jeweller comes, that the value of the jewels may come to light.

(3) The third characteristic of the God-realiser is his great equanimity. He stands in the market-place, like Socrates, without any partiality for anybody : दोनो दीन कि खैर. He has neither friends nor foes :

सुहृन्मित्रार्युदासीनमध्यस्थद्वेष्यबंधुषु ।
साधुष्वपि च पापेषु समबुद्धिर्विशिष्यते ।।,

says the Bhagavadgita. The Stoics and the Epicureans regarded equanimity as their highest virtue, though they used different words to signify this conception, apathia and ataraxia. Kabir advises absolute impartiality to all, and an even balance. Higher and lower classes, Congressmen and Socialists, democrats and communists, would have been all alike to him. He would have wished them all Good-luck !

(4) The fourth mark of such a God-realiser is his absolute self-surrender. Kabir tells us in his Doha मेरा मुझ में कुछ नहीं, that all things come to us from God. Why then not dedicate them back again to God ? The position we enjoy, the power we wield, and the wealth we accumulate are all due to His sweet will; why then not hand back the power, the position, and the wealth to their Dispenser ? The sons and daughters we possess are due to His Grace, why then not make them serve His purpose ? More than this, our feelings and emotions must themselves be handed over to God. We must denude our minds of them, and make God reign in their place.

(5) The last characteristic of a God-realiser is his great altruism. Rahim tells us in his Doha तरुवर फल नहि खात हैं, that accumulation of wealth should be intended for universal welfare; the trees do not partake of their own fruit; the lake does not drink its own water. Inequality will vanish, if material wealth is evenly distributed according to worth, while the distribution of spiritual wealth becomes the chief task of the God-realiser. सम्पत्ति may not mean only material wealth, but it may mean spiritual wealth also. The great Bādarāyaṇa used the word सम्पत्ति to signify spiritual wealth in his famous Vedantic Sutra सम्पद्याविर्भावः स्वेन शब्दात् (बा. सू. ४।४). It thus becomes the duty of the Saint not to keep his spiritual accumulation only for himself, but to utilise it for the upliftment of humanity.

10. *Liberation, Beatification, and Infinitude*— We now pass on to one of the highest problems in the philosophy of religion, and particularly one in which the Dohas might be regarded as having made some contribution. Under this head we shall consider three Dohas of Kabir :

(1) नोन गला पानी मिला,
(2) कबिरा हम गुरुरस पिया,
(3) हद हद पर सब ही गया,

all of which deal with the problem of the spiritual Summum Bonum. Three theories can be advanced on this head. First, the theory of liberation, second, the theory of beatification, and third, the theory of infinitude. These are supported by metaphors, drawn from such ordinary conceptions as the salt-bag, the baked pot, and a game of sport, as is Kabir's usual wont. When a salt-bag is thrown into the water of the ocean, says Kabir, all the salt in the bag is dissolved in the water, so that ultimately nothing remains inside the bag. Even so, when the human body, with all its emotions and passions, is thrown into the ocean of God, the emotions and passions are dissolved in God, and nothing but the body remains. Just, again, as no further salt can be produced inside the bag, similarly, no life-principle can reappear in the body. Reincarnation for man thus becomes impossible, just as reproduction of salt becomes impossible in the salt-bag. This is an excellent illustration of a पूर्णदृष्टान्त from the rhetorical point of view. Further, when Kabir tells us that the salt in the bag is mixed with the water of the ocean, the statement only stands for the union of the individual with the universal spirit – a phenomenon at which Death stands gaping and aghast, because he has no longer any power to bring the body under his control. This metaphor of Kabir is founded on the ancient and most well-known metaphor in the छांदोग्य Upanishad, in the conversation between श्वेतकेतु and आरुणि, where the mixing of the salt with the water is regarded as an illustration for the union of self with God : लवणमेतदुदकेऽवधाय....अंतादाचामेति.... मध्यादाचामेति, कथमिति लवणमिति....स य एषोऽणिमा....तत्सत्यं स आत्मा । तत्त्वमसि श्वेतकेतो. This same idea is re-echoed in the famous Abhanga of Tukaram, which stands on the lips of every devotee of God in Maharashtra :

> लवण जैसें पुन्हा जळाचे बाहेरीं
> येत नाहीं खरें त्यांतूनिया ।
> त्यासारिखे तुम्ही जाणा साधुवृत्ति
> पुन: न मिळती मायाजाळ ॥.

So far, then, about the first aspect of the three-fold problem of the Summum Bonum, namely, the conception of liberation.

Let us now pass on to the problem of beatification. In the Doha कबिरा हम गुरुरस पिया, the slaking of spiritual thirst by ambrosial juice, says Kabir, automatically puts an end to all desires. जुगन जुगन की

तृषा बुझाती, करम भरम अघ व्याधि टरै, says Kabir elsewhere also; but the putting to an end of all desires may mean only desirelessness, unless it becomes the vehicle for some higher conception. At many places in the Vedanta philosophy, liberation is explained as consisting in desirelessness (वासना-त्याग). This is only a negative conception. Mere desirelessness, without a positive content, could not come up to the mark, as is required for the highest emancipation. Kabir tells us that this positive content is beatification. "I have drunk the cup of juice from my teacher", says Kabir; "I am absolutely satiated, and no desire now remains in me to be fulfilled". Satiety, or Beatification, therefore, seems to be the positive content behind desirelessness. Beatification as a result of the desirelessness produced by the ambrosial juice, would really be what an aspirant should seek to have. Then again, Kabir gives us in the Doha the analogy of a baked pot. Just as a baked pot is never made to mount on the wheel again, similarly, he—Kabir—will never be made to mount on the wheel of reincarnation. Redness of the pot is a symbol for perfection attained through beatification. Here again, redness is an indication of the highest Sattva in Kabir, as we have noticed elsewhere. Kabir does not bother himself with the philosophical questions like those of पीलु-पाक or पिठर-पाक. He is satisfied that his pot is fully baked, and, as such, will never be mounted again on the wheel of reincarnation. The close analysis which Kabir has made of desirelessness and beatification will convince us of the robust confidence that runs through the Doha, as well as his complete "knowledge" of the process of liberation. Because he 'knew' the process thoroughly, he became so confident : पाका कलस कुम्हार का, वहुरि न चढ़सी चाक. If we were just to analyse the different attitudes with which philosophers at different times have approached such an ultimate question of 'knowledge', we can say that there are four such attitudes possible,–the attitudes of the Sophists, Socrates, Shuka, and Kabir. If now we were asked to mention tersely the central points in the attitudes, we might say on the whole that the Sophists did not know that they did not know; Socrates knew that he did not know; Shuka did not know that he knew; and Kabir knew that he knew. This "knowledge" gave him the confidence that he had reached the highest state of beatification, and that he would never be born again.

We have, hitherto, considered two conceptions of the spiritual Summum Bonum, namely, liberation and beatification. We shall now consider the third, namely, that of 'sport' which synthesises the other two, namely, liberation and beatification. Kabir has referred in many places to his sport in the spiritual kingdom. We have already met with the Doha in which he has told us, अविनाशी की गोद में "खेलत" दास कबीर. In the present Doha, he tells us बेहद के मैदान में "रमै" कबीरा सोय. He is recreating himself on the playground of बेहद, or the Limitless. The conception of sport seems to underlie this final process of the Summum Bonum according to Kabir. If we analyse the synthetic conception of sport, we shall see that it contains the following three elements, freedom, beatification, and activity; the first two having been discussed already, we now consider the third, which is the essence of sport. As to what relationship the sport of Kabir may bear to the so-called लीला of God, as expounded in the Vedanta Sutra लोकवत्तु लीलाकैवल्यम्, we cannot, unfortunately, discuss here. Philosophers have fought battles royal about what is meant by लीला as applied to God; whether it involves personality, or is used in an impersonal sense, whether it is purposive, or unpurposive. To sit in judgment on the motives of God is a very difficult matter, but to sit in judgment on the motives of the saint may not be impracticable. When Kabir is talking about his spiritual sport, he is suggesting blissful activity, both on his own part, as well as on the part of the world. Tukaram has said, elsewhere, आतां उरलों उपकारापुरता, meaning thereby that, after God-realisation, he was living only for the sake of conferring spiritual benefaction on humanity.

Kabir tells us in the Doha that he is sporting

on the playground of the बेहद, or the Unlimited. We are familiar, and intimately familiar, with the distinction between हद and बेहद in Kabir. हद belongs to the ordinary spiritual teacher, who reflexly mutters some 'mantra' in the ears of his disciple. The Guru of बेहद transcends such a conception: कनफूंका गुरु हदका, बेहद का गुरु और. For a parallel to this conception of हद and बेहद, we have to go to Pythagoras's Limit and Unlimited, the Peras and the Apeiron. We shall come to this presently. In the meanwhile, the purport of the Doha we are discussing is that Kabir tells us that he is playing a game of spiritual cricket on the plains of the Limitless. All the players have only hit up to the boundary, he says, but he alone has been able to hit an over-boundary. What is this over-boundary, and what is the nature of the infinite plain, बेहद का मैदान, on which he is playing?

There have been three classical answers to this problem. One comes from the conception of the Unconditioned in philosophic thought, whether Indian or European. In the Vedanta philosophy we are aware of God's existence as दिक्कालाद्यनवच्छिन्न, unlimited by time, space, and cause. Even so, Bradley's Absolute, like the Absolute of many other idealistic philosophers, is beyond space, time, and causation. Then, secondly, the बेलु and निर्बेलु about which Kannada Mysticism speaks might be likened to the philosophic conceptions of the Unconditioned or the Absolute. In his lectures on Karnatak Mysticism, the present writer has spoken about the relation of बैलु to निर्बैलु, बैलु meaning space and निर्बैलु meaning spacelessness. As however बैलु or space may be taken to be equivalent to the void, what would be the conception of निर्बैलु which transcends the void? It might be a void beyond the void, which may not therefore carry any scientific value. The first void should be enough for us, call it बैलु or निर्बैलु, as you please. The Vachana बैलिगे बैलायितु बैलोळगे which we meet with in Purandardas, may be taken exactly to imply the region in which the mystic may live after the realisation of God. This is the second parallel to Kabir's बेहद का मैदान. The third might be taken from the great Greek Philosophers. We have conceptions such as those of the Unlimited and the Indeterminate in the philosophies of Pythagoras and Aristotle, and, more than this, the conception of the Infinite or the Apeiron in Anaximander, which has been legitimately regarded, as by Windelband, as the first European philosophical conception of God. It is unfortunate that, though Pythagoras and Aristotle came after Anaximander, they could not understand the full significance of Anaximander's Apeiron. Pythagoras did great injustice to it by saying that the conception of the Unlimited was an even, and not an odd number, and therefore capable of multiplicity and evil. Aristotle, who founded his conception of the Indeterminate upon the Apeiron of Anaximander, could not rise to appreciate its full philosophic value. In fact, the conception of the Indeterminate is the weakest spot in Aristotle's philosophical system. The conception of the Apeiron in Anaximander, which stands for the Unitary and Divine Being, marks out Anaximander from a number of other Greek and modern philosophers, who vainly bear the badge of a 'philosophos'. Kabir's conception of वेहद is exactly like that of Anaximander. He tells us in a famous song :

> ज्योति लजाय ब्रह्म जहँ दरसै, आगे अगम अपारा ।
> कह कबीर वहँ रहनि हमारी, बूझै गुरुमुख प्यारा ॥.

This Infinite, and Incomprehensible Beyond in which Kabir lives is exactly the Infinite, the Unitary, and the Divine Being of Anaximander —tò Theîon.

Index of Sources.

PADAS.

CHAPTER I

Group 1.

१ धौखै ही धौखै डहकायो सूरदास

२ केहि समुझावों सग जग कवीर

३ मुसाफिर सोता है कृष्णानंद

Group 2.

४ केशव कहि न जाय तुलसीदास

५ ऊधो धनि तुम्हरो सूरदास

Group 3.

६ कीजै प्रभु अपने सूरदास

७ शंकर रामरूप तुलसीदास

Group 4.

८ ममता तू न गई तुलसीदास

९ क्या तन माँजता रे प्रभुदास

१० जा दिन मन पँछी सूरदास

Group 5.

११ बहुरि नहिं आवना कवीर

१२ दिवाने मन भजन बिना कवीर

Group 6.

१३ करमगति टारे नाहिं टरी कबीर

१४ रे मन जनम अकारथ सूरदास

१५ रे दिल गाफिल कवीर

CHAPTER II

Group 1.

१ छाँडि मन हरिबिमुखनको सूरदास

२ अब मैं नाच्यो बहुत सूरदास

३ करनी बिन कथनी चरनदास

Group 2.

४ सो काफ़िर जो बोलै कृष्णानन्द

५ मन लागो यार फकीरीमें कवीर

६ ब्राह्मण सो जो ब्रह्म चरनदास

Group 3.

७ बिसर गई सब आप. नानक

८ जाके प्रिय न राम तुलसीदास

९ जेहि जय होइ सो तुलसीदास

Group 4.

१० सात्विक श्रद्धा धेनु तुलसीदास

११ पावन पर्वत बेद तुलसीदास

१२ गोपी सुनहु हरिसन्देस सूरदास

१३ ऊधो हमहिं न योग सिखै सूरदास

१४ सुनु मुनि तोहि कहो तुलसीदास

१५ नवधा भगति तुलसीदास

CHAPTER III

Group 1.

१ कत जाइए रे घर रामानन्द

२ ऐसी आरति त्रिभुवन कवीर

३ सोइ सच्चिदानन्दघन तुलसीदास

४ सुनु गिरिजा तुलसीदास

५ जिन्हकै रही भावना तुलसीदास

६ कोई स्याम मनोहर मीराबाई

७ अब कैसे छूटै नामरट रैदास

८ काहे रे बन खोजन जाई नानक

Group 2.

९ तौ निवहै जन सेवक तेरा दादू

१० नरहरि चंचल है मति मोरी रैदास

११ मैं मझधाराका माँझी हूँ अज्ञात

Group 3.

१२ अबकी राखि लेहु — सूरदास
१३ मेरो मन अनत कहाँ — सूरदास
१४ नैनहीनको राह दिखा — अज्ञात
१५ घर तजौं वन तजौं, — अज्ञात
१६ तौक पहिरावौ — अज्ञात
१७ इतनी कृपा हो स्वामी — बहिरो

CHAPTER IV

Group 1.

१ गुरु बिन कौन बतावै — कबीर
२ साधो सो सद्गुरु — कबीर
३ कोई सद्गुरु सन्त कहावै — कबीर

Group 2.

४ अपने घट दियना बारुरे — कबीर
५ नामरूप दुइ ईस — तुलसीदास
६ काहे न रसना रामहि — तुलसीदास

Group 3.

७ अजर अमर इक नाम है — कबीर
८ या विधि मनको लगावै — कबीर
९ चेतना है तो चेतले — नानक
१० भूले मन समझके लाद — कबीर
११ कोरी साल न छाँडै रे — दादू
१२ झीनी झीनी बीनी — कबीर

Group 4.

१३ तो भी कच्चा वे — मत्स्येन्द्र
१४ अगर है शौक मिलनेका — मन्सूर

Group 5.

१५ नौकरी शरिअतसे करना — कबीर
१६ प्रीति लगी तुव नामकी — कबीर

Group 6.

१७ सुना रे मैंने निर्वलके — सूरदास
१८ तुम पलक उघारो — मीराबाई
१९ जोगी मत जा मत जा — मीराबाई

CHAPTER V

Group 1.

१ पायो जी मैंने रामरतन — मीराबाई
२ फागुनके दिन चार रे — मीराबाई
३ साधुकि संगत पाई रे — मीराबाई
४ वन्दउँ श्री हरिपद सुख. — सूरदास
५ अब तो प्रकट भई — सूरदास
६ बिनु पग चलै — तुलसीदास
७ शून्य शिखरमें सुरत — गोरखनाथ
८ झरि लागै महलिया — धरमदास
९ झिलमिल झिलमिल — यारी
१० और देवल जहाँ धुंधली — चरनदास
११ गुरु कृपांजन पायो — एकनाथ
१२ साई अलख पलखमें — महिपति

Group 2.

१३ ऐसा देस दिवाना — चरनदास
१४ जबतें अनहत घोर — चरनदास

Group 3.

१५ महरम होय सो जानै — कबीर
१६ चुवन अमीरस भरत ताल — कबीर
१७ रस गगन गुफामें — कबीर

Group 4.

१८ ऐसो है रे हरिरस कबीर

१९ हो तो कोई पिये रामरस कबीर

२० रामरस मीठा रे कोई पीवै दादू

Group 5.

२१ है कोइ सन्त सहज सुख कबीर

२२ दरस दिवाना वावला कबीर

२३ हमन है इश्कमस्ताना कबीर

२४ मन मस्त हुवा तव क्यों कबीर

Group 6.

२५ रमैया कि दुलहिनि लूटल कबीर

२६ साधो सहज समाधि भली कबीर

Group 7.

२७ जो पीर मेरा बड़ा औलिया मौला

२८ वन्धनोंकी श्रृंखला को सखा

Group 8.

२९ तत्त हिंडोलवा सतगुरु गुलाल

३० क्या वे किसीसे काम नरहरि

३१ आरती कहाँ लौ जोवै रैदास

३२ पावन जस है माधो तेरा रैदास

Group 9.

३३ कहूँ रे जो कहिवेकी होइ कबीर

३४ गुरुने मोहि दीन्ही अजब कबीर

DOHAS.

CHAPTER I

Group 1.

१ सदा नगारा कूचका रहीम

२ पाती झड़ती देखते अज्ञात

३ क्षणभंगुर जीवनकी कलिका अज्ञात

Group 2.

४ कच्चेमें नीका लगै अज्ञात

५ कहँ जाये, कहँ ऊपने अज्ञात

६ हाड़ जरैं ज्यों लाकडी कबीर

CHAPTER II

Group 1.

१ चींटी चावल ले चली कबीर

Group 2.

२ कदली सीप भुजंगमुख अज्ञात

३ जो रहीम उत्तम प्रकृति रहीम

४ कबिरा तेरी झोंपडी कबीर

Group 3.

५ मृदंग कहै धिक् है धिक् है अज्ञात

६ गाया है बूझा नहीं कबीर

Group 4.

७ ऋतु बसन्त याचक भयो अज्ञात

८ सहज मिलै सो दूधसम कबीर

९ तुलसी करपर कर करै तुलसीदास

Group 5.

१० अस्थिचर्ममय देह मम तुलसीपत्नी

११ तुलसी यह जग आयकै तुलसीदास

१२ घर राखे घर जात है तुलसीदास

Group 6.

१३ कबिरा खड़ा बजारमें कबीर

१४ साधु कहावन कठिन है कबीर

१५ चढ़ा मन्सूर सूलीपर अज्ञात

CHAPTER III

Group 1.

१ सन्त सन्त सब एक हैं — कबीर

२ सिंहोंके लेंहडे नहीं — कबीर

Group 2.

३ तुलसी मूरति रामकी — तुलसीदास

४ अन्तर्जामिहु ते बड़ — तुलसीदास

Group 3.

५ सगुनहिं अगुनहिं — तुलसीदास

Group 4.

६ चलती चक्की देखके — कबीर

७ कबीर कूता रामका — कबीर

८ घर घर माँगे टूक — तुलसीदास

९ चित्रकूटके घाटपर — तुलसीदास

१० पीछे माँगै चाकरी — कबीर

११ चलो सखी तहँ जाइए — सूरदास

Group 5.

१२ जो चाहे आकार तू — कबीर

१३ निराकारकी आरसी — कबीर

१४ भजन भरोसे रामके — अज्ञात

CHAPTER IV

Group 1.

१ क्षीररूप सतनाम है — कबीर

२ गुरु तो वही सराहिए — कबीर

३ गुरु कुम्हार सिख कुम्भ है — कबीर

४ कनफूंका गुरु हद्दका — कबीर

५ गुरु गोविन्द दोऊ खडे — कबीर

Group 2.

६ इक लख चन्दा आनि घर — कबीर

७ अगुन सगुन दुइ ब्रह्म — तुलसीदास

८ हम लखि लखिहिं हमार — तुलसी

९ एक छत्र एक मुकुटमनी — तुलसी

१० रामनाम सब कोइ कहै — अज्ञात

Group 3.

११ राम नाम मणिदीप धरु — तुलसी

१२ नाम रामको कल्पतरु — तुलसीदास

१३ शून्य मरै अजपा मरै — कबीर

Group 4.

१४ काल करो सो आज कर — अज्ञात

१५ श्वास श्वास पर हर भजो — अज्ञात

१६ काँकर पाथर जोड़कर — कबीर

Group 5.

१७ माला तो करमें फिरै — अज्ञात

१८ तू रहीम मन आपनो — रहीम

१९ प्रीतम छबि नैनन बसी — रहीम

Group 6.

२० जिन खोजा तिन पाइया — कबीर

२१ रकीबोंने लिखाई हैं रपटें — अकबर

२२ तुलसी ऐसे नामको — तुलसीदास

२३ भाव कुभाव अनख आलस — तुलसी

२४ रहिमन गली है साँकरी — रहीम

Group 7.

२५ सर्गुणकी सेवा करो — कबीर

२६ कविरा धारा अगमकी — कवीर
२७ लाख कोस जो गुरु बसै — कवीर

Group 8.

२८ सर सूखै पंछी उडैं — रहीम
२९ वार वरावर वारि है — अज्ञात
३० एक भरोसो एक वल — तुलसीदास

CHAPTER V

Group 1.

१ लिखा पढीकी वात नहिं — अज्ञात
२ तुलसी या संसारको — तुलसीदास
३ हाथ छुड़ाये जात हो — सूरदास
४ जो देखे सो कहै नहिं — कवीर
५ जों गूंगेके सैनको — कवीर

Group 2.

६ गुण इन्द्री सहजै गए — कवीर
७ हाड़ सूखि पिंजर भए — कवीर
८ सब वाजे हिरदे वजैं — कवीर

Group 3.

९ अलख पुरुष निर्वाण है — कवीर
१० सवद सवदका अन्तरा — कवीर
११ मकड़ी चढ़ती तारसे — अज्ञात

Group 4.

१२ हरि दरिया सूभर भरा — कवीर
१३ बूंद समानी बूंदमें — अज्ञात
१४ सुन्न मण्डलमें घर किया — कवीर

Group 5.

१५ गगन गरजि बरसे अमी — कवीर
१६ धरनी पलक परै नहीं — धरनीदास
१७ पिंजर प्रेम प्रकासिया — कवीर

Group 6.

१८ सुन्न सहज मन सुमिरतें — कवीर
१९ हृदया भीतर आरसी — कवीर
२० लागी लागी सब कहैं — अज्ञात
२१ पियको हेरन मैं गई — अज्ञात

Group 7.

२२ मनुवा मेरो मरि गयो — कवीर
२३ कविरा देखा एक अंग — कवीर
२४ सुरत उड़ानी गगनको — कवीर

Group 8.

२५ वड़ा लुत्फ़ है यार इश्कमें — मन्सूर
२६ दी गई मन्सूरको सूली — अज्ञात

Group 9.

२७ रहिमन बात अगम्यकी — रहीम
२८ बडे बड़ाई ना करैं — रहीम
२९ हीरा तहाँ न खोलिये — कवीर
३० कविरा खड़ा बजारमे — कवीर
३१ मेरा मुझमें कुछ नहीं — कवीर
३२ तरुवर फल नहिं खात हैं — रहीम

Group 10.

३३ नोन गला पानी मिला — कवीर
३४ कविरा हम गुरुरस पिया — कवीर
३५ हद हद पर सबही गया — कवीर

INDEX OF SUBJECTS

(AUTHOR–WISE)

AKBAR

DOHA. Moral requisites of meditation : *IV* 21.

ANONYMOUS

PADAS. Parity between devotee and God : *III* 11 ; Lyrical Prayer (Surdasian) : *III* 14 ; Passionate attachment of the devotee towards God : *III* 15 ; A devotee's preparedness to brave all dangers for the sake of God ; *III* 16.

DOHAS. One goes ahead, another follows : *I* 2 ; Universal reign of uncertainty : *I* 3 ; Decrepitude and death : *I* 4–5 ; Place of company in spiritual life : *II* 2 ; Fine arts and mysticism : *II* 5 ; Charity : *II* 7 ; Suffering as the ladder to God : *II* 15 ; Lying on the lap of the Immutable : *III* 14; A viable and a non-viable Name : *IV* 10 ; Extreme value of the present moment : *IV* 14 ; Taking care of every breath : IV 15; Control of the wanderings of the mind : *IV* 17 ; A devotee's passionate longing for God : *IV* 29 ; Intuition vs. Intellect : *V* 1 ; Music and the Musician : *V* 8 ; The ever ascending ladder of Shabda : *V* 11 ; Coalescence of sound and form experience : *V* 13 ; Realisation of Self : *V* 18–19 ; Discovery of God : *V* 21 ; Moral marks of the God-realiser : *V* 28.

BAHIRO

PADA. Absolute resignation to the will of God : *III* 17.

CHARANDAS

PADAS. Action as the cradle of God : *II* 3 ; Moral and spiritual requirements of Brahminhood : *II* 6 ; Thakurdwar is everywhere : *V* 10 ; Effects of God-realisation : *V* 13–14.

DADU

PADAS. Meaning of a Kafir : *II* 4 ; Philosophical Prayer : *III* 9 ; The Spiritual Charkha : *IV* 11 ; Flavourism : *V* 20.

DHARAMDAS

PADA. Beatificatory spiritual experience: *V* 8.

DHARANIDAS

DOHA. Thirst for the enjoyment of God's splendour: *V* 16.

EKNATH

PADA. Vision of God in all states of consciousness: *V* 11.

GORAKHNATH

PADA. Description of spiritual experience: *V* 7.

GULAL

PADA. Post-ecstatic ejaculation: *V* 29.

KABIR

PADAS. Universal blindness: *I* 2; Transmigration and metempsychosis: *I* 11–12; Helplessness in life's experience: *I* 13; Way of escape from life's miseries: *I* 15; A spiritual Fakir: *II* 5; Conception of God: *III* 2; Characteristics of a Guru: *IV* 1–3; The Name of God: *IV* 4; Internal meditation: *IV* 7; Intense concentration: I*V* 8; Meditation here and now: *IV* 10; A spiritual Charkha: *IV* 12; The militant and the submissive attitudes: *IV* 15–16; Sublimity and ineffability of mystical experience: *V* 15–17; Flavourism and Beatification: *V* 18–19; God-intoxication: V 21–24; Lifting of the cosmic deceit: *V* 25–26; Apostleship and Prophethood: *V* 33-34.

DOHAS. Funeral pyre as inciter to spiritual life: *I* 6; Spiritual welfare and material welfare: *II* 1; Place of company in spiritual life: *II* 4; Music and mysticism: *II* 6; Varieties of obtainment: *II* 8; Suffering as the ladder to God: *II* 13–14; Sainthood, a rare phenomenon: *III* 1–2; Proximity of God saves from annihilation: *III* 6; Limited human freedom: *III* 7; God fore-fulfils the desires of the devotee: *III* 10; Saint as personal, and God as impersonal reality: *III* 12–13; Nature and function of a Guru: *IV* 1–5; Word of Guru alone as dispelling darkness: *IV* 6; Name confers immortality: *IV* 13; Meditation in silence: *IV* 16; Necessity of active effort: *IV* 20; Requisites of meditation: *IV* 25–27; Inter-communicativeness of senses: *V* 4–5; The music and the Musician:

V 6; Realisation of Person and love of Shabda: *V* 9; Metaphysical and Epistemological significance of Shabda: *V* 10; Visual experience: morphic and photic: *V* 12, 14; Supersensuous experiences: *V* 15, 17; Seeing of the face in the mirror of the heart: *V* 20; Motor and tactual experience: *V* 22–24; Moral marks of God-realiser *V* 29–31; Liberation, Beatification, and Infinitude: *V* 33–35

KRISHNANAND

PADA. Sleep of ignorance: *I* 3.

MAHIPATI

PADAS. Mystic's life in a tumult of light and colour: *V* 12; Post-ecstatic ejaculation: *V* 30.

MANSUR

PADA. The Anal-Haq method of meditation: *IV* 14.
DOHA. The Travail of Unison: *V* 26–27.

MATSYENDRANATH

PADA. Place of Yoga in the meditational process: *IV* 13.

MAULA

PADA. Ecstacy and the effacement of the distinction between Self and God: *V* 27.

MIRABAI

PADAS. 'Theos' of Gopis becomes a 'Pan-theos': *III* 6; Dark night of the soul: *IV* 18; The dark night and the dawn: *IV* 19; Possession of the jewel of God: *V* 1; Experience of sound and colour: *V* 2; Doctrine of Approximation: *V* 3.

NANAK

PADAS. God, the source of all virtues: *II* 7; Unity of the internal and the external God: *III* 8; Turning every moment to spiritual use: *IV* 9.

PRABHUDAS

PADA. On the vanity of human life: *I* 9.

RAHIM

DOHAS. Perpetual flux : *I* 1 ; Place of company in spiritual life : *II* 3 ; Mental requisites of meditation : *IV* 18–19 ; Leaving away all egoism : *IV* 24 ; God as the sole resort of the devotee : *IV* 28 ; Ignorando cognosci : *V* 27 ; Spiritual altruism : *V* 32.

RAIDAS

PADAS. Various analogies for the relation of Saint and God : *III* 7 ; Mutual love on mutual inspection : *III* 10 ; Futility of waving lights before an omnipresent God : *V* 31; Post-ecstatic ejaculation : *V* 32.

RAMANAND

PADA. Internal immanence and universal pervasiveness of God : *III* 1.

SAKHA

PADA. Ecstacy and the sustenance of the world : *V* 28.

SURDAS .

PADAS. Illusionism : *I* 1 ; Contradictions of desert and fruit : *I* 5 ; Consciousness of sin : *I* 6 ; Ravages of death : *I* 10 ; Way of escape from submission to death : *I* 14 ; Avoidance of the un-godly : *II* 1 ; Un-godliness, the root of all vices : *II* 2 ; Jnana as the transcendence of Appearance : *II* 12 ; Bhakti as the quest for God : *II* 13 ; Lyrical prayers : *III* 12–13 ; Surrender, the essential condition of Grace : *IV* 17 ; Divine omnipotence and supersensuous experience : *V* 4 ; God as inextricably bound up with every fibre of the body : *V* 5.

DOHAS. Spiritual eudaemonism : *III* 11 ; Internal Perception : *V* 3.

TULSIDAS

PADAS. Philosophical afflatus to spiritual life : *I* 4 ; Consciousness of sin : *I* 7 ; Effects of old age : *I* 8 ; Leaving away of all relations for the sake of God : *II* 8 ; Chariot of spiritual victory : *II* 9 ; Lamp of Jnana : *II* 10 ; Jewel of Bhakti : *II* 11 ; God in relation to the Jnani and Bhakta : *II* 14 ;

Supernal Bhakti as a diamond with nine facets : *II* 15 ; God as 'niranjana' : *III* 3 ; Inscrutability of the reasons for the incarnation of God : *III* 4 ; God as inspiring different emotions in different men : *III* 5 ; Name as schematiser of Nirguna and Saguna : *IV* 5 ; Apostrophe to Tongue : *IV* 6; Mystical transcendence of God : *V* 6.

DOHAS. Charity : *II* 9 : Devotion to God in its social and spiritual aspects : *II* 11-12 ; The Immano-transcendence of God : *III* 3-4 ; Ascending Stages of Philosophy of Devotion : *III* 5 ; God, the source of all honour : *III* 8 ; God as serving the Saints : *III* 9 : Personal and Impersonal God as subordinate to Name : *IV* 7 ; Impossibility of perceiving the Unperceivable : *IV* 8 ; Sovereign status of Name of Rama : *IV* 9 ; Function and power of Name : *IV* 11-12 ; Moral requisites of meditation : *IV* 22-23 ; One-pointed devotion : *IV* 30 ; Divine perception prevented by cataract of ignorance : *V* 2.

TULSI–PATNI

DOHA. An all-absorbing love of God : *II* 10.

YARI

PADA. Manifold spiritual experience : *V* 9.

GENERAL INDEX

[REFERENCES ARE TO MAJOR ITEMS ONLY.]

A

Absolute, the, beyond mere intellectual endeavour, p. 14; beyond space, time, and causation, p. 403.

Advaitism, three varieties of, p. 76, 77; on liberation through knowledge, p. 77: attack by the Gopis, p. 78.

Allahabad, and an English friend, p. 34; and Untakhana, p. 34; and riots, p. 175; Bungalow at, visit of two persons, p. 378.

Anahata, and Purandardas, p. 57; as the horse for the self to ride, p. 166; various kinds of, p. 207, 221; Physiological effects of, p. 218; moral effects of, p. 219; and the Amirasa, p. 224; produced by throttling the goat of Eros, p. 234; lulling a person to Samadhi, p. 253; and the jingling bells, p. 321; as "luminous sound", p. 342; and Shabda distinction between, Pp. 143, 350, 351, 374, 376; meditation in the presence of, p. 362; as a vehicle for God-realisation, 374, 375.

Antaryamin, Ramanuja's great stress on, p. 131; as inferior to Bahiryamin, p. 307;

Aristotle, contribution to Ethics, p. 49; ethos is ēthos, p. 84; doctrine of the mean, p. 91; concept of magnanimity, p. 91;

Aristotle, *contd.*

divine theory, p. 91; on God as transcendent, p. 254; concept of the Indeterminate, in, p. 404, 405;

Augustine St., Attitude to sin, Pp. 20, 23; second founder of Christianity p. 23; Platonic virtues as expressions of love, p. 93; Ignorando Cognosci, p. 394.

Aurobindo, Ghose, Surrender, the plank of integral yoga; Pp. 133, 181; on directing consciousness upwards, p. 154.

B

Badarayana, Ahi-Kundalvat, various interpretations, p. 15; doctrine of vichitravada, p. 111; on the continuance of spiritual meditation to the end of life, p. 160; on no-return to world by life, Pp. 254, 339; on the meaning of Sampatti, p. 397;

Bhagwadgita, as comparing mind to wind, p. 6; description of demoniac heritage, Pp. 53, 54; God-love as the prime virtue, Pp. 60, 61, 84, 85, 94; on illumination as responsible for liberation, Pp. 77, 78: on no contradiction between a Jnani and a Bhakta, p. 78; doctrine of incarnation, p. 110; on God as Sutra, p. 116; on Smarana Mukti, p. 131; on

Bhagwadgita, *contd.*
Sayujya Mukti, p. 132; on Sharanagaman Mukti, p. 133; doctrine of actionlessness p. 139; on vision of the self by self, p. 213; concept of Gunas in, p. 301; on Jnanadeepa, p. 349; on self-realisation, p. 386; on the virtue of equanimity, p. 396.

Bhagavata, the, on mystical relationship between Uddhav and Krishna, p. 75; on body clinging to the self as an Uttariya, p. 235; story about Vyasa and Shuka, p. 319.

Bhakti, the supreme virtue in the Bhagwadgita, p. 61; new nine kinds of, Pp. 69, 81, 82, 83, 92; Jewel of, Pp. 73, 349; Rasa of, p. 113; compared to a chaste woman, p. 310.

Bradley, doctrine of appearance, p. 77; degrees of truth and reality, p. 198; on the Absolute, p. 403.

Brahman, as the target to aim at, p. 177; as enveloped by the self, p. 222; lighting up of the fire of, Pp. 233, 234.

C

Carlyle, on a disbeliever in God as our enemy, p. 60; everlasting no, and everlasting yea, p. 181; on the tiniest particle as filled with God, p. 241; on looking to one's own saving, p. 264; on conscious virtue, p. 395.

Christ Jesus, on renouncing father and mother, p. 60;

Christ Jesus, *contd.*
surrender the chief element in, p. 133; on the prophet's not being honoured in his own country, p. 261; as ascending the cross, p. 393.

D

Death, and old age as incentives, Pp. 24, 29; Stoics' view of, p. 26; Epicureans' view of, p. 26; great impartiality of, p. 31.

E

Emotions, psychic energy substratum of, p. 233; their correspondence with spiritual colours, p. 247.

England, travail during second world war, p. 39; Churchill on the final success of, p. 40; conquest of, by William I, p. 296;

Equanimity, as a result of divine intoxication, Pp. 235, 237; through God-possession, p. 239; creative, p. 250; as a mark of God-realisation, p. 396.

G

Gandhi, Mahatma, Churchill's sarcastic title of Naked Fakir, Pp. 54, 322; remains buried at Rajaghat, p. 55; statuettes of three monkeys, p. 199; on humanity's indifference, p. 261; Gokhale's advice to, p. 394.

God, architectonic skill of, p. 2; as a diamond in the devo-

God, *contd.*
tee's heart, p. 5; handiwork of, p. 11; as our home, p. 11; moral proof of, p. 17; as a great judge, p. 18; resignation to the will of, Pp. 36, 40; as a super-moral being, p. 37; alliance with, p. 41; as the pole-star of attention, p. 43; as the only cynosure of our effort, p. 47; the source of all virtue, p. 57; as the vinculum substantiale, p. 62; as monas monadum p. 62; as Niranjan, Pp. 98, 104, 106, 312; reasons for incarnation of, p. 98; universal pervasiveness of, p. 102; vision of, as putting an end to delusion, p. 103; idea of a Saguna, p. 107; positive and negative attributes of, Pp. 107, 108; and self, identity between, p. 118; sound and form as expressions of, p. 143; as Amolika Vastu, Pp. 191, 192; as a great oarsman, p. 193; transcendent powers of, p. 203; as identical with Rasa, p. 230; found even behind a sesamum, p. 241; as transcendent, p. 254; as walking like a sepoy, p. 255; office of, for the saints, p. 316; as spiritual fulcrum, p. 317; compared to a great expert in the game of chess, p. 325; as impersonal reality, p. 326.

God-love, binding together all saints, p. 48; as the charioteer in the spiritual victory, p. 49; as the supreme virtue according to the Bhagwadgita, Pp. 61, 63, 84, 94, 95; in its individual, social and spiritual

God love, *contd.*
aspects, Pp. 291, 295.

Gopis as not distinguishing between Krishna and Uddhava, Pp. 15, 16; on the injustice of the divine court, p. 16; as having left off their husbands for the sake of God, p. 60; and Krishna, relationship between, p. 75; filled with sorrow at the mention of Nirguna, p. 78; Brija as the alpha and omega of the life of, p. 79.

Grace of God, and self-effort, relation between, Pp. 19, 20; descending on Gajendra, Pp. 182, 183; making possible supersensuous perception, Pp. 199. 201.

Green, T. H. contribution to ethical philosophy, p. 49; Unity of the spiritual principle in nature and in man, p. 59; doctrine of self-realisation, p. 91.

H

Hamsa, and Soham, no distinction between, p. 143; as having reached Manasa sarovar, Pp. 240, 241; derivation according to Yaska, p. 346.

Hanuman, as not prizing precious ornaments, p. 50; according to Valmiki on the four chief sources of power, Pp. 182, 183; Tulsidas's vision of, p. 293.

Herakleitos, apostle of the doctrine of flux, p. 274; author's essay on, p. 331; Anticipating Christianity in his doctrine of

Herakleitos, *contd.*
the kingdom of God as belonging to the child, p. 331.

I

Ida and Pingala, parallel chords of the sympathetic nervous system, Pp. 152, 164 ; the confluence of, Pp. 155, 157, 176 ; as waving lights, Pp. 204, 205.

Incarnation, correct doctrine of, Pp.98, 109, 110 ; ten incarnations, cinematographic vision of, p. 42, 223 ;

J

Jagannathadas, experience of God as walking with him, Pp. 209, 210 ; on escaping from the clutches of death, p. 352 ; motor experience, p. 389.

Jnana, and Bhakti, p. 49 : not antithetical to Bhakti, p. 69 ; compared to a light of great luminosity, p. 70 ; intuitive as realisation of God, Pp. 76, 77.

Jnaneshwara, similarity of ideas between Kabir and, Pp. 2, 44, 45; question of his meeting Kabir, Pp. 4, 45 ; comparing the world to a conflagration, p. 7 ; on suffering as an incentive to spiritual life, p. 35 ; on man's sitting in a wrecked boat in the river of life, Pp. 43, 46 ; on Virahavastha, Pp. 178, 179 ; on ever increasing devotion, p. 180 ; on mystical ensigns, Pp 185, 186; on God as Amolika Ratna, Pp. 191, 192 ; on the difference between

Jnaneshwara, *contd.*
a perfected mystic and God, p. 197 ; on God as walking in front like a torch-bearer, Pp. 255, 389 ; on God and Saint as mirrors, Pp. 329, 386, 387 ; on the forms of spiritual bath, p. 383.

K

Kamal, on the two great saints, Kabir and Namdeo, p 45 ; and Kabir, stories about the relationship between, Pp. 317, 318.

Kant, philosopher and moralist, p. 3 ; cosmo-teleological argument, p. 11 ; on the philosophic consequence of disparity between desert and fruit, p. 17; moral proof of God, p. 18 ; on the kingdom of ends, p. 91 ; unity of apperception, Pp. 92, 150 ; on schematism, p. 147 ; on imagination higher than perception and understanding, p. 313 ; theory of Reciprocal Causation, Pp. 224, 225.

Kashi, Namdeo going on a pilgrimage to, p. 44 ; to Pandharpur. prevalence of the same spiritual ideas, p. 45; described both as Mahashmashan and Anandavana, p. 273.

Krishna, and Uddhava, not distinguished by the Gopis, Pp. 15, 16 ; great friend of Pandavas, p. 37 ; using Shikhandi to kill Bhishma, p. 38 ; Gopis left off their husbands for the sake of, p. 65 ; and Uddhava, their mystical relationship in the Bhagawat, p. 75 ; and

Krishna, *contd.*
Gopis, p. 75; appeal of Gopis to Uddhava for the revelation of, p. 79; appeared once to Gopis in the form of a yogin, p. 186.

L

Lateral, ventricle, Pp. 154, 155, 157; as the seat of the unseen, p, 204; oozing of mellifluous juice in the, Pp. 222, 224; opening of the, p. 225; self flying to the, p. 390.

Leibnitz, Doctrine of Optimism p. 58; Law of sufficient reason, p. 58; his Monadology, p. 62.

M

Meditation, methodology of, Pp. 134, 145; supersensuous effects of, Pp. 198, 201; by the help of the name of God, Pp. 333, 340, 348; requisites of, p. 333; physical requisites of, Pp. 351, 354; mental requisites of, Pp. 354, 356; moral requisites of, Pp. 356, 360; mystical requisites of, Pp. 360, 363.

Mellifluous juice, experience of, p. 216; a mystic being drenched in, p. 218; oozing of, in the lateral ventricle, Pp. 222, 224; consequence of drinking, p. 249; mystic herb as full of, p. 263.

Milton, writing poems about heaven though blind, p. 128; on the two attitudes of joy and pensiveness, p. 172.

Mystical experience, as sui generis, p. 186; varieties of, Pp. 189, 191, 216; sublimity and ineffability of, Pp. 190, 220; riot of, p. 204; social aspect of, p. 251; as enjoyment of Sahaja Samadhi, Pp. 243, 244; law about the correspondence between mystical experience and the quality of the heart, p. 246; as going beyond the three states of consciousness, p. 255; and fine arts, p. 287; Criteria of, (Introd.)

N

Name of God, 'Sat nama', p. 34; and form of God, relation between, Pp. 134, 144, 145, 146, 147, 314; as bringing self and God together, p. 145; as schematizer between Saguna and Nirguna, Pp. 147, 148, 312; as symbol of ultimate reality, p. 148; meditation by means of the, Pp. 340, 348; pinnacle of Tulsidasa's philosophy of devotion, Pp. 309, 310; illuminator, witness and interpreter, p 312; sitting in a judicial tribunal over Saguna and Nirguna, p. 313; superior to Nirguna and Saguna, Pp. 313, 342; fundamental vehicle of meditation, p. 315; as ladder to reach God, Pp. 346, 347; as the atom bomb of spiritual experience, p. 347.

Namdeo, Pilgrimage to North India, particularly to Kashi, p. 44; Namdeo and Kabir relation between, p. 45; experience of God as eating and speaking with him, p. 209; as having received divine juice, p. 231.

Narsi Mehta, poet of Gujarat, resemblance in his teaching with Tulsidas on God-love, Pp. 63, 64, 65, 66; independent parallelism of thought between him and Tulsidas, p. 66.

O

Optimism, eschatological, p. 26; doctrine of Leibnitz, p. 58; Robert Browning on, p. 58; God-centred, p. 97.

P

Pandharpur, to Kashi, prevalence of the same spiritual thoughts from, p. 45; practice of putting on Bukka, p. 323.

Patanjali, enumeration of Yamas and Niyamas, p. 67; on requirements of meditation, p. 135; characteristics of meditational process, Pp, 159, 160; on the supersensuous avenues opening to a mystic, Pp. 199, 200; concept of Parama Guru, p. 240; on the vision of one's own form, p. 251; 386.

Pearls, experience of the showers of, p. 208.

Philosophers, and moralists, p. 3; as coming to the fair of life simply to look on, p. 10; in King Janaka's court, p. 113; classification of, Pp. 279, 280; and market place, p. 295.

Philosophy, an ironical definition of, p. 12; and mysticism, controversy between, p. 103; of an idler, p. 243.

Plato. on man's blindness, Pp. 12, 14; contribution to ethics, p. 49; on learning and teaching philosophy, p. 56; on the cardinal virtues, Pp. 85. 90, 91; on the charioteer controlling the unruly horse, p. 176; on the idea of the Good, p. 198.

Pralhad, as disobeying his father, p. 37; as having left off his father for the sake of God, Pp. 60, 65; as having received divine juice, p. 231; on the locus of God, p. 306.

Preetam, Gujarati poet, on invincible courage for the spiritual path, Pp. 174, 175; on throwing ourselves in the conflagration of God-love, p. 229: on the way of the brave, p. 357.

Prema, Narada on the concept of, p. 86; and Prana as the warp and woof of the spiritual garment, p. 165; and Preeti, personal and impersonal love of God, p. 327.

Purandardas, on an ass not knowing the fragrance of the musk it carries on its back, p. 50; description of a Brahmin Pp. 56, 57; comparison of moments to drops from a broken pitcher, p. 160; on his experience of God as walking with him, Pp. 209, 210; on the interchange of physiological function, p. 374; on motor relationship of God and Saint- p. 389; on God as a void beyond the void, p. 404.

R

Rama, Indra having a superb devotion to, p. 20; coronation of, and stellar conjunction, p. 36; pursuing a Hema Mriga, p. 38; incidents of, serving as mines of jewels, p. 73; as a complex of all Rasas, p. 114; wanting to cross the Ganges, p. 123; engaged in giving tilak, p. 293; derivation of the word according to Tulsidas, p. 345.

Ramadas, on the great impartiality of death, p. 31; on suffering as an incentive, p. 35; on seeking the friendship of God alone, p. 60; on Viveka-Vairagya, p. 71; on God as not to be found in water and stones, p. 101; spiritual teacher as God's replica, p. 144; on the futility of the repetition of Mahavakya, p. 171; on the listlessness of people, p. 261; as a shouting philosopher, Pp. 279, 280; on instantaneous liberation, p. 336; advice not to lose a single breath, p. 352.

Ramanand, reflexly uttering Rama Rama, p. 100; experience of colour & fragrance, p. 102.

Ramanuja, on the reality of the world, p. 15; Ramanand belonging to the school of, p. 100; doctrine of Prapatti, p. 133; doctrine of Antaryamin, p. 307.

Rasas, new and old schemes of, Pp. 111, 112, 113, 114; as the quality oozing from God, p. 230; Upanishadic doctrine of, p. 231.

Reality, self a child in the cradle of, p. 252; terrace of, p. 299; as both centrifugal and centripetal, p. 317.

Reciprocal Causation, between meditation on name and the love of God, p. 97; between fearlessness and joy, p. 139; between Anahat and Amirasa, Pp. 224, 225.

S

Saint, a member of the Theopolis, p. 57; and God, parity between, p. 99; as Khaggavishan, Pp. 236, 303; as a celestial tree overladen with Ambrosial fruit, p. 251; his luminosity as transcending the earthly limitations, p. 251; calling himself merely a bondsman of his spiritual teacher, p. 254; as personal and God as impersonal reality, p. 326; elevation of, to the pedestal of God-head, p. 327; spirit of, merging with absolute spirit, p. 322; and God, unison between, p. 329.

Saints, company of, as the welfare state, p. 48; together tied only by the bond of God-love, p. 48; as experiencing divine juice, p. 230; living in a state of God-enjoyment, p. 242; world as indifferent to the, p. 261.

Saint of Nimbargi, on the dedication of our life and actions to God, p. 163; on progressive realisation, p. 197; on the futility of burning huge quantities of camphor, p. 258; drawing God to the bar of his

Saint of Nimbargi, *contd.* spiritual teacher, p. 340; on Name as Kalpataru, p. 349; story about inter-incommunicativeness of senses in ordinary experience narrated by, p. 371.

Saint of Umadi, on a combination of Prem and Prana, p. 166; d poem from the posthumous aiary of, p. 245; on Kakadarati, p. 248; teaching about charity, Pp. 290, 291; narration of a story about Kabir and God, p. 339; on intercommunicativeness of senses in mystical experience, Pp. 373, 374

Samadhi, three types of, p. 140; theory of, Pp. 243, 244.

Samadhi, Alankara, illustration, p. 182; state of, Pp 245, 249; Anahata lulling a person to, p. 253; of Mahatma Gandhi on the Rajaghata, p. 322; and tomb of Kabir at Magahar, p. 330.

Samkhya philosophy, on suffering as an incentive to spiritual life, p. 35; Kabir speaking in terms of, p. 263; on Prakriti ceasing to exist as soon as she is seen by her lord, Pp. 387, 388.

Sanskrit, Subhashita, on a short-dated human life, p. 194; verse on sleep as Samadhi, p. 243; verse on momentariness, p. 276; verse on the lotus of life torn away by an elephant of Death, p. 284; verse on the rarity of sainthood, p. 303; verse on the cataract of ignorance, p. 341.

Sāngarupaka, on God-love as the charioteer, p. 49; on devotion to God as a diamond with nine facets, p. 49; on the chariot of spiritual victory, Pp. 66, 67; on the comparison of Jnana to a lamp, p. 68; on the comparison of Bhakti to a jewel, Pp. 68, 69.

Sarvajna, experience of God as walking with him, Pp. 209, 210; epigrammatic Kannada saint, p. 270; on the formless taking on the form of a saint, p. 328.

Self, effort of, and grace, Pp. 119, 120; as central telephone exchange, Pp. 150, 152; as enveloping Brahman, p. 222; spiritual bath of the, Pp. 205, 207; as a child in the cradle of reality, p. 252; flying into the empyrean, p. 283; as the supreme object of love, p. 253; becoming dissociated and transcendent, p. 254; as a messenger riding on the 'Turangama', of Shabda, Pp. 116, 362; as enjoying beatific sleep, p. 384.

Self and God, identity between, Pp. 118, 170; brought together by the Name, p. 143.

Self-realisation, doctrine of, Pp. 15, 91, 250, 385, 388; song of, p. 252.

Self-surrender, highest type of liberation, p. 133; doctrine of, p. 181; mark of God-realisation Pp. 396, 397.

Shabda, the spiritual teacher making his consciousness enter into, p. 141; and Anahata, Kabir on, p. 143; rope of, p.

Shabda, *contd.*
243; physical influence of, p. 245; as producing light, p. 341; as substance, Pp. 376, 379; as self-immanent, p. 378; as criterion of itself, p. 379.

Shankara, as enjoying the Chabi of Rama with 15 eyes, p. 21; approached by Madan, p. 234; living in a cemetery, p. 273; as uttering the name of Rama with full faith, p. 358.

Shankaracharya, on an unreal cause producing terror, p. 13; on an unreal cause producing a beneficial effect, p. 13; analogy of Rajjusarpa, p. 13; on the unreality of the world, p. 15; philosophical prayer of, p. 119; doctrine of Sayujyamukti, p. 132; on Kevala Kumbhaka, Pp. 140, 141; on the place of Anahata in realisation, p. 363.

Shesha, taking the burden of the world on the head, p. 184; according to Kanakadasa, intervening between Shiva and Vishnu, p. 313.

Shvetashvataropanishad, on mystical ensigns, p. 185; catalogue of photic experiences, p. 208; on the experience of spi-ritual fragrance, p. 385.

Sidgwick Henry, contribution to ethical philosophy, p. 49; on philosophic intuitionism, p. 91.

Sin, problem of, p. 3; consciousness of, p. 18; as a propaedeutic to a spiritual life, p. 19; attitude of Surdas and Virgil towards, Pp. 19, 20; of Duryodhana and Richard III, Pp.

Sin, *contd.*
19, 20; of Indra and Augustine, p. 20.

Spinoza, intellectual love of God, p. 91; on substance, Pp. 146, 378; postulating an original hammer, Pp. 240, 379; on God as identical and coexistant with the world., p. 307; on the difference between God and Dog, p. 320.

Spiritual, capital, man as bringing with him, p. 8; principle in nature and in man (Green), p. 59; illumination, process by which attained, Pp. 70, 72; virtues, Pp. 89, 95, 95; energy, colour and fragrance as manifestations of, p. 103; gravitation, law of, p. 142; Charkha: description of the, p. 163; communion, ascending ladders of, p. 188; bath, Pp. 205, 207; path, nature of the, p. 213; realisation, psychological and moral effects of, p. 224; mine, concept of a, Pp. 232, 235; colours and their correspondence with Gunas, states of consciousness and emotions, p. 247; consciousness, Pp. 248, 249; and secular work, combination of, p. 257; fulcrum, God as a, p. 317; from, Vice-Chancellor's chair not incompatible with the vision of a, p. 326; fragrance, experience of, Pp. 384, 385; juice, experience of, p. 384; cricket, game of, p. 403.

Spiritual experience, microcosmic aspect of, p. 57; geometrical progression in, p. 193; supersensuous character of

Spiritual experience, *contd.* Pp. 368, 371; psychology of, Pp. 368, 374.

Spiritual life, secret of, p. 7; ethical approach to, p. 15; sin as a propaeduetic to. p. 19; the place of company in, p. 283.

Spiritual Teacher, worship of, as an impenetrable armour, p. 68; as higher than the Godhead. p. 55; characteristics of a, Pp. 134—144; as a great oarsman, p. 193; nature and function of a, Pp. 334—340.

Stoics, on death as an incentive to spiritual life, p. 26; on nature, p. 35; and Epicureans on desirelessness, p. 219; on the virtue of Epoche, p. 239; on philosophers as never afraid of death, p. 272; on equanimity, p. 376.

Sukadev, Grace of, enabling his disciple to see the spiritual territory, p. 217; as having received divine juice, p. 231.

T

Tukaram, Guru's Mantra given to him in a dream, p. 14; on action and not words, p. 52; on devotees who left off every thing for the sake of God, Pp. 65, 66; lyrical prayer of, p. 119; attitude of submission in, p. 179; on being able to look at God's face, p. 200; experience of God as walking with him, Pp. 209, 210; on God making His home even in a sesamum, p. 241; on having

Tukaram, *contd.* seen the banner of God, p. 245; on his apostleship. p. 262; as a weeping philosopher, p. 289; on his being the dog of God, Pp. 320, 351; on the difference between Rama and Atmarama, Pp. 347, 348; on devotion as an emergent, p. 364; on God as running after him, p. 389; on God whirling round him in a circle, p. 389; tactual experience, p. 391; union of self with God, p. 399; on his living only for benefactions to humanity, p. 402.

U

Uddhava, and Krishna not distinguished by the Gopis, Pp. 15, 16; misunderstood by poet-saints, Pp. 5, 75; his mystical relationship with Krisnna in the Bhagavata, p. 75; as a great devotee, Pp. 2, 75: Advaitism of, p. 76.

Unison, between saint and God, p. 329; eschatological, p. 331; travail of, Pp. 391, 393.

Upanishads, on God-love as the bond of substantiality between relatives, p. 63; on the Niranjana concept of God, p. 104; positive and negative attributes of God, Pp. 107, 108; on Samipya, p. 132; on Sayujya, p. 132; on controlling the horse of mind by the reins of reason, p. 176; on concentrated attention, p. 177; on God as supreme resplendence, p. 223; on God as Rasa, p. 231; song of universal unity, p. 237;

Upanishads, *contd.*
conception of 'Bhooman' Pp. 250, 251; on the saint's splendour enveloping the universe, p. 251; on self as the supreme object of love, p. 253; on second birth, p. 277; on necessity of self-effort, p. 351; on perception and audition by means of the self, p. 373; Arachromorphism, p. 379; vision of the self in a flood of light, p. 386; on motor experience, p. 389.

V

Valmiki, Tulsidas, literary Avatara of, p. 32; devotee greater than God, p. 96; his Ramayana on four kinds of power, p. 182; as uttering the name of God with irradiated faith, p. 358.

Vijayadasa, Lyrical prayer of, p. 119; on the window of the

Vijaya Dasa, *contd.*
lateral ventricle as opened by the Grace of God, Pp. 154, 155.

Virtues, moral, cultivation of, p. 48; God-devotion as a supreme virtue Pp. 70, 72; and vices, inventory of, Pp. 88, 89; classification of, p. 88; individual, Pp. 89, 95; social, Pp. 89, 95, 96; spiritual, Pp. 89, 95, 96.

Vithalpant, Ramanand, the teacher of, p. 100; father of Nivrittinath and Jnanadeva, p. 100.

Y

Yoga, fire of, p. 72; and absolutism, place in the meditational process, Pp. 135, 168, 172; kept aflame by the saint in the midst of enjoyment, p. 138.